Profit and Principle

Profit and Principle

The New Rules of Wealth in an Age of Conscience

Zayn Elric

Mindful Pages

Published in 2025

ISBN: 9789371770378 (PB)
ISBN: 9789371770873 (eBook)

Published by

Mindful Pages
Imprint of Alpha Editions LLC
312 W. 2nd St #1834
Casper, WY 82601, USA

This book was developed using advanced writing tools to support the drafting and ideation process. All content has been thoughtfully curated, refined, and reviewed to ensure quality and relevance.

Content

Introduction
Why Conscience Compounds

For as long as capital has been exchanged, human beings have debated whether money is best understood as a tool of morality or as a force indifferent to it. We inherit a long tradition of suspicion about bringing ethics into finance. From the stockbroker's floor to the dinner-table conversation, the assumption lingers that profit and principle are natural adversaries—that to choose one is, inevitably, to sacrifice the other. To many, ethical investing still sounds like a concession: a choice for softer returns, a luxury for the wealthy, or, at best, a symbolic gesture against a tide of profit-seeking too vast to influence.

And yet, another voice has grown louder in the past two decades, not from idealists alone but from sober analysts, pension funds, and even central bankers. It suggests that conscience, far from being a drag on returns, can compound alongside them—that values shape risk, reputation, and resilience in ways markets cannot ignore forever. When looked at closely, moral failures have a stubborn way of becoming financial failures. Tobacco, asbestos, fossil fuels, predatory lending—all were once formidable engines of wealth, only to be undermined by the very harms they inflicted. What looked profitable in the short term proved ruinous in the long run.

This book begins from a simple but demanding claim: that conscience, when disciplined and embedded in investment practice, does not weaken wealth but strengthens it. Principle and profit, rightly understood, are not parallel tracks destined never to meet. They are threads in the same fabric. Woven carefully, they reinforce each other; neglected, they unravel together. This is not a call for moral grandstanding. Nor is it an invitation to accept diluted returns as the cost of personal virtue. It is, instead, an argument for clarity—for a rigorous, intellectually honest framework through which investors can align capital with principle without abandoning prosperity.

The False Trade-Off

One of the most persistent myths in finance is that ethical choices inevitably cost money. This is the false trade-off that frames much of the public debate. On one side, sceptics warn that divesting from profitable industries is naïve, tantamount to moral exhibitionism at the expense of returns. On the other, defenders of ethical investing sometimes reinforce the caricature by appealing to virtue for its own sake, leaving economic performance as an afterthought. Between them lies a conceptual stalemate that serves no one.

The evidence increasingly undermines this binary. Historical divestment campaigns, whether against South African apartheid or the tobacco industry, did not simply cleanse consciences—they reshaped industries, altered risk profiles, and forced revaluations of entire markets. The rise of environmental, social, and governance (ESG) indexes—despite their imperfections—has shown that portfolios attentive to ethics can perform competitively, sometimes even outperforming their conventional peers. These are not accidents of history. They reveal a deeper truth: markets are slower to price moral risk than they are to reward short-term exploitation, and investors who ignore this lag eventually pay for it.

A Mirror of Values

Every pound or dollar invested is a signal. It communicates priorities, sometimes more honestly than words do. We may pride ourselves on progressive values, yet hold shares in companies whose practices contradict them. Our investments, like our consumption habits, are mirrors of what we truly endorse. If money is speech, then portfolios are essays written in numbers, silently declaring what we deem acceptable or intolerable.

The parallels with ethical consumerism are striking. Boycotts, climate strikes, and anti-sweatshop movements have shown how social pressure can alter corporate behaviour faster than regulators often manage. Capital allocation works on an even grander scale. Pension funds, endowments, and even modest individual investors, when their assets are pooled, exert influence disproportionate to their size. The question is no longer whether money reflects values, but which values it will reflect, and with what consequences.

Navigating the Ethical Terrain

Yet acknowledging this truth is not the same as knowing how to act on it. Ethical investing has become a domain crowded with jargon, competing frameworks, and well-meaning but inconsistent metrics. ESG, impact, values-based, sustainable—each term promises clarity but often breeds confusion. The alphabet soup of ratings, with their opaque methodologies, can obscure more than they illuminate. Regulation, too, is evolving unevenly, with the European Union pressing ahead with taxonomies and disclosure rules while other jurisdictions lag. For investors, the challenge is not merely to select a label but to develop a framework that is personally coherent, strategically resilient, and resistant to marketing gloss.

This book does not offer a checklist of "good" and "bad" investments, nor does it suggest a single definition of what conscience in capital must mean. Instead, it equips readers to interrogate the terrain with greater clarity, to discern the strengths and limits of existing frameworks, and to move beyond labels toward a more rigorous and personal alignment of money and morality.

The Moral Margin

The heart of this argument rests on understanding risk differently. Reputational damage, environmental liability, exploitative labour practices—these are not merely ethical failings. They are latent financial liabilities. They may not appear in quarterly reports, but they lurk beneath the balance sheet, waiting to surface. Markets, obsessed with the near term, consistently misprice such slow-burning threats. For the patient investor, this creates opportunity: aligning with ethics is not just a matter of virtue, but of prudence.

The looming carbon bubble illustrates this perfectly. Vast fossil fuel reserves sit on the books of major corporations as assets, yet if the world honours its climate commitments, many of these reserves will never be extracted. They will become stranded, turning today's wealth into tomorrow's liability. Here, the moral imperative and the financial calculus converge. To dismiss conscience in this case is to ignore a risk that could dwarf many of the shocks markets currently fear.

The Psychology of Conscience and Capital

But if the economic case is strong, why do so many investors resist aligning their portfolios with their principles? The answer lies partly in psychology. Humans are adept at compartmentalising. We drive electric cars but invest in oil majors. We decry labour abuses but hold fast-fashion shares. This cognitive dissonance allows us to preserve self-image while avoiding discomfort. Add to this the phenomenon of moral licensing—where token acts of virtue are used to justify broader inaction—and it becomes clear why greenwashing thrives. Ethical investing, to be meaningful, must contend with these biases and habits, not just market data.

This book therefore insists on the importance of designing not just better financial strategies, but better behavioural ones. Bringing investments into harmony with conscience requires more than information; it requires deliberate practice, new habits, and the courage to confront one's own contradictions.

Lessons from History

There is reassurance, however, in recognising that this struggle is not new. Long before ESG became a buzzword, religious communities and reformers wrestled with how to align money with morality. Quakers and abolitionists refused to profit from the slave trade. Campaigners against apartheid pressured investors to divest from South Africa. Public health advocates confronted tobacco giants with the power of capital withdrawal. Each of these cases reminds us that ethics often precede economics: what society deems intolerable eventually reshapes markets, though not without resistance.

History's lesson is twofold. First, values-based investing is not a modern fad but a recurring force in financial history. Second, ignoring the moral undercurrents of capital is rarely costless in the long term. Investors who wait for regulators or markets to catch up often discover that conscience has already begun to compound elsewhere.

The Instruments of Conscience

Today, investors have tools at their disposal that past reformers could scarcely imagine. Green bonds finance renewable infrastructure. Socially oriented exchange-traded funds allow broad, accessible participation. Shareholder activism has demonstrated that even minority stakes can push corporate behemoths to change direction. Community and local investing channels capital into places overlooked by global markets, marrying impact with return. The range of instruments available reflects not just innovation, but demand: investors are asking for ways to invest without leaving their conscience at the door.

The Company's Response

Corporations, too, are adjusting—sometimes reluctantly, sometimes proactively. Shareholder resolutions, activist campaigns, and reputational pressures have forced boards to treat ethical issues as core financial concerns. The cost of inaction is visible in declining market valuations, consumer boycotts, and mounting regulatory scrutiny. Intangible reputation has become a tangible balance sheet item, shaping valuations as surely as factories or patents once did. The old doctrine that boards need only maximise shareholder value is being reshaped into a broader fiduciary duty—one that recognises ethical concerns as inseparable from financial performance.

Building a Framework

Against this backdrop, the purpose of this book is practical. It offers readers a framework for clarifying their own values, ranking their non-negotiables, and translating abstract principles into concrete portfolio decisions. It does not shy away from dilemmas: when the most ethical choice appears less profitable, when small local impact conflicts with global scale, when imperfect companies seek investment while making incremental progress. These are not reasons to abandon conscience, but invitations to exercise it more thoughtfully.

The task is not easy, but nor is it insurmountable. Just as compounding interest rewards patience, so too does compounding conscience reward consistency. Every decision, however small, builds momentum. Over time, aligned capital does more than preserve wealth; it reshapes it, embedding values into the very architecture of future markets.

A Promise of Clarity

This book is written in the conviction that ethical investing is neither sentimental nor utopian. It is, when done rigorously, both rational and transformative. Its aim is not to prescribe a single set of values but to equip you, the reader, with the clarity to align your capital with your conscience without sacrificing prosperity. It is an invitation to look at wealth not only as a store of value but as a statement of values, to recognise that the future of finance will be written not only in profit and loss but in the principles it chooses to uphold.

Conscience compounds. Not automatically, and not without effort, but reliably when paired with discipline, patience, and clarity. The wealth built on such a foundation is more than numerical—it is durable, defensible, and, ultimately, meaningful.

Chapter 1
The False Trade-Off

The story of modern investing is littered with a single, stubborn idea: that to bring conscience into finance is to invite compromise. This assumption, that ethical choices must inevitably lower returns, has been repeated so often it has hardened into orthodoxy. It shapes conversations in boardrooms, whispers through pension trustee meetings, and echoes in the disclaimers attached to socially responsible funds. It is a myth so entrenched that many investors dismiss values-driven finance before ever examining its evidence. Yet myths, however persistent, eventually encounter reality, and reality tells a different story.

The belief that values erode returns rests on a narrow view of how profit is generated. It assumes that companies can isolate financial outcomes from their social and environmental impacts, that the ledger of costs and benefits is sealed within quarterly earnings. But financial history is littered with evidence that morality and markets are more entangled than sceptics admit. Consider the trajectory of the tobacco industry. For decades it delivered staggering profits, defended by powerful lobbies and deeply ingrained cultural habits. Yet the long arc of medical science, regulatory tightening, and shifting social attitudes turned those same profits into liabilities. Litigation costs mounted, reputational capital crumbled, and an industry once untouchable became a pariah, shrinking in value as conscience caught up with capital. To describe ethical considerations as external to financial performance is, therefore, to ignore how markets actually evolve.

This is where ESG indexes complicate the old narrative. Their track record, though imperfect and often overstated, challenges the assumption of weaker returns. Numerous studies show that portfolios weighted towards environmental, social, and governance criteria perform on par with, and in many cases slightly better than, their traditional counterparts. The resilience of ESG funds during downturns has been particularly striking, suggesting that what looks like a concession to principle is often an unrecognised form of risk management. Investors who exclude polluting industries, for example, are not simply expressing virtue; they are pre-emptively insulating themselves from regulatory crackdowns, lawsuits, and consumer revolts. What detractors dismiss as moral indulgence often proves to be pragmatic foresight.

Why, then, does the myth of lower returns endure? Partly because it is psychologically comforting. It permits a convenient detachment: investors can tell themselves that conscience is incompatible with serious wealth-building and so avoid confronting uncomfortable contradictions in their own portfolios. But it also survives because the financial industry has for too long promoted a binary framing of the debate: profit versus principles, as though investors were forced to choose between mutually exclusive goods. This binary trap is seductive because it simplifies decision-making. Either one is pragmatic and profit-driven, or principled and idealistic. Yet reality rarely conforms to such neat dichotomies. The very act of investing already embeds values—choices about industries, practices, and futures deemed worthy of capital. To deny this is to accept the default ethic of maximisation at all costs, an ethic that carries its own moral commitments, however unacknowledged.

The problem with binary thinking is not just that it distorts perception, but that it blinds investors to hidden risks and overlooked opportunities. A company delivering high returns by exploiting labour may look attractive today, but if consumer outrage or regulatory intervention shifts tomorrow, those returns can evaporate. Likewise, a renewable energy start-up may seem speculative in its early years, but if cultural momentum, technological innovation, and public policy converge, its growth can outpace legacy competitors. By insisting on a false choice between conscience and capital, investors often misprice both the dangers of short-term exploitation and the rewards of long-term responsibility. The binary trap does not merely oversimplify; it misleads.

History provides ample evidence of what happens when markets underestimate the force of ethics. Asbestos was once hailed as a miracle material, cheap, versatile, and seemingly indispensable. For decades it enriched those who mined, manufactured, and marketed it. Then came the revelation of its health consequences: mesothelioma, asbestosis, lung cancer. The industry that had once seemed untouchable collapsed under the weight of lawsuits and regulatory bans. Similarly, fossil fuels, the backbone of industrial growth for over a century, now face mounting scrutiny as the realities of climate change bear down. Stranded assets—oil reserves that cannot be burned without catastrophic consequences—hang like shadows over balance sheets. What was once a source of assured prosperity has become a zone of extraordinary uncertainty. The pattern is clear: industries built on practices society later judges unacceptable eventually confront not just ethical condemnation but material decline.

This is not to claim that every ethically questionable enterprise will collapse, nor that every values-driven initiative will thrive. Markets are complex, subject to contingencies no framework can fully predict. But to ignore the recurring pattern of collapse is to risk repeating it. Investors who clung to tobacco stocks long after the tide had turned, or who refused to divest from asbestos until bankruptcy was inevitable, paid dearly for mistaking short-term profitability for enduring value. The lesson is that markets are slow to price moral risk, and those who align their strategies earlier often avoid compounded losses later.

To see this clearly requires a new lens—one that treats conscience not as a sentimental overlay but as an analytic tool. This lens recognises that markets, left to their own devices, are often myopic. They reward exploitation in the present and only later, sometimes decades later, reckon with its costs. Investors who rely solely on traditional measures of performance are, therefore, often ill-equipped to anticipate these shifts. Conscience, in this context, becomes a form of foresight. It identifies where societal pressure, regulatory action, and scientific discovery are likely to converge into financial consequences. It treats values as signals of future risk and opportunity, not distractions from them.

Such a reframing does not absolve investors of hard choices. There will still be moments when an industry's profitability collides with one's ethical boundaries, when patience is required, or when compromises must be weighed. But it does reposition the debate. No longer is it a contest between heart and head, virtue and pragmatism. Instead, it is an invitation to see capital as inseparable from the values that shape its trajectory. To invest without this awareness is to risk being blindsided; to invest with it is to accept that conscience compounds, just as returns do, over time.

The chapters that follow will dismantle the false trade-off more thoroughly, examining why the myth persists, how binary thinking distorts perception, and what lessons investors can draw from industries that collapsed under the weight of their own moral contradictions. More importantly, they will argue that ethical clarity is not a luxury but a necessity—a way of future-proofing wealth against the inevitability of moral reckoning. By the end of this exploration, it should be clear that the supposed choice between profit and principle is not only misleading but dangerous. The true risk lies not in aligning with conscience, but in ignoring it until it is too late.

The Myth of Lower Returns

Few ideas in finance have proved as resilient as the conviction that ethical choices carry a financial penalty. Suggest to a traditional investor that divesting from fossil fuels, armaments, or tobacco might enhance rather than erode long-term returns, and the reaction is often one of scepticism, if not outright dismissal. The presumption runs deep: moral restraint narrows opportunity, and narrower opportunity must inevitably lead to diminished gain. It is a belief shaped by decades of financial orthodoxy and reinforced by a culture that has long regarded markets as amoral mechanisms. Yet when this belief is interrogated with evidence, history, and logic, it reveals itself to be not a universal law but a convenient fiction.

The roots of this myth lie partly in how markets are framed. For much of the twentieth century, the dominant narrative in corporate finance held that the sole responsibility of a company was to maximise shareholder value. Ethical considerations were to be managed outside the ledger—left to governments, charities, or individuals. Within such a paradigm, any deviation from profit-maximisation appeared as a dilution of purpose. If a fund manager excluded lucrative sectors on ethical grounds, the rationale seemed emotional rather than economic. Even the language of "socially responsible investing" was interpreted by many as a form of charity: worthy, perhaps, but financially indulgent. What this view neglected was how thoroughly financial outcomes are entangled with social and environmental dynamics. To dismiss ethics as external to profit is to misunderstand the very conditions under which profit is created and sustained.

The tobacco industry offers a telling case. For decades, tobacco companies delivered consistent dividends and reliable growth. On paper, there was no rational case for exclusion; the products were addictive, demand was stable, and lobbying ensured political protection. But the ethical questions surrounding smoking did not remain external for long. Mounting evidence of health harms led to litigation costs in the billions, escalating regulation, advertising bans, and reputational collapse. What looked like steady profitability in the short term became, over decades, a declining proposition. The ethical critique, dismissed initially as moralism, eventually revealed itself as financial foresight. Investors who had divested early were not sacrificing returns—they were sidestepping liabilities.

This pattern has repeated itself across industries. Asbestos, once a staple of construction, was lauded for its versatility and durability. But the medical consequences—lung cancer, mesothelioma—turned its apparent strength into fatal weakness. Companies once profitable became mired in lawsuits, bankruptcies, and bans. Fossil fuels, the industrial powerhouse of the modern world, now confront a similar reckoning. Oil and coal reserves booked as assets may never be exploited if climate targets are to be met. These stranded assets, combined with shifting consumer behaviour and regulatory pressure, suggest that what once guaranteed prosperity may soon represent risk. Here, again, the ethical critique of carbon dependency is not simply a moral plea—it is an economic warning.

The rise of environmental, social, and governance (ESG) investing has brought empirical weight to the dismantling of the myth. ESG funds, though often maligned for inconsistency in measurement, have consistently demonstrated that aligning capital with ethical considerations need not harm returns. Indeed, a substantial body of research shows that ESG portfolios have performed comparably to, and in many cases outperformed, traditional benchmarks. During periods of market stress, they have displayed greater resilience. The financial crisis of 2008, and more recently the volatility of the COVID-19 pandemic, revealed that companies attentive to governance, environmental stewardship, and social responsibility were better positioned to withstand shocks. What had been dismissed as an ethical premium turned out to function as a form of risk insurance.

It is worth asking why these results surprise so many. The assumption of lower returns rests on a narrow, short-termist definition of profitability. If an investor looks only at the immediate earnings generated by a company, ethical exclusions will indeed appear as foregone opportunities. But if one broadens the horizon to account for litigation risk, regulatory change, shifting consumer expectations, and reputational fragility, the picture alters dramatically. Companies that profit by externalising costs—whether through pollution, unsafe labour, or deceptive practices—are not avoiding costs altogether. They are simply deferring them, shifting them onto society in ways that eventually resurface as financial liabilities. Ethical investors, by anticipating these liabilities, are not reducing opportunity but refining it, distinguishing between ephemeral profit and sustainable value.

Historic divestment movements illustrate this dynamic with clarity. The campaign against apartheid South Africa in the 1980s is often remembered for its moral stance, but its financial logic is equally instructive. Companies operating in South Africa faced boycotts, sanctions, and reputational harm that compromised their global competitiveness. Universities, pension funds, and sovereign wealth vehicles that divested were not simply expressing virtue; they were managing exposure to political risk and reputational contagion. When apartheid eventually fell, those who had aligned capital with conscience found themselves vindicated both morally and financially. Similarly, divestment from the tobacco industry, once derided as symbolic, reshaped valuations by increasing the cost of capital for tobacco firms and signalling the direction of regulatory pressure. The combination of ethical conviction and financial prudence generated outcomes stronger than either could alone.

Of course, critics of ESG and ethical investing raise legitimate questions. They argue that the methodologies behind ESG ratings are inconsistent, that funds sometimes exclude profitable industries without clear standards, and that ethical screens can create concentration risk by narrowing the investable universe. These critiques cannot be dismissed; they highlight the immaturity of measurement frameworks and the risk of overpromising. Yet they do not restore the myth of lower returns. They merely remind us that ethical investing, like all investing, requires discernment, scrutiny, and adaptation. Poorly designed strategies will underperform, just as conventional funds can. The question is not whether ethics inherently drag on returns, but whether investors are willing to integrate them with rigour rather than rhetoric.

The persistence of the myth is also cultural. Finance has long cultivated an image of itself as value-neutral, concerned only with numbers, ratios, and returns. To admit that conscience may be a driver of profit is to blur the line between morality and markets, a boundary many professionals have been trained to defend. Yet this boundary is more illusion than reality. The very idea of shareholder value is itself a value judgement: a decision to prioritise one constituency over others. Once recognised, it becomes harder to claim that ethics are external to finance. They are already embedded, whether acknowledged or not.

Perhaps the most compelling reason to reject the myth is the logic of compounding itself. Returns are not generated in isolation but over time, across shifting landscapes of risk and opportunity. An investment that appears optimal today may become untenable tomorrow if built on practices that society will not tolerate indefinitely. Conscience compounds because it anticipates the trajectory of those tolerances. It recognises that what is permissible now may become unacceptable later, and that markets, slow to adjust, will punish laggards. Ethical investing, when disciplined, is not a trade-off but a strategy for resilience. It is a recognition that financial performance and social legitimacy cannot be divorced forever.

The assumption that ethics erode returns has survived not because it is true, but because it has been convenient. It has allowed investors to ignore uncomfortable contradictions, to treat profitability as immune to morality, and to preserve a narrative of markets as neutral engines of wealth. Yet the evidence of history, the performance of ESG portfolios, and the logic of deferred costs all point in the same direction: ethical alignment is not a concession but a source of strength. To persist in the belief that conscience weakens capital is to cling to a myth that serves neither investors nor society. The reality is more demanding, but also more promising: that profit and principle, when woven together with discipline, reinforce each other across time.

The Binary Trap

Few mental models have done more damage to intelligent investing than the insistence that one must choose between profit and principle. The idea that wealth and conscience are adversaries—locked in an unavoidable zero-sum contest—has shaped decades of debate around ethical investing. It is a framing that flatters itself as hard-headed realism, a belief that tough-minded investors know that moral concerns dilute returns, while idealists settle for less. But the "profit versus principles" binary is neither hard-headed nor realistic. It is a distortion that obscures how markets truly operate, blinds investors to long-term risks, and conceals opportunities available only to those willing to think beyond the false dichotomy.

The persistence of this binary owes much to cultural conditioning. For over half a century, business schools, financial media, and corporate boardrooms were steeped in the doctrine of shareholder primacy. The canonical text was Milton Friedman's 1970 proclamation in the New York Times that the sole social responsibility of business was to increase profits. Within that worldview, to consider environmental stewardship, labour conditions, or community welfare was to indulge in "distractions." The binary was simple: maximise returns or compromise them. This reductionist framing became the default lens through which ethical investing was assessed. A pension fund debating divestment from fossil fuels, for example, was cast as weighing moral purity against fiduciary responsibility, as if these were inherently opposed. Yet the simplification hides more than it reveals.

One reason the binary trap endures is that it offers psychological comfort. It simplifies a complex landscape into a single dramatic choice. Investors need not wrestle with ambiguity, conflicting time horizons, or systemic risks; they can dismiss ethical considerations as inherently costly and move on. But this simplification comes at a steep price. By portraying conscience as the enemy of profit, the binary blinds investors to the ways in which ethical lapses become financial liabilities. Reputational scandals, regulatory crackdowns, consumer boycotts—these are not external shocks imposed from nowhere. They are foreseeable consequences of ignoring principles. The binary model treats them as anomalies rather than predictable features of the market's moral gravity.

Take the case of the garment industry. For years, investors enjoyed high margins from fast-fashion retailers reliant on cheap labour in underregulated regions. From the binary perspective, to raise concerns about working conditions was to indulge in moral idealism, inevitably at odds with financial pragmatism. Then came the Rana Plaza disaster in Bangladesh in 2013, where the collapse of a factory building killed over 1,100 workers. What had been dismissed as an external "ethical" concern suddenly translated into lawsuits, regulatory investigations, consumer outrage, and a wave of reputational damage that affected not only the companies sourcing from the building but the sector as a whole. The binary model, by excluding ethical questions from financial analysis, left investors unprepared for the market consequences of exploitation exposed to daylight.

The trap also obscures hidden opportunities. Consider the rapid expansion of renewable energy. For years, clean energy investments were dismissed as idealistic, incapable of competing with established fossil fuel giants. Investors committed to renewables were caricatured as sacrificing profit for principle. Yet those who entered early captured extraordinary growth as costs of solar and wind plummeted, technology improved, and public policy shifted. What appeared to be a moral gamble turned into a financial windfall. The binary framing blinded many to this transition, encouraging them to cling to legacy industries long after their prospects dimmed. By forcing investors to see profit and principle as opposing camps, the binary suppressed recognition of how they can converge.

The influence of binary thinking extends beyond portfolio choices to how investment debates are staged. When university endowments discuss divestment, opponents frequently frame the question as whether students' moral concerns should be allowed to "undermine" financial performance. Rarely is the inverse considered: whether clinging to industries facing ethical and regulatory headwinds might itself undermine returns. When sovereign wealth funds weigh investments in oil-rich states with human rights controversies, critics of divestment depict the decision as politics intruding upon rational finance. Yet they seldom acknowledge that reputational risk, geopolitical instability, and consumer sentiment are themselves financial variables. By defining ethics as external, the binary trap ensures that such risks are under-analysed and underpriced.

Philosophically, the binary rests on an impoverished understanding of value. It assumes that profit is measurable, objective, and real, while principles are subjective, sentimental, and illusory. But this distinction collapses under scrutiny. Profits are not independent of social context; they are shaped by law, culture, and legitimacy. A company may generate profit by exploiting loopholes or externalising costs, but if those practices become politically untenable, the profits evaporate. Principles, far from being ethereal, can determine which revenue streams endure and which collapse. To pretend otherwise is to mistake the current market equilibrium for an eternal law.

The binary trap also thrives on temporal myopia. In the short term, exploitation can indeed appear profitable. Polluting industries may enjoy low costs until regulators intervene. Companies that ignore labour rights may reduce expenses until scandals erupt. In such narrow windows, the binary seems plausible: principles appear costly, profits plentiful. But stretch the horizon and the logic reverses. Ethical lapses compound into crises, while principled strategies build resilience. The binary framing conceals this temporal asymmetry, seducing investors with short-term gains at the expense of long-term viability.

It is not only detractors of ethical investing who fall prey to the binary. Advocates too sometimes reinforce it inadvertently, portraying ethical choices as noble sacrifices, proof that one is willing to accept lower returns for higher values. This posture may be rhetorically satisfying, but it concedes too much to the binary. It affirms that profit and principle are fundamentally at odds, when the evidence shows otherwise. A more productive approach recognises that alignment between the two is neither automatic nor impossible, but contingent on foresight, discipline, and strategy.

The way forward requires rejecting the binary and embracing a more integrated lens. Rather than treating ethics as an optional add-on, investors must recognise them as embedded in financial systems, shaping risk, regulation, and consumer behaviour. This does not mean all ethical investments will outperform, nor that values alone guarantee success. It means that excluding ethics from financial analysis guarantees blindness to material risks and emerging opportunities. Ethical clarity is not a luxury—it is a form of strategic vision.

The binary trap persists because it is easy, but investing has never rewarded simplicity. Markets punish complacency and reward those who see what others ignore. To escape the binary is to acknowledge that profit and principle are not enemies but variables in the same equation, whose interactions define the future of wealth. Investors who remain trapped in outdated dichotomies will misprice assets, underestimate liabilities, and miss transformations already underway. Those who move beyond it will see what the binary obscures: that the deepest risks and the richest opportunities often share the same moral contours.

Case Studies of Collapse

Few lessons are more sobering for investors than watching industries once deemed untouchable fall into structural decline. Tobacco, asbestos, and fossil fuels were not fringe businesses operating on the margins of society; they were at the very heart of global economies, providing steady cash flows, political influence, and apparent immunity from disruption. Yet each, in its own way, illustrates how ethical concerns, when paired with scientific discovery, cultural momentum, and regulatory intervention, can unravel business models that once seemed invincible. These collapses are not mere historical curiosities—they are warnings about how markets misprice moral risk until it becomes unavoidable.

Tobacco provides perhaps the clearest example of how long-term decline can be disguised by short-term profitability. For much of the twentieth century, tobacco was regarded as a financial stalwart. The addictive nature of nicotine provided extraordinary customer loyalty, marketing ingenuity kept brands culturally embedded, and shareholder dividends were among the most reliable in the market. For decades, any suggestion of moral hazard was brushed aside. Investors reassured themselves that as long as demand persisted and governments benefited from tax revenues, tobacco companies would continue to deliver. But science had already begun rewriting the terms of the debate. As early as the 1950s, evidence linking smoking to lung cancer mounted. By the 1990s, litigation in the United States and beyond brought the industry to account, culminating in the Master Settlement Agreement of 1998, which imposed $206 billion in damages over 25 years and strict limits on advertising. The reputational damage was irreparable: tobacco firms became pariahs in many institutional portfolios, excluded from pension funds, endowments, and sovereign wealth strategies. Although the industry still generates profits today, its long-term trajectory is one of contraction, regulatory suffocation, and cultural rejection. Investors who once viewed tobacco as a safe harbour discovered that ethical liabilities can metastasise into enduring financial headwinds.

Asbestos tells a parallel story, though one compressed into a shorter and more catastrophic arc. Marketed for decades as a miracle material—fire-resistant, cheap, and adaptable—its uses spanned construction, automotive, and manufacturing industries worldwide. The financial prospects seemed unassailable. Yet behind this apparent resilience lay an unacknowledged human cost. Medical evidence linked asbestos exposure to mesothelioma, asbestosis, and lung cancer, diseases with devastating latency periods. By the time the science was undeniable, millions of workers had been exposed, and liability claims mounted on an unprecedented scale. The 1982 bankruptcy of Johns-Manville, then the largest asbestos manufacturer in the United States, shocked financial markets. Once a blue-chip stock, the company was overwhelmed by lawsuits, forced into a trust structure that would eventually pay tens of billions to victims. The fallout spread globally as governments banned asbestos use, reputational stigma grew, and companies abandoned the material altogether. Investors who clung to the industry on the assumption that profitability outweighed principle faced catastrophic losses. The asbestos collapse is a stark illustration that profits built on hidden harms cannot be insulated from eventual accountability.

The fossil fuel industry represents the most pressing and contemporary case of collapse-in-progress. For over a century, oil, coal, and gas defined industrial growth, geopolitical power, and shareholder wealth. Few industries commanded more political leverage or infrastructural dependence. The narrative of fossil fuels as indispensable has underpinned trillions in market valuation. Yet climate science and the ethics of intergenerational responsibility have transformed the calculus. If global commitments under the Paris Agreement are honoured, much of the world's proven fossil fuel reserves cannot be extracted without breaching catastrophic warming thresholds. These reserves—currently listed on company balance sheets as assets—risk becoming stranded, their value written down to zero. Analysts estimate that trillions of dollars could be wiped from market capitalisations if decarbonisation accelerates.

The financial implications are already visible. Coal, once the backbone of electricity generation, has entered a secular decline in much of the developed world, driven not only by environmental regulation but also by the rapid cost reduction of renewables. Oil majors, once unquestioned as blue-chip investments, have faced shareholder revolts demanding climate accountability, exemplified by the 2021 Engine No. 1 campaign that secured seats on ExxonMobil's board. Banks and insurers are tightening lending to fossil projects, while sovereign wealth funds such as Norway's have begun large-scale divestments. Public sentiment, too, is shifting: fossil fuels are no longer seen as symbols of progress but as relics of an unsustainable model. The ethical critique—that it is indefensible to profit from destabilising the climate—has merged with financial prudence, reshaping risk assessments across capital markets.

What unites tobacco, asbestos, and fossil fuels is not merely their profitability turned sour, but the mechanism by which decline unfolded. In each case, industries externalised costs—health, safety, or environmental damage—that were initially ignored by markets. Investors convinced themselves that as long as regulation lagged and demand persisted, the profits were secure. What they underestimated was the compounding power of ethics. Once scientific consensus crystallised, once cultural rejection gained momentum, and once regulatory action aligned with public sentiment, the deferred costs returned with multiplied force. *Markets can delay moral reckoning, but they cannot avert it indefinitely.*

These cases also reveal a subtler truth: decline rarely arrives as a sudden collapse. Tobacco companies continued to post profits long after health risks were publicised. Asbestos remained in widespread use for decades after dangers were identified. Oil and gas firms still dominate energy markets despite decades of climate research. This lag fosters complacency. Investors mistake delayed consequences for permanent immunity, convincing themselves that ethical critiques are irrelevant to balance sheets. Yet the eventual revaluation, when it comes, is often brutal. The decline of asbestos was abrupt once lawsuits reached critical mass. Tobacco's long contraction has been financially painful for late divestors. Fossil fuels may yet face a disorderly transition if policy and technological shifts converge faster than markets anticipate.

For investors, the lesson is not to romanticise principle as a guarantee of financial reward, but to recognise that ethical concerns function as early warning systems. They flag risks long before traditional financial analysis does. By the time regulation, litigation, or consumer revolt materialises, much of the damage is already priced in. Those who heed the warnings early avoid compounded losses; those who dismiss them as irrelevant often discover they were staring at material risk all along. *Ethics, in this sense, are not externalities but predictive signals of where value will erode and where it will endure.*

The collapses of tobacco, asbestos, and fossil fuels demonstrate that industries built on harms society cannot tolerate indefinitely are inherently unstable. Profitability does not shield them from accountability; it merely delays the reckoning. For the discerning investor, these cases are not cautionary tales from a bygone era but templates for identifying future vulnerabilities. The question is not whether conscience will compound into financial consequence, but how quickly—and whether one's portfolio is prepared for that inevitability.

Why Investors Need a New Lens

Markets pride themselves on efficiency, on the notion that prices reflect all available information and adjust rapidly when conditions change. Yet history repeatedly shows that they are slow to account for one particular category of risk: the moral consequences of business practices. Ethical liabilities do not appear neatly on quarterly statements, nor are they modelled with the precision of currency fluctuations or commodity prices. They simmer below the surface, ignored by those convinced they are immaterial, until suddenly they erupt into regulatory upheaval, consumer backlash, or legal catastrophe. Investors who dismiss such risks often find themselves holding assets that erode quietly at first and then collapse swiftly, their losses magnified by the delay in recognition. *Moral risk, like interest, compounds over time; the difference is that it compounds against rather than in favour of the inattentive.*

The tendency to discount moral risk stems from the time horizons built into modern markets. Fund managers judged on quarterly performance, analysts issuing twelve-month price targets, and corporate executives incentivised by annual bonuses all share an inherent bias towards the immediate. In this compressed frame, an industry exploiting cheap labour or externalising environmental costs may look efficient, even exemplary. What is harder to capture in spreadsheets is how these practices generate liabilities that accrue invisibly until they manifest in lawsuits, boycotts, or regulatory bans. Because the timing of such events is uncertain, markets often treat them as remote possibilities rather than inevitabilities. This underpricing persists until the evidence becomes undeniable, by which time the losses have already been baked in.

Consider the trajectory of the opioid crisis in the United States. For years, pharmaceutical companies generating enormous revenues from addictive painkillers were lauded by analysts for their growth. Warnings from public health officials and community advocates were treated as external to financial analysis, relevant to policymakers but not to investors. Yet when lawsuits multiplied and settlements reached into the tens of billions, valuations fell sharply. The companies did not become riskier overnight; the risk had been there all along, simply ignored. What markets belatedly recognised was that the profits were built on a foundation of harm that could not be sustained indefinitely. Investors relying on traditional lenses were caught off guard, while those attentive to moral risk saw the liabilities looming years before they materialised.

The same lag can be seen in the fossil fuel sector. Climate science has for decades demonstrated the dangers of unmitigated carbon emissions. Activists, scientists, and forward-looking policymakers warned that a significant portion of proven reserves could never be burned if catastrophic warming was to be avoided. Yet markets persisted in valuing oil and coal companies as if those reserves were guaranteed assets. Only recently, as stranded asset risk became impossible to ignore, have investors begun revaluing these firms downward. Even so, large swathes of the financial industry continue to act as though climate liabilities are speculative, rather than structural. This lag represents a collective failure of imagination: the inability to see that ethical constraints on extraction are not abstract ideals but concrete determinants of future cash flows.

One reason investors need a new lens is that traditional financial metrics often disguise moral risk by externalising it. A balance sheet records revenues and expenses but not the health costs imposed on communities, the carbon emitted into the atmosphere, or the human suffering embedded in supply chains. Yet these externalities are not costless; they are simply deferred. When governments tighten regulations, when consumers mobilise, or when courts impose damages, those costs migrate back onto the company's accounts, often in magnified form. Treating them as irrelevant because they are not yet quantified is not rational analysis but wilful blindness. The new lens requires recognising that what is excluded from financial statements may matter more than what is included.

Critics often argue that investors should focus on what is measurable and leave moral considerations to policymakers. But this stance rests on a misunderstanding of how policy itself evolves. Political action rarely emerges spontaneously; it is driven by shifting public sentiment, activism, and the gradual erosion of legitimacy for harmful practices. By the time regulation is enacted, the underlying ethical critique has usually been building for years. Investors who wait for laws to codify risks are already late. Those who track cultural momentum—whether the rise of climate strikes, consumer boycotts, or campaigns against sweatshops—can anticipate the regulatory wave before it breaks. *Moral risk is not noise at the margins; it is often the leading indicator of where policy and markets will converge.*

It is also crucial to recognise that the failure to price moral risk is not neutral—it actively redistributes value. When a company profits by externalising costs, those profits are sustained by pushing liabilities onto workers, communities, or the environment. Investors benefit in the short term, but only by assuming that those costs will never return. History shows otherwise. Tobacco companies externalised healthcare costs until lawsuits forced reimbursement. Asbestos producers externalised worker safety until litigation bankrupted them. Fossil fuel firms continue to externalise climate costs, but the bill is already arriving through floods, wildfires, and droughts that are transforming insurance markets and infrastructure spending. The redistribution is temporary; the reckoning is inevitable. A new lens insists on accounting for these hidden transfers before they ricochet back as losses.

The implications extend beyond risk management to opportunity recognition. Just as markets are slow to penalise harmful practices, they are often slow to reward businesses aligned with emerging ethical priorities. Renewable energy, plant-based proteins, fair-trade goods—each began as niche sectors dismissed as uncompetitive. Investors who recognised that cultural momentum, regulatory incentives, and technological innovation would eventually converge on these industries captured outsized returns. Here too the new lens provides an edge: by identifying where moral and market forces reinforce each other, it highlights opportunities invisible to those clinging to the old binary of profit versus principle.

The philosophical underpinning of this shift is straightforward but profound: value is not merely a financial construct, it is a social one. Markets assign prices, but societies assign legitimacy, and the two are inseparably linked. A company can generate impressive profits, but if its social licence erodes, those profits will not endure. Legitimacy is intangible until it is lost, at which point its absence devastates valuations. The new lens treats legitimacy as a core asset, not a peripheral concern, recognising that it determines both the sustainability of profits and the durability of wealth.

Investors who resist this perspective often do so out of habit rather than evidence. The efficient market hypothesis, though powerful in certain contexts, does not absolve one from considering risks that markets are demonstrably slow to price. Efficiency does not mean omniscience; it means consensus. If the consensus overlooks moral risk, the market will underprice it until reality forces adjustment. The question is whether an investor prefers to be part of that late adjustment, or to anticipate it and position accordingly.

The demand for a new lens is not an appeal to sentimentality but to discipline. It requires expanding the analytical frame to include variables traditionally dismissed as intangible, recognising that those variables—public trust, cultural legitimacy, ethical accountability—shape financial outcomes as decisively as interest rates or inflation. It demands a longer horizon, one that sees beyond the next quarter to the compounding effects of deferred costs. And it insists on humility: the recognition that markets, for all their power, are often the last to acknowledge what societies have already decided is intolerable.

Investors who continue to operate with outdated lenses risk repeating the mistakes of the past: overestimating industries that appear profitable because their harms are hidden, and underestimating the resilience of enterprises aligned with societal values. Those who adopt a new lens—one that treats moral risk as material, legitimacy as a core asset, and conscience as a form of foresight—will not only protect themselves from compounded losses but also position themselves to capture the wealth that emerges when principle and profit converge.

Chapter 2
Capital as a Mirror of Values

Few forces in modern life reveal priorities as starkly as money. We may profess one set of values in conversation, display another in consumption, and yet embed an entirely different set in the way we allocate capital. A portfolio, unlike rhetoric, cannot be persuaded, embellished, or selectively edited; it is a ledger of choices that reveals what an individual or institution ultimately endorses. This does not mean that every investor sets out consciously to fund or withhold from particular industries. But it does mean that whether intentional or not, capital is always a signal. Where money flows, legitimacy follows. Where it retreats, industries falter. In this sense, financial markets are not neutral arenas but mirrors—reflecting, amplifying, and sometimes distorting the values of those who participate in them.

That capital sends signals is not merely a metaphor; it is observable in the way industries respond to patterns of allocation. When institutional investors divested from South Africa during apartheid, they were not merely making symbolic gestures. They were raising the cost of capital for companies complicit in the system, shrinking their access to global finance, and forcing boards to reconsider the risks of maintaining operations under political scrutiny. Similarly, the wave of divestments from tobacco, while often framed as moralistic, reduced the social legitimacy of the industry to the point where many firms were unable to recruit graduates from top universities or secure mainstream advertising slots. The signal mattered not only because of the money withdrawn, but because of the reputational shift it conveyed: *this is no longer acceptable, and capital is moving accordingly.* Investors who assume that money is passive overlook the performative power of allocation.

The link between consumption and investment strengthens this claim. Ethical consumerism is now an established phenomenon, with individuals choosing fair-trade coffee, boycotting fast-fashion brands implicated in labour abuses, or shifting to electric vehicles in response to climate concerns. These choices, while individually modest, accumulate into market shifts that reshape supply chains and corporate strategy. Yet consumer choices pale in comparison to the influence of investment capital. Where a single purchase influences a day's revenue, an allocation of millions to or away from a sector affects valuations, lending capacity, and strategic direction for years. Ethical investing is the logical extension of ethical consumerism, magnifying the same logic: when enough individuals and institutions reallocate, industries are reshaped more swiftly than regulation alone could manage.

Examples abound. Renewable energy, once dismissed as uncompetitive, has surged not only because of technological improvements but because investors reallocated trillions away from coal and oil, signalling confidence in clean energy's future. This reallocation accelerated cost declines by financing scale, thereby hastening the very competitiveness that sceptics doubted. Similarly, companies implicated in supply chain abuses have found themselves subject to activist pressure not only from consumers but from investors filing shareholder resolutions or threatening divestment. The mechanism is the same: capital moves towards what it deems viable and acceptable, leaving behind industries whose practices carry mounting liabilities. Regulation often follows this shift, codifying into law what capital has already begun to enforce through allocation.

Cultural momentum amplifies these dynamics, pushing investors to reconsider where they place their capital. Movements such as #MeToo, climate strikes, and anti-sweatshop campaigns were not confined to street protests or social media hashtags; they penetrated boardrooms and investment committees. After #MeToo, companies facing revelations of harassment or toxic culture saw not only public backlash but stock volatility, as investors recalibrated governance risk. Climate strikes heightened awareness that younger generations viewed fossil fuel expansion as incompatible with a liveable future, prompting pension funds and universities to divest under pressure from their beneficiaries. Anti-sweatshop activism, sustained over decades, shifted apparel companies from indifference to auditing, certification, and in some cases relocation of production. What is striking is not simply that these movements influenced consumer behaviour, but that they altered investor sentiment. When cultural legitimacy collapses, capital flees. *Money does not like uncertainty, and cultural rejection is one of the most destabilising forms of uncertainty an investor can face.*

The influence of individuals in this process is often underestimated. It is tempting to believe that only vast institutional investors can move markets, while individuals are mere spectators. Yet the structure of modern finance belies this assumption. Pension funds, index funds, and mutual funds pool the contributions of millions of individuals, who may never imagine themselves as market participants yet collectively wield enormous power. When university students demand that endowments divest from fossil fuels, or when pensioners challenge their funds' exposure to harmful industries, the aggregated capital of modest contributors becomes a formidable force. The rise of retail investing platforms has only accelerated this leverage, allowing individuals to direct their allocations more consciously and to coalesce around collective demands. An individual may not sway a multinational directly, but the pooled effect of individuals shaping the mandates of large funds absolutely can.

The case for recognising capital as a mirror of values is not rooted in idealism alone but in pragmatic foresight. Investors who deny the signalling function of their money risk underestimating reputational liabilities, regulatory shifts, and cultural turning points that alter valuations. Those who embrace it recognise that every allocation is both a financial choice and a value statement, whether acknowledged or not. To claim neutrality is to accept the prevailing ethic of maximisation at any cost, which is itself a choice with consequences. To act consciously is to acknowledge the leverage inherent in capital and to wield it with intention.

This chapter therefore begins from a simple yet demanding premise: portfolios are not only collections of assets but declarations of values. Whether managed by a global pension fund or held by an individual investor, they reflect and shape the moral architecture of markets. To view them as mere financial instruments is to miss their performative power. The chapters that follow will interrogate how money functions as a signal, how the logic of consumption extends into investment, how cultural movements alter the cost of capital, and how even modest investors exert disproportionate influence. By recognising capital as a mirror of values, we gain not only a clearer picture of ourselves but also a sharper understanding of the market forces that will determine which industries thrive and which collapse.

Money as a Signal

A portfolio speaks louder than a manifesto. We may articulate our principles with eloquence, but the real measure of what we endorse is where our money goes. This is not an abstract moral statement; it is an observable fact of how markets function. Capital is both permission and endorsement. When it flows into a company, it lowers its cost of capital, enables expansion, and signals confidence. When it retreats, it raises costs, restricts growth, and signals rejection. Money, whether placed deliberately or passively, is a form of speech. And unlike words, it leaves a durable imprint on balance sheets, valuations, and corporate strategy.

Investors often underestimate the expressive nature of capital because they view money as neutral. The prevailing assumption is that cash, unlike speech or behaviour, does not carry meaning; it is simply a medium for exchange. Yet in practice, the allocation of capital is deeply interpretive. To invest in a defence contractor is to affirm that one's wealth is aligned with the economics of conflict. To hold shares in a fossil fuel company is to support, however indirectly, a future tied to carbon extraction. To allocate to a renewable energy fund is to advance the transition towards a different energy regime. One may not intend these statements, but they are made nonetheless. *Intent is irrelevant to impact: capital functions as a signal whether or not investors acknowledge it.*

The rise of socially responsible investing underscores this point. When university endowments, pension funds, or sovereign wealth funds announce divestment from certain industries, the dollar value of the withdrawal is often modest relative to global capital markets. Yet the symbolic power is immense. The South African divestment campaign in the 1980s is a case in point. The immediate financial effect on apartheid-era firms was limited, but the reputational damage was devastating. Corporations feared being blacklisted, talent pipelines dried up, and governments took notice. What mattered was not only the absence of money but the message it carried: participation in an immoral system was no longer tolerable. Capital became a megaphone through which values were broadcast, reshaping global political pressure.

This signalling power operates even when investors claim neutrality. Passive index funds, for instance, are often presented as impartial vehicles that simply reflect the market. Yet by virtue of their size, they become some of the largest shareholders in major corporations. Their presence—or silence—on issues like executive pay, climate disclosure, or governance failures sends unmistakable signals to boards. When these funds abstain from pressing for accountability, they tacitly endorse the status quo. Conversely, when they adopt stewardship guidelines, their influence can accelerate change. The myth of neutrality conceals the reality that *every allocation, even passive, is an implicit statement about what deserves capital and what does not.*

The comparison to consumption is illuminating. Ethical consumerism—whether through boycotts, fair-trade purchases, or sustainability choices—has shown how spending habits reflect personal values. Buying organic food or electric vehicles signals endorsement of certain practices, while rejecting products associated with sweatshops or deforestation signals disapproval. But consumption operates on the level of immediate revenue. Investment, by contrast, shapes strategic capacity. A company can weather short-term boycotts if its investors remain loyal, but if its access to capital shrinks, its long-term survival is imperilled. Thus, *investment signals carry deeper weight than consumption signals: they not only express values but alter the structural conditions of business itself.*

The implications for investors are profound. It is tempting to believe that one can separate personal values from financial strategy, keeping morality in the realm of philanthropy and leaving markets to operate in a purely economic register. Yet this separation is illusory. To invest without considering values is to allow the default ethic of profit maximisation at any cost to govern one's capital. Silence, in this context, is not neutrality; it is complicity. Portfolios therefore serve as diagnostic tools: they reveal priorities more candidly than any statement of belief. A portfolio heavily weighted towards extractive industries, for example, speaks volumes about what its holder values in terms of risk tolerance, time horizon, and ethical boundaries, whether they admit it or not.

This is not merely a theoretical point. The reputational risk faced by large institutions illustrates the consequences of ignoring the signalling function of money. When Norway's sovereign wealth fund, one of the world's largest, divested from coal, it was not simply reallocating capital. It was affirming a principle: coal is incompatible with long-term stewardship. Other funds followed, not necessarily because the financial case was immediately compelling but because the reputational cost of holding coal after Norway's exit had risen dramatically. The domino effect was not triggered by regulation but by signalling. A single fund's choice altered the perceived legitimacy of an entire sector.

At the individual level, the same dynamics hold. Retail investors may feel their capital is too modest to carry weight, yet when aggregated through pension systems, index funds, and mutual vehicles, their preferences define entire markets. The shift towards ESG-themed funds reflects not only institutional mandates but also consumer demand from individuals who refuse to separate their values from their portfolios. Each choice, while small, contributes to the momentum that redefines industry norms. Just as consumer boycotts gain strength through collective action, investor choices gain significance through pooling. The cumulative effect is that *individual allocations, multiplied across millions, become signals powerful enough to steer corporate behaviour.*

The expressive role of money also reveals tensions worth acknowledging. Critics argue that signalling through divestment or ESG allocation can be superficial, serving as moral theatre rather than substantive change. If one investor sells fossil fuel shares, another buys them; the company remains funded. Yet this critique overlooks the dynamics of stigma and cost of capital. While ownership shifts hands in any divestment, the marginal price is affected, and as stigma accumulates, entire sectors face rising borrowing costs and falling legitimacy. This, in turn, constrains their ability to expand or retain talent. Even if the immediate financial effect is muted, the long-term structural impact is significant. Signalling is not instantaneous in its consequences, but it compounds over time.

There is also the risk of incoherence. Investors may claim values publicly while holding portfolios that contradict them privately. Corporations face similar hypocrisy when their sustainability reports trumpet climate commitments while their pension plans remain invested in oil majors. This dissonance is not without consequence. Activists and journalists are increasingly adept at exposing the gap between words and allocations. When the revelations surface, reputational damage can exceed any short-term gain. Here again, money is a signal: it betrays dissonance between stated and actual priorities, undermining credibility.

Philosophically, the recognition that money signals values challenges long-standing myths about markets. The myth of neutrality, the myth of value-free profit, the myth that financial activity can be divorced from moral context—all collapse under scrutiny. Markets are not detached from society; they are embedded within it, and capital allocation is one of the most consequential forms of moral expression available. The question for investors is not whether money will send a signal, but which signal it will send, and whether they are comfortable with what it says about them.

Understanding money as a signal also reframes fiduciary duty. Traditionally, fiduciaries were instructed to maximise returns for beneficiaries without regard to extraneous concerns. Yet if values shape long-term risk and opportunity, then ignoring them is itself a breach of duty. Trustees who treat climate risk, labour exploitation, or governance failures as irrelevant are not safeguarding beneficiaries; they are exposing them to compounded losses. A new conception of fiduciary responsibility recognises that money's signalling power is not peripheral but central to prudent stewardship.

Ultimately, the recognition that investments express values requires a shift in mindset. Portfolios are not static collections of financial instruments; they are narratives, telling stories about what their holders endorse, tolerate, or reject. They are visible statements of priorities, carrying weight beyond the spreadsheets that track them. Investors who acknowledge this reality can harness money's signalling function consciously, aligning capital with principle without abandoning prudence. Those who deny it are still sending signals, but unintentionally, leaving their values to be inferred—and often misinterpreted—by the markets that respond to them. *Money will always speak. The only question is whether we are willing to own what it says.*

From Consumption to Allocation

When people think of shaping industries through personal choice, they often picture what they buy: the coffee labelled fair trade, the electric car parked in their driveway, the decision to avoid fast fashion or plastic packaging. These consumption decisions are visible, emotionally resonant, and easier to narrate in everyday life. Yet the influence of consumption, powerful though it may be, pales in comparison to the force exerted through investment. Where spending directs the revenue of a single transaction, investment determines the strategic direction of entire industries. A consumer boycott may damage sales; the reallocation of capital can transform a sector's cost of capital, research budgets, and long-term viability. Ethical consumerism signals preference. Ethical investing determines survival.

The distinction between the two is not simply one of scale, but of mechanism. Consumption decisions are reactive: individuals respond to the goods and services presented to them, rewarding some and rejecting others. Investment decisions are proactive: they shape which products and services come into existence at all. A coffee purchase affirms one supply chain; an investment in a coffee company shapes whether its plantations expand, diversify, or disappear. *Allocation is the upstream counterpart to consumption—it governs not only what is bought but what is possible to buy.* Recognising this relationship is critical for understanding how capital flows can reshape industries faster than regulation, and with more lasting consequences.

The renewable energy sector provides one of the clearest demonstrations of this dynamic. Consumers can choose to install solar panels or subscribe to green energy tariffs, but the affordability and availability of those options depended on decades of capital allocation. Investors poured billions into solar and wind, financing technological improvements and scaling up manufacturing capacity. The result was a dramatic decline in costs, which in turn made renewable energy competitive in markets where regulation lagged. Policymakers later codified these shifts through subsidies and targets, but the decisive momentum came from capital flows that made clean energy commercially viable. Without that investment, consumer demand would have remained aspirational. It is allocation, not regulation alone, that enabled renewables to cross the threshold from niche to mainstream.

The fashion industry offers another example, though in reverse. For years, consumers expressed outrage over sweatshop conditions, unsafe factories, and exploitative wages. Campaigns pressured brands, and scandals like the Rana Plaza collapse in 2013 triggered temporary spikes of attention. Yet systemic change has remained limited, precisely because capital has not followed consumer sentiment with the same force. Private equity firms and investors in fast-fashion giants continue to reward rapid turnover and low costs, financing an economic model that undermines the very reforms consumers demand. This divergence highlights the asymmetry: consumption may voice disapproval, but as long as capital remains aligned with exploitative business models, systemic change stalls. *It is not until investors withdraw or redirect funds that corporations face genuine structural pressure to evolve.*

The tobacco industry shows how allocation can accelerate decline even where regulation moves slowly. Long after smoking bans became common in public places, tobacco companies remained profitable and continued to enjoy loyal consumer bases. What shifted their trajectory was not simply legislation but the withdrawal of institutional capital. Pension funds, sovereign wealth vehicles, and university endowments began divesting, raising the cost of capital and reducing the industry's legitimacy. Banks hesitated to underwrite expansion, talent pipelines dried up, and the reputational stigma of being associated with tobacco spread far beyond consumption choices. What mattered was not whether consumers stopped smoking overnight but whether capital providers signalled that future growth was unacceptable. Allocation changed the terms of viability.

Philosophically, the distinction between consumption and allocation reveals a deeper truth about markets. Both are expressions of values, but they operate on different timelines and with different magnitudes of impact. Consumption expresses values daily, at the level of individual preference. Allocation expresses values over decades, at the level of systemic architecture. A single purchase reflects taste or principle; a portfolio reflects structural endorsement. For this reason, investors cannot meaningfully claim neutrality. To allocate capital without considering ethical consequences is to shape markets unconsciously, often in ways that contradict stated personal or institutional values. Portfolios reveal priorities more starkly than shopping baskets because they expose what an individual or institution is willing to underwrite for the long term.

The interplay between consumption and allocation also creates feedback loops. When enough consumers adopt sustainable products, investors see growth potential and direct capital accordingly, accelerating the scaling of new industries. Conversely, when capital flows into certain sectors, it lowers costs and expands availability, making ethical consumption easier for individuals. Electric vehicles illustrate this dynamic. Early adopters were limited by high costs and lack of infrastructure, but as investors financed battery technology, charging networks, and production facilities, prices fell and accessibility increased. Today, the transition to electric transport is no longer confined to niche markets but represents a mainstream shift—one catalysed by capital but reinforced by consumer adoption.

Cultural movements often bridge the gap between consumption and allocation, pressuring investors to act where consumer activism alone falls short. The climate strike movement, led by students, mobilised public sentiment and consumer awareness, but its enduring impact came when institutional investors began divesting from coal and pressuring oil majors to disclose carbon risks. #MeToo, though originating in social activism, reshaped how investors assessed governance risk and workplace culture, leading to shareholder resolutions and leadership changes in companies implicated. These movements succeed not only in altering what people buy but in compelling capital providers to reconsider what they fund. *The shift from consumption to allocation marks the difference between symbolic protest and structural change.*

Critics sometimes argue that investment-driven change is illusory, pointing out that divested assets are often bought by less scrupulous investors, leaving companies funded regardless. Yet this critique misunderstands how capital markets respond to stigma. Even if assets are reallocated, the marginal price is affected. Companies facing sustained divestment experience higher borrowing costs, reduced market confidence, and declining ability to recruit talent. Over time, these pressures compound, reshaping strategy. In this sense, the act of allocation is not merely financial but reputational. It signals to boards, regulators, and society at large that certain practices are no longer tolerated, shifting incentives for adaptation.

The lesson for investors is not that consumption is irrelevant but that it is incomplete without allocation. To buy ethically sourced products while investing in companies that undermine those very values is to undercut one's own influence. Conversely, aligning consumption with allocation magnifies impact, creating coherence between daily choices and long-term capital flows. For institutions, the stakes are even higher: their investment decisions can accelerate industrial transitions more decisively than most policy interventions. For individuals, the power lies in recognising that their pooled capital—through pensions, funds, or savings vehicles—shapes markets whether they choose consciously or not.

Ultimately, the parallel between ethical consumerism and ethical investing underscores the primacy of capital as a driver of change. Regulation matters, but it is slow, contested, and often reactive. Capital allocation, by contrast, is immediate, dynamic, and cumulative. Where it flows, innovation accelerates; where it retreats, decline hastens. Ethical consumption may raise awareness, but ethical allocation builds futures. Investors who recognise this distinction understand that every pound, dollar, or euro they allocate is not just a financial choice but a structural one—a decision about which industries will thrive, which will adapt, and which will be left behind.

Cultural Momentum

Markets like to imagine themselves as self-contained systems governed by efficiency and rational calculation. Prices, we are told, move on fundamentals: earnings forecasts, interest rates, supply and demand. Yet history shows that markets are not insulated from society's moral pulse. They absorb, amplify, and respond to cultural currents in ways that can dramatically alter the value of entire industries. The most powerful shocks to corporate behaviour in recent decades did not originate with regulators or economists but with social movements. Climate strikes, #MeToo, and anti-sweatshop campaigns began as expressions of collective conscience, but they matured into forces that reshaped investor sentiment and corporate governance. What begins in the streets or online can migrate rapidly to boardrooms and balance sheets. *Cultural momentum is not noise outside the market; it is a driver within it.*

The climate movement illustrates this dynamic vividly. For decades, climate science warned of existential risks, yet markets priced fossil fuel companies as if their reserves were unassailable assets. What shifted the calculation was not a sudden revelation of data but the crescendo of cultural mobilisation. The student-led climate strikes and campaigns like Fridays for Future reframed climate change from an abstract environmental concern into a generational moral demand. Pension funds, university endowments, and asset managers faced direct pressure from their beneficiaries: why should we profit from an industry undermining our future? As divestment campaigns grew, investor sentiment shifted. The cost of capital for coal producers rose, oil companies faced mounting shareholder resolutions, and insurers began refusing to underwrite new projects. Here, cultural energy translated into financial revaluation. The signal was not only that carbon-heavy assets posed environmental risks but that their legitimacy as investments was eroding.

The #MeToo movement followed a different trajectory but produced similar market consequences. Initially catalysed by high-profile allegations in media and entertainment, the movement quickly expanded to encompass systemic workplace harassment across industries. For investors, this was not simply a moral awakening but a governance crisis. Companies implicated in scandals faced leadership upheavals, reputational damage, and in some cases stock declines as lawsuits and regulatory investigations mounted. Boards were forced to reconsider how culture, long dismissed as an intangible, could become a financial liability. Investors who had previously regarded social issues as peripheral to financial analysis found themselves recalibrating risk models: *to ignore workplace culture was to misprice governance risk.* Shareholder proposals demanding diversity disclosures, harassment policies, and cultural audits gained traction. Capital began to enforce what culture had already declared: tolerance of misconduct was incompatible with long-term value creation.

Anti-sweatshop activism, while older, offers a parallel story. Campaigns in the 1990s exposed the labour conditions behind major apparel brands, from child labour to unsafe factories. Initially dismissed as activist noise, these campaigns escalated into reputational crises for companies reliant on low-cost outsourcing. Consumers boycotted, but more importantly, investors began questioning whether companies entangled in labour scandals faced sustainable growth prospects. After the Rana Plaza disaster in 2013, which killed more than 1,100 garment workers, the pressure intensified. Investor coalitions demanded supply chain transparency and auditing, recognising that reputational damage could erode brand value and profitability. Funds that had previously overlooked such risks began screening for labour practices, not out of charity but out of recognition that *ethical lapses were material risks.* Again, cultural mobilisation prefigured financial revaluation.

What unites these cases is the way cultural energy transformed the definition of fiduciary responsibility. Investors who once claimed that their sole duty was to maximise returns could no longer ignore how social legitimacy shapes financial outcomes. A pension fund ignoring climate activism risked stranded assets; an asset manager overlooking harassment scandals risked governance collapse; a brand investor indifferent to labour abuses risked reputational contagion. Fiduciary duty itself was reinterpreted, not by statute but by social momentum, to encompass a broader understanding of risk. Cultural movements did not merely demand change; they altered the calculus of prudence.

This raises a crucial point: cultural momentum often moves faster than regulation. Legislators are slow, constrained by political compromise and lobbying. Cultural movements, by contrast, mobilise rapidly, spread globally, and reframe narratives in ways regulation cannot match. Investors who wait for law to catch up find themselves already exposed. By the time governments legislate carbon disclosures, much of the market has already priced in the stigma of carbon-heavy portfolios. By the time regulators mandate workplace harassment reporting, investors have already pressured boards to act. *Cultural legitimacy is often the earliest and most accurate signal of where regulation will eventually land.*

Critics sometimes argue that markets should remain insulated from social movements, that to let culture dictate capital allocation is to politicise finance. Yet this critique ignores that markets have always been political, always embedded in social norms. What changed is that cultural scrutiny has grown sharper, globalised by digital platforms, and more willing to link consumption and investment. A scandal once confined to local newspapers can now trigger global divestment campaigns within days. Investors who resist this reality are not defending neutrality but clinging to a fiction. Neutrality in the face of cultural momentum is simply delayed recognition of risks others already see.

There is also a positive dimension. Cultural momentum does not only penalise; it creates opportunity. Companies that anticipate cultural demands—by investing in clean energy, building inclusive workplaces, or ensuring ethical supply chains—gain reputational advantages that translate into financial resilience. Tesla, though volatile, captured disproportionate investor enthusiasm in part because it symbolised alignment with climate aspirations. Unilever gained credibility with investors by embedding sustainability into brand narratives long before it was fashionable. Companies that read cultural currents early benefit not only from consumer loyalty but from investor confidence. *Cultural momentum, when engaged constructively, becomes a tailwind rather than a headwind.*

The lesson is clear: investors cannot afford to treat cultural movements as background noise. They are early warning systems, revealing where legitimacy is eroding and where it is accruing. To ignore them is to accept exposure to compounded losses, as industries facing cultural rejection eventually see it reflected in regulation, litigation, and consumer desertion. To engage with them is to recognise that markets are not insulated from society but entwined with it. Capital flows accordingly: not in defiance of culture but in response to it.

Cultural momentum is therefore not peripheral to investment strategy but central. Movements like climate strikes, #MeToo, and anti-sweatshop campaigns have demonstrated that social legitimacy can be as decisive as earnings or cash flow in determining value. They show that investors who wait for numbers alone will miss the story already being written in society. And they remind us that capital, like culture, compounds: small shifts in sentiment today become decisive transformations tomorrow. For investors, the question is not whether cultural momentum matters, but whether they are prepared to recognise it early enough to act.

The Individual's Leverage

It is tempting to believe that power in financial markets resides exclusively with the giants: trillion-dollar asset managers, sovereign wealth funds, or pension systems that move capital in volumes beyond the imagination of any individual saver. This perception feeds the narrative that small investors are passengers on a ship charted by institutions, unable to influence its course. Yet this assumption overlooks a crucial reality: *the collective weight of modest investors, channelled through pooled capital, is one of the most powerful forces in modern markets*. The leverage of individuals does not lie in isolated choices but in the aggregation of their capital, which ultimately determines the mandates, strategies, and governance of the largest funds in existence.

The scale of this aggregation is staggering. Consider the global pensions industry. The average worker may never think of themselves as an investor, yet their retirement contributions feed into funds that collectively manage tens of trillions of dollars. The California Public Employees' Retirement System (CalPERS), one of the world's largest pension funds, owes its size to millions of ordinary workers whose pooled savings became a financial colossus. Similar dynamics apply in Europe, where state pension systems and occupational schemes have grown into dominant institutional investors. Each individual contribution is modest, but together they define the investment strategies that shape corporate priorities globally. The crucial insight is that the capital stewarded by the world's largest funds is not owned by faceless institutions; it is owned by individuals whose voices, when mobilised, can direct policy.

This leverage becomes visible when beneficiaries assert their influence. University endowments, which pool alumni donations and tuition revenues, provide a striking example. Student campaigns demanding fossil fuel divestment reframed endowment management as a moral issue, challenging administrators to reconcile institutional values with investment practice. What began as campus activism evolved into a global divestment movement, influencing funds worth hundreds of billions. The individual student had no direct access to markets, but through collective mobilisation, they altered the mandates of funds large enough to shake energy markets. Similar stories unfold in pension funds where beneficiaries—teachers, municipal employees, healthcare workers—press trustees to align portfolios with climate or social justice goals. The message is clear: pooled savings are not abstract numbers but aggregated agency.

Index funds further amplify this phenomenon. The rapid growth of passive investing means that retail investors now hold stakes in nearly every major listed company, albeit indirectly. When individuals buy into index-tracking funds through retirement accounts or brokerage platforms, they effectively become part-owners of global corporations. Their combined weight gives firms like BlackRock, Vanguard, and State Street their unprecedented voting power in shareholder meetings. These asset managers may appear to act autonomously, but their clout is derived entirely from the aggregation of individual capital. This reality means that the preferences of ordinary investors, whether expressed or not, shape corporate governance indirectly. If investors demand that their fund managers vote on climate resolutions or diversity measures, the effect reverberates through boardrooms worldwide. *The silence of individuals sustains the status quo; their voices can redirect it.*

Case studies highlight how modest actors have punched far above their weight. In 2021, the small activist hedge fund Engine No. 1, with just a fraction of ExxonMobil's market capitalisation, successfully secured three seats on the company's board. The campaign was possible only because large institutional investors—who themselves represent millions of individuals—supported the resolution under pressure from their stakeholders. The fund's success demonstrated that even tiny players can catalyse change when they mobilise cultural momentum and align with the latent power of pooled capital. What appeared at first as a mismatch in scale was, in reality, a demonstration of how individual leverage, strategically aggregated, can overcome entrenched corporate inertia.

The influence of individuals is not limited to headline campaigns. It is embedded in the structure of everyday capital flows. When retail investors choose ethical exchange-traded funds (ETFs) over traditional benchmarks, they shift demand in ways that alter capital allocation across sectors. A surge of inflows into ESG-focused funds not only boosts valuations of included companies but pressures excluded firms to reform in order to regain access to this growing pool of capital. These decisions are rarely dramatic; they happen quietly in brokerage accounts and workplace retirement schemes. Yet their cumulative effect is profound. A single investor moving a modest sum has little impact, but millions doing so at scale reconfigure the financial architecture. *The market does not respond to intention in isolation; it responds to aggregated flows, and those flows are built from individual decisions.*

Philosophically, the idea of individual leverage challenges the fatalism that often paralyses small investors. It reframes the question from "What difference can I make?" to "What difference do I already make, whether I acknowledge it or not?" Because pooled vehicles dominate capital markets, every contribution participates in shaping outcomes. The only real choice is whether to exercise that influence consciously or to let it be wielded passively by default strategies that may conflict with one's values. This recognition shifts responsibility: the modest investor is not powerless but complicit. Portfolios are not silent; they speak through the aggregation of their capital.

The democratic character of this leverage is striking. Political systems often dilute individual voices, making reform appear distant and inaccessible. Financial systems, by contrast, aggregate capital mechanically. Every contribution, however small, enlarges the pool through which institutions wield influence. This does not mean outcomes are guaranteed—power still resides in intermediaries who may resist change—but it does mean that the structure of markets amplifies rather than diminishes collective weight. When beneficiaries coordinate, they can set agendas that once seemed reserved for elites. From climate disclosures to board diversity, issues once dismissed as marginal have become mainstream precisely because individuals asserted their leverage through the funds that manage their capital.

Critics may counter that most individuals are disengaged, indifferent to how their money is invested, and unlikely to mobilise in significant numbers. While true in part, this scepticism underestimates two trends. First, awareness is growing rapidly. The proliferation of ESG-labelled products, shareholder activism, and transparency campaigns has brought investment choices into public discourse in ways unthinkable a generation ago. Second, digital platforms have reduced barriers to mobilisation. Whether through online petitions, shareholder coalitions, or social media campaigns, individuals now have unprecedented capacity to pressure funds and corporations directly. The inertia of disengagement remains strong, but the infrastructure for mobilisation is stronger than ever.

The implications for corporate direction are undeniable. Firms can no longer assume that their largest shareholders will remain passive. Even if intermediaries like asset managers are cautious, they are increasingly responsive to the voices of their underlying investors. Companies facing controversies—from carbon emissions to labour practices—must now consider not only regulatory and reputational risks but the possibility that shareholder coalitions representing millions of ordinary people will challenge their leadership. The old assumption that small investors were irrelevant has given way to a recognition that their pooled capital is the ultimate source of institutional clout.

To see the individual's leverage clearly is to abandon the myth of insignificance. Every paycheque contribution to a pension, every choice of a mutual fund, every passive allocation to an index becomes part of a vast current that shapes markets. That current can sustain harmful industries or redirect capital towards more sustainable, equitable futures. The choice is not whether individuals matter—they do—but whether they are willing to recognise their power and use it intentionally. In the aggregate, modest investors are not passengers; they are co-pilots. The corporate world is already adjusting to this reality, even if many individuals have yet to fully grasp it. *Leverage is not the privilege of the few; it is the latent force of the many, waiting to be claimed.*

Chapter 3
Mapping the Ethical Terrain

Few domains in modern finance are as crowded with competing claims, technical jargon, and contested definitions as ethical investing. Investors looking to align their portfolios with principle are confronted not with a clear map but with a thicket of acronyms, frameworks, and labels, each offering to capture what it means to be responsible. ESG, impact investing, socially responsible screening, values-based funds—the vocabulary itself can obscure more than it clarifies. The complexity is not accidental. It reflects the deeper challenge of translating moral commitments into financial practice, of codifying values in systems designed primarily for profit maximisation. To navigate this landscape requires discernment: the ability to distinguish substance from branding, and to move beyond formulaic checklists toward a framework that is both intellectually honest and personally resonant.

The first obstacle is definitional. Environmental, Social, and Governance (ESG) investing has emerged as the most widely used umbrella, embraced by institutions from asset managers to pension funds. Its strength lies in integration: ESG factors are treated as financially material risks and opportunities, incorporated into conventional analysis. Yet this pragmatic framing, while appealing to fiduciaries, is also its blind spot. ESG is not inherently ethical; it is evaluative. A fossil fuel company may score well on governance and safety standards, even as its core business remains environmentally destructive. Investors attracted by high ESG ratings may assume alignment with principle, only to find they are supporting companies fundamentally at odds with their stated values. Impact investing, by contrast, promises intentionality. It directs capital towards enterprises designed to deliver measurable social or environmental benefits alongside financial returns. Its strength is clarity of mission. Its limitation is scale: impact funds often remain niche, small in comparison to the trillions governed under ESG mandates. Values-based investing adds another layer, explicitly aligning portfolios with ethical, religious, or philosophical commitments. Its clarity is admirable, but its rigidity can deter investors wary of limiting diversification. These approaches, taken together, show that *the very act of defining ethical investment is fraught with trade-offs: clarity often comes at the expense of breadth, breadth at the expense of conviction.*

Metrics complicate the picture further. Investors are now confronted with an alphabet soup of ESG ratings from agencies whose methodologies diverge wildly. A single company may score highly with one rater and poorly with another, not because of fraud but because of differing assumptions, weightings, and definitions of materiality. Volkswagen, for example, held strong ESG scores shortly before its emissions scandal, revealing how metrics can obscure rather than illuminate risk. Such inconsistencies do not render metrics useless, but they demand critical literacy. An investor who treats ratings as gospel will misinterpret them; one who interrogates their assumptions can use them as tools rather than crutches. *The key is not to seek certainty in numbers but to recognise their constructed nature, their susceptibility to both methodological bias and corporate lobbying.*

Metrics are maps, not territories—they guide but never fully capture the terrain.

Regulation is beginning to impose order on this fragmented landscape, though not without controversy. The European Union's taxonomy for sustainable activities represents one of the most ambitious attempts to define what counts as "green," establishing thresholds for sectors from energy to agriculture. The United States, through the Securities and Exchange Commission, has moved to tighten disclosure rules around climate risks and ESG claims. These interventions matter because they shift the baseline: they redefine what companies must reveal and what investors can reasonably expect. Yet regulation, too, is double-edged. On the one hand, it raises standards and reduces greenwashing; on the other, it risks ossifying definitions that may lag behind evolving science or ethical norms. Natural gas, controversially included as a "transitional" activity under parts of the EU taxonomy, exemplifies this tension. Investors seeking certainty may welcome regulatory clarity, but they must remain alert to the political compromises embedded within it.

To approach this terrain with confidence, investors must ultimately move beyond labels. ESG, impact, values-based—each framework offers insights, but none substitutes for personal clarity. A checklist may indicate compliance, but it cannot substitute for conviction. Ethical investing cannot be outsourced entirely to agencies, regulators, or product providers. It requires a degree of introspection: What principles matter most to me or my institution? Which trade-offs am I willing to accept? How do I balance diversification with integrity? These questions cannot be answered by ratings or taxonomies; they demand judgement. And it is precisely this exercise of judgement that transforms ethical investing from a branding exercise into a disciplined practice.

The task ahead, then, is to chart a path through competing frameworks without succumbing to either cynicism or naivety. Cynicism sees all labels as marketing ploys, dismissing the possibility of meaningful alignment between capital and principle. Naivety embraces labels uncritically, mistaking the appearance of ethics for their substance. The challenge—and opportunity—is to navigate between these extremes, recognising the value of frameworks while refusing to be confined by them. This chapter begins that work: clarifying approaches, interrogating metrics, analysing regulation, and encouraging readers to articulate a framework that reflects not only market trends but personal conscience. Ethical investing, at its best, is not about adopting someone else's definition of responsibility but about constructing one's own, informed by evidence, tempered by humility, and committed to coherence. To map the ethical terrain is not simply to catalogue its features but to decide where, and how, one wishes to travel across it.

ESG vs. Impact vs. Values-Based Investing

For decades, financial markets treated ethics as something external to investment, the domain of philanthropy or policy rather than portfolio construction. That view no longer holds. Today, investors are confronted with a spectrum of frameworks—ESG integration, impact investing, and values-based approaches—each claiming to reconcile profit with principle. At first glance, these frameworks appear interchangeable, yet their underlying logic differs significantly. Understanding their distinctions is not merely a matter of terminology; it is essential to navigating an investment landscape where the boundaries of responsibility are hotly contested. The stakes are high: confusion can lead to superficial alignment or unexamined contradictions, while clarity enables investors to align capital with both conscience and prudence.

Environmental, Social, and Governance (ESG) investing has become the lingua franca of the industry, embraced by asset managers, rating agencies, and regulators. Its appeal lies in its pragmatic framing: ESG factors are treated not as moral imperatives but as material risks and opportunities. A company with poor labour practices may face lawsuits, reputational damage, and operational disruption; one with robust governance may avoid scandals and attract long-term investors. By embedding these considerations into financial analysis, ESG reframes responsibility as risk management. This positioning explains its rapid adoption: fiduciaries can claim alignment with sustainability without departing from their duty to maximise returns. But here lies the central paradox. *ESG is descriptive rather than prescriptive: it measures how companies manage non-financial factors, not whether their core business is compatible with a sustainable future.* An oil major with excellent disclosure and safety records can achieve a high ESG score despite perpetuating dependence on fossil fuels. Thus, while ESG is invaluable for sharpening risk awareness, it is insufficient as a framework for aligning investments with deeper ethical commitments.

Impact investing responds to this limitation by shifting the emphasis from process to purpose. It is defined not only by the consideration of non-financial factors but by the explicit intention to generate measurable social or environmental outcomes alongside financial returns. Where ESG integration may justify holding a polluter with strong governance, impact investing directs capital only toward enterprises designed to produce positive externalities. A microfinance institution expanding access to credit, a renewable energy start-up decarbonising electricity grids, or a healthcare company delivering affordable vaccines are classic impact cases. The defining feature is intentionality: investors select these opportunities precisely for their expected social outcomes, and they demand evidence of those outcomes. This brings both strength and constraint. The strength lies in clarity of mission; the constraint lies in scalability. Impact investing often operates in niche markets, private equity, or venture capital, where measurement can be intensive and liquidity limited. It appeals strongly to foundations, family offices, and mission-driven investors but remains less dominant in mainstream portfolios.

Values-based investing represents yet another approach, one that predates the modern ESG and impact frameworks. Rooted historically in religious or ethical traditions, it reflects the principle of avoiding industries or practices inconsistent with deeply held beliefs. Quaker investors in the eighteenth century refused to finance the slave trade; more recently, funds aligned with Islamic finance exclude alcohol, gambling, and interest-bearing securities. Today, values-based approaches extend to a wide array of concerns: from fossil fuels to firearms, from animal welfare to human rights. The strength of this model lies in its moral clarity. It enables investors to align their capital with their conscience without compromise. Yet it can also create rigidity, limiting diversification and potentially excluding companies undergoing meaningful transition. Moreover, values-based screens can sometimes result in paradoxes: excluding one harmful industry while remaining exposed to others, or relying on narrow definitions that fail to capture systemic risks.

What unites these frameworks is their effort to bridge the gulf between finance and ethics, yet their differences matter enormously. ESG, with its focus on risk, helps investors understand how externalities affect companies; impact investing, with its emphasis on intentional outcomes, directs capital toward solutions; values-based investing, with its clarity of exclusions, protects investors from complicity in practices they reject. Each carries blind spots. ESG can be technocratic and susceptible to greenwashing, as companies optimise disclosures without changing fundamentals. Impact investing can struggle with measurement, as social outcomes are often difficult to quantify or compare across contexts. Values-based investing can be rigid, prioritising purity over pragmatic influence. To treat these approaches as interchangeable is to obscure their strengths; to understand their distinctions is to use them in complementary ways.

Real-world examples illustrate how these approaches diverge in practice. Consider renewable energy. An ESG investor may hold a utility company transitioning slowly toward renewables, valuing its improving governance and disclosure. An impact investor might finance a start-up dedicated exclusively to solar microgrids in underserved regions, seeking measurable reductions in carbon emissions and energy poverty. A values-based investor might exclude all fossil fuel holdings outright, refusing to finance transition laggards regardless of their governance scores. Each approach channels capital differently, and each reflects different interpretations of responsibility. None is inherently superior; the key lies in aligning method with intention.

Critics often argue that these frameworks complicate investing unnecessarily, that capital should flow purely on the basis of risk-adjusted returns. Yet this objection assumes that financial returns exist in isolation from societal context. In practice, every allocation carries implicit values: silence on ethics is simply complicity with prevailing norms. The question is not whether to integrate values but how. ESG, impact, and values-based investing provide tools—imperfect, but useful—for making explicit what has always been implicit.

Philosophically, the distinctions highlight deeper questions about the role of capital in society. Should investors merely avoid harm, as values-based approaches often emphasise? Should they mitigate risks and reward good governance, as ESG encourages? Or should they actively seek to create positive externalities, as impact frameworks demand? These are not merely technical debates; they are questions about the purpose of investment itself. For some, the priority is coherence with personal or institutional ethics. For others, it is harnessing finance as a tool for societal transformation. For many, it is a balancing act: using ESG integration to manage risk, values-based screens to protect conscience, and impact allocations to catalyse change. *The sophistication of an ethical investor lies not in choosing one model but in understanding when and how to use each.*

As markets mature, the boundaries between these approaches are blurring. Some funds integrate ESG analysis while also committing to impact measurement; others combine values-based exclusions with ESG scoring. Regulators, too, are beginning to shape definitions, demanding greater clarity to prevent greenwashing. Yet the essential distinctions remain: risk management, intentionality, and exclusion are different logics, and recognising them prevents confusion. For investors navigating this terrain, clarity is both a defensive tool and a source of opportunity. To know the strengths and blind spots of each framework is to avoid superficial alignment and to build portfolios that reflect both principle and prudence.

Ethical investing is not a monolith. It is a contested space where multiple models compete to define what responsibility looks like. ESG, impact, and values-based investing each provide partial answers, shaped by history, culture, and institutional incentives. By cutting through jargon and clarifying distinctions, investors can make deliberate choices rather than drifting into default positions. Ultimately, the measure of success is not whether one adopts the latest label but whether one's portfolio genuinely reflects the values one claims to hold—and does so with rigour, coherence, and transparency. *Frameworks are tools, not ends in themselves; the real task is to use them wisely, with eyes open to both their utility and their limits.*

Metrics and Their Limits

Few tools have risen as rapidly in prominence, and as sharply in controversy, as Environmental, Social, and Governance (ESG) ratings. In the span of two decades, what began as niche indicators produced by specialist firms has become a multi-billion-dollar industry, with major financial institutions, regulators, and corporations leaning heavily on these metrics to demonstrate responsibility. Today, ESG ratings are routinely cited in prospectuses, used as benchmarks for investment products, and treated as shorthand for ethical credibility. Yet beneath their glossy surface lies a deep and unresolved tension: the alphabet soup of ratings often obscures more than it illuminates. *A company can receive an "A" for sustainability from one rater and a "C" from another, not because of malfeasance but because of divergent methodologies.* For investors seeking clarity, this inconsistency is not a minor irritation; it is a fundamental signal that metrics, while useful, are far from definitive.

The problem begins with what ESG ratings are designed to measure. Contrary to popular assumption, most ratings do not assess whether a company is "good" for the world. They evaluate how well a company manages risks and opportunities related to environmental, social, and governance factors. This distinction is critical. A tobacco company, for example, may receive strong ESG scores if it demonstrates robust governance, transparent disclosures, and effective risk management—despite selling products that contribute to millions of preventable deaths annually. Ratings are therefore not moral absolutes but relative performance assessments. They ask: compared with peers, how well does this firm manage the risks inherent to its industry? For investors unaware of this nuance, the shock can be profound. What appears to be a seal of ethical approval may in fact be little more than a risk-adjusted performance grade.

Discrepancies between rating agencies deepen the confusion. A 2020 study from the Massachusetts Institute of Technology highlighted correlations between major ESG raters as low as 0.3, compared to the near-perfect alignment typical of credit rating agencies. Tesla exemplifies the divergence. Some agencies award it high environmental scores for its role in advancing electric vehicles, while others penalise it for supply chain controversies and governance lapses. ExxonMobil, conversely, has sometimes scored more favourably on ESG metrics than Tesla because of its rigorous reporting and governance frameworks, despite its central role in fossil fuel extraction. These inconsistencies reveal the subjective judgments embedded within ESG methodologies. What one agency sees as evidence of sustainability, another interprets as evidence of risk. The result is that ratings can become less a reflection of objective truth and more a mirror of methodological assumptions.

The opacity of these methodologies compounds the problem. Most rating agencies guard their formulas closely, offering only high-level explanations of weighting systems. An investor may know that environmental factors account for 40 per cent of a score and governance 30 per cent, but the underlying judgments about which indicators to prioritise remain hidden. Should water use weigh more heavily than carbon emissions? Should labour practices outweigh board diversity? These are normative decisions, yet they are often presented as technical facts. *By cloaking value judgements in the language of quantitative rigour, ESG ratings risk misleading investors into believing they are dealing with neutral science rather than contested interpretations.*

Another limitation lies in the incentives of companies themselves. Once ratings become benchmarks, firms quickly learn how to "game" them. Corporations invest heavily in sustainability reporting, knowing that disclosure often influences scores as much as actual performance. Volkswagen's high ratings before the diesel emissions scandal are a cautionary tale: the company excelled at reporting and governance structures, even as it systematically cheated on emissions tests. Critics argue that ESG metrics can therefore incentivise cosmetic compliance rather than substantive change. When investors reward companies primarily for disclosure, they risk encouraging the proliferation of glossy sustainability reports without corresponding improvements in practice.

This does not mean metrics are worthless. On the contrary, they can provide valuable insights when read critically. They highlight trends, flag controversies, and allow for comparisons across industries. For instance, an ESG score may reveal which companies in a sector are lagging on worker safety or which are leaders in renewable energy adoption. The challenge is to resist treating them as verdicts. An informed investor uses ESG ratings as one input among many, interrogating their assumptions rather than outsourcing ethical judgement to an opaque algorithm. *The key is literacy: understanding what ratings measure, what they omit, and how to interpret them without surrendering discernment.*

Regulatory momentum is beginning to address some of these weaknesses. The European Union's Sustainable Finance Disclosure Regulation (SFDR) and the development of a taxonomy for sustainable activities are designed to standardise definitions and increase transparency. Similarly, the U.S. Securities and Exchange Commission has proposed rules to prevent misleading ESG claims in fund marketing. These efforts will not eliminate subjectivity—no taxonomy can capture every nuance of responsibility—but they may reduce the most egregious inconsistencies. Still, investors should be wary of overconfidence. Regulation can provide a floor, but it cannot substitute for critical engagement. The inclusion of natural gas in parts of the EU taxonomy demonstrates the compromises inherent in political processes. What regulators define as "sustainable" may not align with evolving science or personal conscience.

Ultimately, the alphabet soup of ESG metrics underscores a larger truth: ethical investing cannot be reduced to numbers alone. Ratings can guide, but they cannot decide. They offer data points, not moral compasses. The danger lies in mistaking metrics for meaning, in confusing compliance with conviction. Investors who rely uncritically on scores risk supporting companies that excel at disclosure while neglecting substance, or overlooking firms making genuine progress that do not fit neatly into existing frameworks. *The responsibility of the ethical investor is not to discard metrics but to read them critically, to understand their limits, and to situate them within a broader framework of values and analysis.*

The future of responsible investment will likely continue to involve ratings, but their role must be recalibrated. Instead of serving as definitive labels of virtue, they should be treated as imperfect tools—helpful for comparison, insufficient for conviction. The real work lies in moving beyond the comfort of numerical certainty toward the discomfort of judgement. Ethical investing requires grappling with complexity, acknowledging trade-offs, and making decisions that reflect both evidence and conscience. Metrics can inform that process, but they cannot resolve it. They are signposts, not destinations. Recognising their limits is not a weakness of responsible investment; it is the first step toward practising it with integrity.

The Role of Regulation

The debate over what constitutes "ethical" investment has never been settled by markets alone. For decades, investors relied on voluntary codes, self-regulation, and the fragmented efforts of rating agencies to define responsibility. That era is ending. Governments and regulators are now moving decisively to standardise definitions, enforce disclosures, and reshape the boundaries of acceptable practice. This shift is not peripheral—it is transforming the very meaning of ethical capital. *What once was an investor's personal interpretation is increasingly mediated by legal frameworks that determine how ethics are measured, disclosed, and marketed.*

The European Union's taxonomy for sustainable activities stands as the most ambitious attempt to impose order on this contested landscape. Launched in 2020 and phased in over subsequent years, the taxonomy seeks to define, in granular detail, which economic activities can be considered environmentally sustainable. It is no longer sufficient for a company to market itself as "green"; it must demonstrate alignment with technical screening criteria covering sectors from energy and transport to agriculture and manufacturing. These criteria are not symbolic. They determine access to financing, eligibility for investment products, and ultimately, market competitiveness. For instance, a utility company seeking to raise capital for renewable projects must prove compliance with the taxonomy's thresholds for emissions intensity. Investors, in turn, must disclose how their portfolios align with these criteria. The taxonomy therefore moves the conversation from aspiration to accountability: sustainability is no longer a matter of narrative but of measurable compliance.

Yet the taxonomy also illustrates the compromises inherent in regulation. Political negotiations led to the inclusion of natural gas and nuclear energy as "transitional" activities, provoking fierce debate. Critics argue that this weakens credibility by allowing carbon-intensive industries to retain sustainable labels. Proponents counter that a pragmatic taxonomy must accommodate transition pathways rather than impose purist exclusions. The controversy reveals a deeper truth: *regulation codifies political choices as much as scientific ones.* Ethical definitions are not neutral—they are shaped by the interplay of environmental science, industrial lobbying, and geopolitical interests. For investors, the lesson is clear: regulatory frameworks provide clarity, but they also embed compromises that must be scrutinised rather than accepted blindly.

In the United States, the Securities and Exchange Commission has moved in a parallel direction, albeit with a different emphasis. Its proposed climate disclosure rules, first outlined in 2022, require public companies to report not only direct emissions (Scope 1) and purchased energy emissions (Scope 2), but in some cases, the more complex supply chain and customer emissions (Scope 3). This represents a seismic change in corporate reporting. For decades, firms could treat climate risks as peripheral; now they are expected to disclose them as material financial risks. The SEC has also begun scrutinising ESG-labelled funds, requiring greater transparency about investment strategies to prevent greenwashing. In effect, the regulator is tightening the definition of what it means for a fund to market itself as "sustainable." Just as consumer protection laws guard against misleading advertising, securities law is extending those principles into the realm of ethical finance.

Global convergence is uneven but accelerating. In Japan, the Financial Services Agency has updated stewardship codes to emphasise sustainability, while in China, green bond standards are evolving to exclude "clean coal" projects. International initiatives like the International Sustainability Standards Board (ISSB) are attempting to harmonise disclosures across jurisdictions, seeking to prevent a patchwork of competing frameworks. For multinational corporations and global investors, this harmonisation is not simply a matter of efficiency. It is essential for comparability. Without it, a company might be considered "sustainable" in one jurisdiction and "unsustainable" in another, leaving investors unable to reconcile divergent definitions.

The regulatory turn is reshaping the incentives of both companies and investors. Firms that once treated sustainability as a reputational issue now face hard compliance costs and legal liabilities. Failure to disclose accurately can invite lawsuits, penalties, and exclusion from investment universes. Conversely, companies that anticipate regulatory trends can position themselves as leaders, gaining access to capital at lower costs. Investors, too, must adapt. No longer can they rely solely on voluntary disclosures or third-party ratings; they must ensure that their portfolios comply with evolving legal standards. This redefines fiduciary duty itself. Where once it was interpreted narrowly as maximising financial returns, fiduciaries are now compelled to integrate sustainability factors because regulators have deemed them material.

Ethical considerations are becoming inseparable from financial obligations.

This regulatory momentum raises philosophical questions. Who decides what is ethical? Should governments codify sustainability, or should investors and civil society retain flexibility to define it themselves? Regulation offers clarity, but it risks narrowing the scope of ethical debate. By defining certain activities as "sustainable" and others as not, regulators can entrench particular worldviews while marginalising alternatives. The EU taxonomy's treatment of nuclear power illustrates this tension: to some, it represents a pragmatic low-carbon technology; to others, it is an unacceptable risk. Regulation resolves such debates by fiat, but resolution is not the same as consensus. For investors committed to ethical integrity, the challenge is to use regulation as a floor, not a ceiling—to treat compliance as necessary but not sufficient.

Historical parallels suggest why regulation matters. Consider the evolution of financial accounting. In the early twentieth century, investors relied on voluntary disclosures, leading to rampant inconsistencies and occasional fraud. The creation of standardised accounting rules underpinned the growth of modern capital markets, providing comparability and trust. Sustainability disclosures are at a similar inflection point. Voluntary reporting has produced insights but also confusion and manipulation. Standardisation, however imperfect, is necessary to move from rhetoric to rigour. Just as accounting standards did not eliminate judgement but provided a common language, so too sustainability regulation will not eliminate ethical ambiguity but will anchor it in shared metrics.

For investors, the practical implications are profound. A fund manager constructing an ESG product today cannot rely on marketing spin; they must demonstrate how holdings align with regulatory criteria. An individual investor reviewing their pension must recognise that their fund's sustainability claims are now subject to legal scrutiny. A corporation considering a bond issuance must evaluate whether its projects qualify as green under official taxonomies. In each case, the presence of regulation shifts the balance from voluntary ethics to enforceable standards. The conversation has moved from "Should companies disclose?" to "How must they disclose?" and "What qualifies as compliant?" The boundaries of responsibility are no longer purely self-determined; they are increasingly legislated.

The evolving role of regulation does not diminish the importance of conscience in investing; it heightens it. *Regulation provides the scaffolding, but investors must decide how to build within and beyond it.* A taxonomy may define thresholds, but it cannot capture the full complexity of moral risk. Disclosure rules may standardise data, but they cannot dictate interpretation. The ultimate responsibility lies with investors to engage critically, recognising that what is legally sustainable may not always be ethically sufficient. To invest responsibly in this new era requires both compliance with evolving regulation and the courage to interrogate its limits. Ethical capital is being reshaped not only by markets and culture but by law. Understanding that transformation is indispensable for anyone seeking to align profit with principle.

Beyond Labels

The modern investor is surrounded by labels. ESG ratings, impact scores, sustainable fund badges, green bond certifications—the marketplace has become crowded with markers designed to convey responsibility. At first glance, these labels appear to simplify an otherwise complex terrain, offering shortcuts for aligning money with values. Yet their proliferation risks creating the very opposite: confusion, complacency, and misplaced trust. *An investor can too easily conflate a label with genuine alignment, mistaking marketing gloss for moral clarity.* The temptation to outsource judgement to a checklist is understandable, but it comes at the cost of depth and discernment. Ethical capital demands something more demanding, and more rewarding, than ticking boxes.

The allure of labels lies in their promise of certainty. For busy professionals or institutions managing large portfolios, the ability to screen investments based on predefined criteria is convenient. A fund labelled "sustainable" or "low-carbon" seems to remove the burden of analysis. Yet labels rarely capture nuance. Consider two funds that both market themselves as ESG leaders. One may focus heavily on governance quality, overweighting technology firms with robust board structures but significant energy use; the other may prioritise environmental criteria, investing in renewable energy but tolerating weaker governance in emerging markets. Both can wear the same ESG badge, yet their underlying philosophies and exposures diverge dramatically. For investors who rely on the label alone, this divergence remains hidden. *The label signals virtue, but the reality may be a compromise misaligned with the investor's deeper principles.*

The danger extends beyond misinterpretation. Labels can breed complacency, encouraging investors to believe that responsibility has been outsourced to regulators, rating agencies, or fund managers. Yet responsibility in investing cannot be delegated so easily. A pensioner who entrusts their savings to a "sustainable" fund may still find themselves financing oil companies or fast-fashion retailers if the label's criteria are loose. Conversely, a company pioneering meaningful climate solutions may be excluded from certain funds because it operates in a sector deemed "brown" by default. Labels provide structure, but they cannot substitute for context. The investor who accepts them uncritically risks complicity in contradictions.

Historical experience illustrates this point. During the divestment campaigns against apartheid South Africa, many funds initially resisted exclusion, arguing that their portfolios already complied with general governance standards. It was only when investors applied their own values, explicitly demanding disinvestment, that meaningful change occurred. The lesson is clear: *ethical momentum arises not from generic labels but from conscious alignment with principle.* Labels may provide the scaffolding, but the architecture of responsible investment must be built by investors themselves.

This does not mean labels are useless. They serve as entry points, making responsible investing accessible to those who might otherwise be daunted. A first-time investor may not have the capacity to analyse the emissions profile of every company in their pension fund, but they can choose a climate-focused option as a starting point. Similarly, institutions can use regulatory labels, such as those under the EU taxonomy, to demonstrate compliance and improve transparency. The key is to treat these tools as beginnings, not endpoints. A label can highlight where to look, but it cannot tell an investor what matters most to them. That requires reflection and intentionality.

Philosophically, this raises a deeper question: what does it mean for capital to reflect principle? A checklist can tell us whether a fund excludes coal, or whether it meets certain governance standards. But it cannot tell us whether those exclusions align with an individual's moral priorities or whether governance standards capture the investor's vision of justice. *Principle is not universal; it is personal.* One investor may prioritise climate mitigation, another gender equality, another indigenous rights. The act of aligning capital with principle therefore requires a willingness to articulate, and sometimes to wrestle with, what those principles actually are. Labels can only gesture at such priorities; they cannot define them.

Consider the example of fossil fuel exclusion. A fund labelled "fossil-free" may exclude oil and gas majors but continue to invest in companies reliant on coal-fired electricity in their supply chains. An investor with a strict climate priority may find this unacceptable; another, more pragmatic, may accept it as a transition compromise. Both positions are legitimate, but neither can be resolved by the label alone. Similarly, a "socially responsible" label may include technology firms praised for workplace diversity while overlooking their roles in enabling surveillance or data exploitation. The ethical weight of these trade-offs cannot be outsourced. They require active engagement.

The strategic investor recognises this and moves beyond labels to develop a personal framework. Rather than asking, "Does this fund have the right badge?" the more powerful question becomes, "Does this portfolio reflect the values I wish to uphold?" This reframing demands effort. It requires interrogating fund holdings, questioning methodologies, and identifying non-negotiables. Yet it also empowers investors to take ownership of their capital's impact. When done thoughtfully, this process transforms investing from passive compliance into active stewardship.

The corporate world is acutely aware of how labels influence perception. Companies increasingly tailor their reporting to secure favourable scores, knowing that investors equate high ESG ratings with sustainability leadership. This dynamic creates a feedback loop where disclosure is optimised for metrics rather than substance. An oil company can score highly by producing transparent reports on emissions, even if those emissions remain substantial. Meanwhile, a smaller company genuinely reducing its carbon footprint may lack the resources to produce glossy disclosures and therefore scores poorly. *If investors rely on labels, they risk rewarding appearances over outcomes.* Moving beyond labels means asking whether the underlying reality matches the advertised virtue.

Regulation, too, plays a role in this tension. Frameworks like the EU taxonomy and SEC disclosure rules aim to standardise what labels mean, reducing the scope for greenwashing. Yet regulation is by definition political, subject to compromise and lobbying. An activity classified as "sustainable" under law may not align with an investor's conscience. The inclusion of nuclear energy and natural gas in parts of the EU taxonomy is one example. Compliance is not the same as conviction. Ethical investors must treat regulation as a floor, not a ceiling—necessary for comparability, but never sufficient for principle.

The future of responsible investment will likely bring more labels, not fewer. As demand for ethical products grows, so will the incentive to categorise, certify, and brand. This makes the imperative of moving beyond labels all the more urgent. Investors who wish to align capital with principle cannot afford to stop at the surface. They must cultivate the discipline of critical reading, the patience to dig into details, and the courage to make choices that reflect their values even when labels are silent or misleading. *The task is not to abandon labels but to transcend them—to use them as tools without mistaking them for truths.*

In practice, this means embracing a dual mindset: sceptical of shortcuts, but pragmatic about tools. Labels can narrow the field, but discernment must refine it. Checklists can screen for red flags, but strategy must determine alignment. By moving beyond labels, investors reclaim agency in defining what ethical capital means for them. They refuse to be passive consumers of sustainability marketing and instead become active architects of portfolios that embody principle. In doing so, they elevate the conversation from compliance to conscience, from superficial branding to substantive impact. That is the challenge—and the opportunity—of ethical investing in its most mature form.

Chapter 4
The Moral Margin

Markets like to present themselves as efficient arbiters of value, pricing in every risk, every opportunity, every conceivable outcome. Yet time and again, history proves otherwise. The financial system is extraordinarily good at capturing short-term signals—earnings guidance, interest rate shifts, consumer sentiment surveys—but notoriously poor at recognising slow-moving currents that reshape the landscape over decades. Among the most consistently mispriced of these forces are moral risks: the reputational, environmental, and governance failures that may appear peripheral in quarterly results but eventually metastasise into liabilities of staggering magnitude. When these failures are ignored, investors do not simply miscalculate risk—they ignore an ethical dimension that, in time, shows itself in the balance sheet. *Ethics neglected today often becomes cost compounded tomorrow.*

Consider the case of reputational collapse. Once, tobacco companies were among the most reliable dividend payers in global markets, prized for their predictability and pricing power. Few anticipated that decades of mounting public health evidence, coupled with legal action and shifting norms, would erode the foundations of the industry. Litigation settlements, advertising bans, and declining consumer acceptance did not materialise overnight; they built slowly, almost invisibly, until the industry's long-term decline became irreversible. Investors who had dismissed the ethical debate as immaterial to financial returns discovered that morality had been a proxy for hidden liabilities all along. What appeared to be a resilient cash machine was, in truth, a structure hollowed out by cumulative social condemnation.

This dynamic is not confined to tobacco. Environmental degradation, poor labour practices, and exploitative governance follow a similar trajectory. Oil majors that once boasted of their unassailable reserves now confront the reality that a significant proportion of those reserves may never be monetised. Textile brands that outsourced production to the cheapest suppliers learned, through disasters like Rana Plaza, that the human cost of negligence carries reputational and financial penalties. Corporations that tolerated corruption or opaque governance structures found themselves shut out of capital markets when scandals erupted. These examples underline the same point: *what appears as ethical critique today often becomes financial reality tomorrow.* The moral margin is where investors fail to see that values and valuation are inseparable.

Why, then, do markets consistently misprice morality? The answer lies partly in the tyranny of short-term reporting. Public companies are judged quarter by quarter, incentivising executives to deliver immediate gains at the expense of long-term stewardship. Climate liability, supply chain exploitation, or inadequate governance controls may not manifest as urgent threats within a three-month horizon, allowing managers to defer meaningful action. Meanwhile, investors who themselves face performance pressure in short measurement cycles are reluctant to penalise companies for risks that may not crystallise for years. The result is a collective blindness: morality is recognised as risk only when its consequences become unavoidable. But by then, the cost of inaction has already compounded.

The advantage belongs to those who resist this short-term bias. Long-term investors—sovereign wealth funds, pension schemes, endowments—are uniquely positioned to treat ethical alignment not as a concession but as a strategic advantage. By recognising that moral risks compound just as financial returns do, they can anticipate future liabilities before they surface in earnings reports. A pension fund that adjusts its portfolio to account for climate risk today is not acting out of charity; it is safeguarding beneficiaries against the wealth destruction that will follow if carbon-intensive assets become stranded. Similarly, an endowment that excludes companies with poor governance structures is protecting itself from the future shocks of mismanagement scandals. Patience, in this sense, is not passivity but prescience. It allows investors to harvest the dividends of foresight in markets addicted to immediacy.

Few case studies illustrate this more starkly than the looming carbon bubble. For decades, fossil fuel companies have been valued on the assumption that their reserves—oil fields, coal mines, gas deposits—would eventually be extracted and sold. Yet climate science and international agreements increasingly suggest that a substantial portion of these reserves must remain untouched to avoid catastrophic warming. The moment this reality is priced in, the supposed assets become liabilities: capital tied up in projects that cannot deliver returns. Investors who ignored the moral argument for decarbonisation are now confronted with the financial one: stranded assets represent not hypothetical risks but tangible losses. What was once derided as an activist fantasy is now acknowledged, even by central banks and regulators, as a systemic risk to global markets. *The carbon bubble is not just an environmental story; it is a parable of how moral imperatives ignored become economic inevitabilities.*

The moral margin, then, is not an abstract concept. It is the space where investors who dismiss ethical critique miscalculate value, where short-term gains obscure long-term fragility, and where patience is not merely a virtue but a competitive edge. This chapter invites readers to examine how risks framed as "ethical" are in fact financial time bombs, how markets repeatedly underestimate their significance, and how those willing to adopt a longer horizon can position themselves not only on the right side of history but on the right side of compound returns. To understand the moral margin is to recognise that principle and profit are not in opposition but entwined—and that ignoring one imperils the other.

Risk as Ethics in Disguise

One of the most striking features of modern finance is how often its greatest surprises are, in truth, ethical failures hiding in plain sight. The collapse of reputation, the exposure of environmental damage, the unravelling of governance scandals—these are not random events that suddenly erupt into markets. They are the natural consequences of decisions that ignored moral responsibility until the costs became too large to contain. *Every scandal once looked like a business strategy; every liability was once defended as efficiency.* What investors call "risk" is often the financial echo of ethical neglect.

Take the case of reputational damage. For decades, corporations treated their brands as marketing tools rather than fragile assets. But when public trust fractures, the market quickly reveals the cost of betrayal. Volkswagen's emissions scandal wiped billions from its valuation, not because investors suddenly discovered that cars pollute, but because the deliberate deception of regulators and customers undermined its social licence to operate. Reputation, in this case, was not a soft intangible—it was collateral for the company's entire business model. When that collateral was squandered, risk and ethics converged. The same is true of the banking sector's mis-selling scandals in the United Kingdom, which cost institutions not only fines but long-term trust erosion. Ethical shortcuts yielded temporary gains, but at the expense of enduring value.

Environmental risks follow a similar pattern. For years, extractive industries operated on the assumption that ecological damage was an externality, a problem for governments or communities rather than balance sheets. Yet oil spills, deforestation, and carbon emissions have returned to the corporate ledger in the form of lawsuits, clean-up costs, regulatory penalties, and investor divestment. BP's Deepwater Horizon disaster is a case in point: what began as lax safety oversight in pursuit of efficiency cascaded into one of the largest financial settlements in corporate history. *The supposed efficiency of ignoring ethical safeguards became, in retrospect, the most expensive decision management ever made.* Investors who framed environmental stewardship as "non-financial" discovered too late that it was the most financial risk of all.

Governance risks are perhaps the most transparent expression of ethics disguised as finance. Boards that tolerate corruption, fail to ensure accountability, or allow excessive executive power often preside over companies that later implode. Enron remains the archetype, but its lessons are frequently ignored. In more recent years, Wirecard's spectacular fraud in Germany exposed the weakness of oversight in a supposedly well-regulated environment. Investors seduced by impressive growth metrics neglected to interrogate the ethical rot beneath the surface. Once again, what appeared as governance failure was in fact moral failure—the inability or unwillingness to confront dishonesty, self-dealing, and negligence until it metastasised into collapse.

The pattern is consistent: reputational, environmental, and governance risks are not technical anomalies; they are the market's delayed recognition of ethical choices. *Risk is ethics in disguise because markets only attach numbers to consequences once the moral failure can no longer be ignored.* Investors who dismiss ethical considerations as external to financial analysis are not being pragmatic; they are choosing blindness. And blindness has a cost. The question is not whether values matter, but when they will surface as valuation.

The difficulty for investors lies in timing. Moral failures often unfold slowly, accumulating over years before bursting into public consciousness. Quarterly reporting, the dominant rhythm of capital markets, discourages management from addressing long-term vulnerabilities. Climate liability, labour exploitation, or weak governance structures rarely produce immediate financial stress, allowing executives to frame them as tolerable or irrelevant. But as these failures accumulate, they eventually tip into crises that markets cannot ignore. *What looks like a stable equilibrium is often moral erosion beneath the surface.* Investors who mistake silence for stability are setting themselves up for compounding losses.

Yet this is also where foresight creates opportunity. Those who recognise the ethical roots of risk are better positioned to anticipate where hidden liabilities may emerge. A retailer with opaque supply chains in countries notorious for labour violations is not merely facing an ethical question—it is carrying latent reputational and regulatory risk. A technology company accused of privacy breaches is not merely sparking philosophical debates about surveillance—it is exposing itself to lawsuits, consumer backlash, and trust erosion. A mining company ignoring indigenous rights is not simply confronting social criticism—it is inviting legal injunctions and project delays that jeopardise profitability. By reading ethics as a leading indicator, rather than waiting for markets to quantify them as risk, investors can avoid traps and align themselves with resilience.

Philosophically, this requires a reframing of what risk means. Traditional finance tends to treat risk as volatility, the fluctuation of prices over time. But volatility is not the same as vulnerability. A company whose share price swings because of macroeconomic forces is not necessarily weak; a company whose culture tolerates exploitation or deception is brittle, even if its share price appears stable. *The deeper definition of risk is the exposure to moral failure that will eventually materialise in financial terms.* To ignore this is to mistake calm waters for safety, unaware of the cracks in the hull below the surface.

Importantly, the integration of ethical considerations into risk assessment is not about altruism. It is about accuracy.

Investors who ignore the moral dimension are not being hard-headed realists; they are engaging in selective fantasy, choosing to focus only on what markets already quantify. Yet the greatest losses in history—from asbestos liabilities to financial crises triggered by reckless lending—have come from precisely this failure to recognise that ethics is embedded in risk. By contrast, investors who interrogate the ethical underpinnings of corporate behaviour are not diluting their financial discipline—they are sharpening it.

The challenge is to operationalise this insight without falling into tokenism. It is easy to reduce ethics to compliance checklists, to treat reputational, environmental, and governance risks as boxes to be ticked. But genuine risk analysis requires nuance. It means asking whether a company's governance structure fosters independent oversight or simply formalises rubber-stamping. It means examining not just whether an environmental policy exists, but whether it materially reduces exposure to liability. It means evaluating whether reputational strength is rooted in authentic trust or fragile marketing campaigns vulnerable to exposure. These questions require patience, scepticism, and willingness to probe beyond glossy reports. *Ethical analysis is not about perfection; it is about probability—the likelihood that a company's failures will migrate from hidden to visible, from tolerable to catastrophic.*

Ultimately, the investor who recognises that risk is ethics in disguise is better equipped to navigate the future. They understand that markets reward denial until the moment they punish it, often brutally. They see that the boundary between values and valuation is illusory. And they accept that every investment decision is not merely a financial allocation but an ethical wager: a bet on which failures will remain hidden and which will be exposed. To approach markets with this awareness is to move from reactive to proactive, from blindsided to prepared. It is to see that the numbers on a balance sheet are not separate from the values embedded in a company's choices. They are reflections of one another—two sides of the same reality, converging over time.

Why Markets Misprice Morality

Few features of modern finance are as paradoxical as its ability to process complex data in milliseconds while consistently overlooking the most predictable risks of all. Markets are lauded as efficient, yet they repeatedly misprice the consequences of moral failure—climate liability, labour exploitation, governance neglect—treating them as distant concerns until they abruptly reshape valuations. This is not simply a technical glitch; it is a structural blindness, hard-wired into systems that prize quarterly results above long-term resilience. *The very rhythm of financial reporting—its three-month drumbeat—distorts how investors perceive, prioritise, and price morality.*

Quarterly reporting, originally intended as a mechanism of transparency, has become a straitjacket for corporate behaviour. Executives are incentivised to maximise earnings over ninety-day windows, often at the expense of long-term stewardship. Investments in safety, sustainability, or workforce wellbeing are easy to defer because their payoff rarely fits within a single quarter. Cutting corners, by contrast, provides immediate boosts to margins. The market, conditioned to react to earnings per share and short-term guidance, rewards this behaviour in the moment. But the deferred costs—lawsuits, fines, reputational collapse—arrive later, often years later, by which time the managers responsible may have already moved on. *The mispricing of morality, therefore, is not about ignorance of risk but about the misalignment of time horizons.*

Take the slow-burn nature of climate risk. For decades, fossil fuel companies were valued primarily on their reserves, with analysts assuming these resources would eventually be extracted and monetised. The moral argument—that much of this carbon must remain underground to avoid catastrophic warming—was dismissed as activist rhetoric. Yet as climate science became mainstream and international agreements tightened, the financial implications of stranded assets became undeniable. Investors who had relied on quarterly earnings to judge the health of oil majors overlooked the longer horizon in which those profits were being generated on a foundation of unsustainability. The carbon bubble was mispriced not because the data were unavailable but because the timescale of moral reality clashed with the timescale of financial reporting.

Labour exploitation tells a similar story. Multinational corporations often outsource production to low-cost suppliers in jurisdictions with weak labour protections. In the short run, this drives impressive margins and reassures investors watching quarterly performance. Yet over time, tragedies such as the Rana Plaza collapse in Bangladesh reveal the true cost of those efficiencies: reputational damage, legal liabilities, and investor pressure to overhaul supply chains. Markets treated these practices as tolerable until the ethical failure was broadcast in blood and rubble. Only then did the share prices of implicated firms adjust, belatedly reflecting risks that had been visible to anyone willing to look beyond the quarterly cycle. *The lesson is clear: when labour is devalued, risk is mispriced, and morality reasserts itself with interest.*

Part of the problem lies in how financial models quantify risk. Analysts are comfortable measuring volatility or discounting cash flows, but they struggle to assign numerical values to moral exposures. What is the cost of ignoring indigenous land rights until litigation halts a mining project? How should one price the reputational fallout of systemic harassment scandals within a company? These are difficult to model with precision, so they are often excluded altogether. This omission is then rationalised as pragmatism, when in reality it is a form of wilful blindness. *Markets do not misprice morality because it is unknowable—they misprice it because it is inconvenient to measure.*

Philosophically, this mispricing reflects a deeper tension between efficiency and responsibility. Shareholder primacy, the dominant ideology of late-20th-century capitalism, trained managers to prioritise financial returns above all else. Ethical concerns were reframed as externalities—issues for governments, NGOs, or civil society to manage. But externalities do not remain external forever. Pollution turns into regulation. Exploitation turns into litigation. Deception turns into scandal. Each time, the costs flow back into the company, erasing the gains that were once celebrated in quarterly results. *The market's mistake is not failing to recognise morality but failing to see its inevitability as a financial reality.*

There are, however, investors who resist this structural short-termism. Sovereign wealth funds, pension schemes, and endowments—institutions with inherently long horizons—have begun to integrate moral risk into their frameworks, not out of charity but out of prudence. The Norwegian Sovereign Wealth Fund, for example, has excluded companies that fail to meet standards on environmental and human rights grounds, recognising that such exposures jeopardise long-term returns. Similarly, university endowments have faced pressure from students and faculty to divest from fossil fuels, forcing boards to reconcile immediate returns with intergenerational responsibility. These cases illustrate how investors with longer horizons are less likely to misprice morality, because their measurement of risk extends beyond the next ninety days.

Yet even these institutions face pressure from the broader market ecosystem. Active fund managers, judged against benchmarks on an annual basis, are reluctant to lag peers by excluding profitable but ethically compromised firms. Corporate boards, dependent on share price performance, hesitate to invest in sustainability initiatives that may depress short-term earnings. Rating agencies and sell-side analysts, tasked with producing digestible recommendations, prioritise near-term financial metrics over complex ethical exposures. The result is a self-reinforcing cycle: everyone recognises the existence of long-term moral risks, but few are willing to bear the short-term cost of acknowledging them. *Markets misprice morality not because no one sees it, but because no one wants to be the first to pay for it.*

This raises the question of accountability. If quarterly reporting structures are hard-wired into the system, can markets ever price morality accurately? Some argue that regulatory intervention is the only way to break the cycle. Mandatory disclosures on climate risk, labour practices, and governance structures can shift what is considered material, forcing companies to integrate ethics into financial reporting. The European Union's taxonomy for sustainable activities and the U.S. Securities and Exchange Commission's proposed rules on climate disclosure represent early attempts to hard-code morality into market mechanics. Critics dismiss these as bureaucratic overreach, but without such interventions, the default trajectory is continued short-termism and continued mispricing.

At its core, the mispricing of morality is a story about time. Ethical failures are rarely dramatic in their early stages. They are quiet, cumulative, and easy to ignore in favour of the next quarterly announcement. But over time, they harden into financial truths that no investor can escape. Climate change will not bankrupt fossil fuel firms tomorrow, but it is already reshaping their future. Labour exploitation may not dent profits today, but it seeds scandals that will erupt tomorrow. Governance failures may appear invisible in the short run, but they eventually unravel in spectacular collapse. *The market's failure is not in missing the signal but in refusing to extend its horizon long enough to acknowledge it.*

To understand why markets misprice morality is to see that the problem is not ethics competing with finance, but finance refusing to adjust its lens. Quarterly reporting blinds investors to risks that unfold over years, sometimes decades, but this blindness is voluntary. The data exist, the warnings are clear, the patterns are known. What is required is not more information but more courage: the willingness to act before the crisis, rather than after. Investors who cultivate this discipline are not moralists at the expense of returns. They are realists, unwilling to be duped by a system that confuses immediacy with truth. In the long run, morality and markets do not diverge—they converge. The only question is whether investors recognise it in time, or whether they wait until the convergence bankrupts them.

The Advantage of Patience

The greatest paradox in finance is that the forces most easily measured are rarely the ones that matter most in the long run. Markets obsess over speed—how quickly information is priced, how fast trades can be executed, how immediately returns can be realised. Yet the most durable forms of wealth are rarely captured in days or weeks; they emerge over years, sometimes decades. Patience, unfashionable in the frenzied tempo of global markets, is not a weakness but a competitive edge. When applied to ethical investing, it becomes a decisive advantage, allowing investors to reap the compounding benefits of aligning principle with profit while short-term traders remain trapped in the volatility of headlines and quarterly guidance. *The investor who can wait, who can see past the noise of the moment, captures truths the market insists on postponing until they are undeniable.*

The short-term trader views the world in compressed intervals. A company is judged by its next earnings call, a stock by its movement between morning and afternoon sessions. Ethical alignment in such a framework often appears as a cost rather than a benefit. Investments in cleaner technology, fair wages, or supply chain transparency are discounted because they do not immediately increase margins. Worse, they may depress them in the near term. The short-term trader, conditioned to exploit fluctuations, cannot monetise these decisions quickly. But the long-term investor recognises that such choices are not marginal—they are foundational. The upfront costs of ethical alignment are investments in durability, reducing exposure to regulatory shocks, reputational crises, and consumer backlash. What looks like a drag on performance in the short run becomes a moat in the long run.

Consider the fate of tobacco. For much of the 20th century, tobacco companies produced staggering returns. Short-term investors profited handsomely from steady cash flows and aggressive marketing campaigns, even as mounting medical evidence revealed the product's dangers. By the 1990s, lawsuits, regulations, and social condemnation converged, permanently reshaping the industry. Long-term investors who failed to anticipate the moral tide paid dearly, watching valuations erode over decades. By contrast, those who had the patience to accept lower immediate yields in exchange for reallocating capital to emerging sectors—healthcare, technology, or consumer goods—outperformed in the long horizon. *Patience, in this sense, is the ability to trust time's alignment with ethics, to see moral risk not as external to markets but as the very soil from which future returns grow.*

The same logic applies to climate risk. Fossil fuel companies continue to generate short-term profits, their valuations buoyed by energy demand and geopolitical cycles. For the impatient trader, these earnings are irresistible. Yet the long-term investor asks a different question: can these profits be sustained in a world that must decarbonise? The answer becomes clearer each year as governments legislate, technologies advance, and public sentiment shifts. Patience is what allows an investor to step back and see the trajectory rather than the fluctuation. By reallocating capital to renewables, energy storage, or efficiency technologies, long-term investors accept the possibility of underperformance in the present but position themselves to capture the inevitability of transition. Here, patience is not passivity but foresight.

Behavioural finance sheds light on why patience is so difficult. Humans are wired to overweight the immediate and discount the distant. Loss aversion makes short-term dips feel unbearable, while confirmation bias leads investors to seek evidence that supports quick wins. This is why markets habitually misprice slow-moving moral risks: they are invisible to the impatient. The advantage of patience, then, is not merely financial but psychological. Long-term investors cultivate habits that counteract these biases, resisting the temptation to panic at volatility or chase the illusion of rapid gains. They replace reaction with reflection, aligning their decision-making with the slower but surer rhythms of compounding. *Patience is discipline applied over time, and in markets it becomes a rare form of intelligence.*

Philosophically, patience reframes the meaning of investment itself. The short-term trader treats capital as a tool for speculation, its purpose exhausted once a gain is realised. The long-term investor treats capital as a force for shaping the future, an expression of priorities that extends beyond personal wealth. Ethical alignment, therefore, is not an add-on but an inevitability: if one believes the future will punish exploitation and reward sustainability, then patience is simply the practice of waiting for that truth to manifest. The investor's role is not to predict the exact moment when the market will catch up, but to hold a position long enough that it cannot help but do so.

History confirms that markets eventually converge with morality, but rarely on the timetable traders demand. Asbestos was once a miracle material, used in everything from construction to consumer products. Its dangers were documented as early as the 1930s, yet the industry thrived for decades, buoyed by short-term profits. When the lawsuits came, they were catastrophic, bankrupting companies and wiping out billions in value. The patient investor who had exited earlier may have appeared overly cautious for years, but their prudence was vindicated. More recently, companies implicated in systemic harassment or abusive labour practices have seen valuations collapse only after scandals erupted, long after the warning signs were visible. In each case, patience allowed certain investors to avoid the trap of chasing quarterly performance at the expense of structural reality.

The practical implications are profound. Pension funds, endowments, and sovereign wealth funds—institutions with multi-generational horizons—are natural beneficiaries of patience. Their mandate is not to maximise next quarter's returns but to preserve and grow wealth for decades. Ethical alignment aligns seamlessly with this mission, ensuring that today's capital decisions do not create tomorrow's liabilities. By contrast, hedge funds and high-frequency traders, by design, cannot capture the same advantages. Their strategies thrive on volatility and arbitrage, but they are structurally incapable of waiting for moral risk to mature into financial risk. The advantage of patience, therefore, is not evenly distributed. It accrues most powerfully to those who can afford to wait—and who have the courage to align with principle while markets remain distracted by immediacy.

The rise of ESG and impact investing provides empirical support. Meta-analyses of sustainable funds over the past decade show that, while short-term performance varies, long-term outcomes tend to match or outperform traditional benchmarks. The reason is not mystical; it is practical. Companies that respect stakeholders, manage environmental impacts, and govern transparently are less exposed to shocks. They may not deliver explosive quarterly growth, but they compound steadily, weathering crises with resilience. For the patient investor, these are precisely the characteristics that sustain wealth across generations. *Patience, in this sense, is the quiet amplifier of ethical alignment, transforming moral foresight into financial durability.*

To embrace patience is to reject the tyranny of immediacy that defines much of modern finance. It is to acknowledge that markets, left to their own devices, will always lag morality, and that catching up is often painful. Investors who cultivate patience step outside this cycle. They refuse to be hostage to the noise of the present and instead commit to the clarity of the future. Ethical alignment, seen through this lens, is not a sacrifice but a strategy—a way of ensuring that when the market finally prices morality correctly, they are already positioned to benefit. Patience, therefore, is not only a virtue but an advantage, perhaps the last true arbitrage left in global finance: the arbitrage of time.

Case Study: The Carbon Bubble

Few metaphors in modern finance carry as much quiet menace as the idea of a carbon bubble. It suggests not only the overvaluation of assets tied to fossil fuels but also the inevitable reckoning when the weight of physical reality collides with the assumptions of financial models. At its core lies a simple but devastating calculation: the world already possesses more proven reserves of coal, oil, and gas than can ever be safely burned if humanity is to keep climate change within tolerable bounds. To invest as though these reserves will all be monetised is to ignore both scientific limits and political commitments. The consequence is stranded assets—resources that remain on corporate balance sheets but can never be exploited without catastrophic cost. *The carbon bubble is therefore not merely an environmental problem; it is a financial time bomb created by the refusal to integrate moral imperatives into economic reasoning.*

The genesis of the concept can be traced to the early 2010s, when think tanks such as Carbon Tracker began highlighting the "unburnable carbon" problem. Their reports compared the carbon embedded in proven reserves with the carbon budget consistent with the Paris Agreement's goal of limiting global warming to well below 2°C. The numbers were stark. Energy companies were sitting on reserves equivalent to several times the safe threshold. If governments honoured their climate pledges, vast swathes of these assets would become effectively worthless. Yet equity markets continued to capitalise fossil fuel firms as though demand would remain strong and politically unchallenged for decades. This disconnect between valuation and reality is precisely what defines a bubble: inflated prices sustained by denial until they collapse under the weight of truth.

Examples of stranded assets are already visible. In the United States, coal once provided more than half of electricity generation. Today, it accounts for less than a quarter, displaced by natural gas and renewables. Entire coal mines, valued as productive assets only a decade ago, now sit mothballed. In 2020, Peabody Energy, once the world's largest private-sector coal company, lost over 90 per cent of its market capitalisation compared to its peak. The collapse was not sudden; it unfolded over years as regulatory pressure, cleaner alternatives, and shifting public sentiment converged. The short-term trader might have profited intermittently during the decline, but the long-term investor who ignored climate risk was left holding depreciating assets. *The lesson is clear: markets rarely price morality until it is forced upon them, and by then the correction is brutal.*

Oil and gas face a similar trajectory. For much of the 21st century, they have appeared more resilient than coal, buoyed by continued demand and political inertia. Yet the structural risks are mounting. European supermajors such as BP and Shell have already written down billions of dollars in assets, acknowledging that part of their reserves may never be extracted profitably. These impairments are harbingers of a larger reckoning. If the world moves decisively towards net zero, as major economies from the EU to China have pledged, then a significant portion of fossil fuel reserves—currently counted as assets—will instead become liabilities. Valuations built on their monetisation will prove illusory. Investors who mistake current profitability for future security are betting against both policy momentum and physics itself.

What makes the carbon bubble particularly instructive is that it illustrates how *moral imperatives ignored in the present become financial disasters in the future*. Unlike other market risks, this one has been flagged in advance with unusual clarity. Scientists have quantified the limits; policymakers have codified them into treaties; activists have translated them into cultural pressure. The evidence is overwhelming. Yet inertia, vested interests, and the allure of short-term gains sustain the bubble. This mispricing persists because financial markets are conditioned to discount the distant, focusing on the next quarter rather than the next decade. But carbon is not patient. Each year of delay compounds the eventual cost, as the transition must become sharper, more disruptive, and more punishing to incumbents.

Investor sentiment is already beginning to shift. The divestment movement, once dismissed as symbolic, has grown into a force with trillions of dollars in commitments. Universities, pension funds, and even sovereign wealth funds have begun to exit fossil fuel holdings, citing both ethical concerns and financial prudence. Shareholder activism has pressured energy companies to disclose climate risks, stress-test their portfolios, and commit to decarbonisation pathways. BlackRock, the world's largest asset manager, has warned of the dangers of stranded assets, signalling that mainstream finance can no longer ignore the carbon bubble. Yet despite this progress, global capital flows still disproportionately favour fossil fuels. The inertia demonstrates how deeply engrained the short-termist mindset remains.

The bubble metaphor is useful but incomplete. Traditional bubbles—whether dot-com stocks or housing in 2008—eventually burst, redistributing capital painfully but visibly. The carbon bubble is more insidious. Its unwinding may occur unevenly, through gradual write-downs, tightening regulation, or sudden geopolitical shocks. This uncertainty makes it harder to anticipate and easier for investors to rationalise away. Yet the endpoint is inescapable: reserves that cannot be burned are worthless as fuel. For companies whose valuations depend on extracting and selling them, this is existential. For investors, it is a warning that delayed recognition of moral imperatives magnifies financial loss. *The market always catches up to reality, but those who wait for the reckoning pay the highest price.*

What the carbon bubble ultimately reveals is that ethics and economics are not parallel tracks but converging lines. The moral imperative to avoid catastrophic climate change is not external to finance; it defines the boundaries within which finance must operate. Investors who treat climate risk as a political debate or a public relations issue misunderstand its nature. It is a constraint on business models as binding as geology or physics. The companies and portfolios that acknowledge this early, adapt their strategies, and reallocate capital accordingly will not only mitigate risk but capture opportunity. Those that persist in denial will face declining valuations, stranded assets, and reputational damage that no short-term profit can offset.

In this sense, the carbon bubble is not merely a cautionary tale about fossil fuels. It is a template for understanding how all moral risks translate into financial costs when ignored. Whether labour rights, data privacy, or social justice, the principle holds: what begins as an ethical critique matures into regulatory action, cultural rejection, and eventually market repricing. Carbon is simply the most urgent and global of these risks, and therefore the most visible. But the broader lesson is that patience and principle are not luxuries in investing; they are necessities. To anticipate moral risk is to protect capital. To deny it is to inflate bubbles whose collapse is both inevitable and devastating.

The carbon bubble forces a reckoning with time itself. Investors are invited to choose between fleeting gains sustained by denial and durable wealth grounded in alignment with reality. The former is tempting but fragile; the latter demands patience but delivers resilience. As the world accelerates towards decarbonisation, the question is no longer whether the bubble will deflate, but who will bear the cost when it does. For those attentive to both conscience and capital, the answer is already clear: the prudent investor escapes the wreckage not by luck, but by recognising that *ignoring moral imperatives is the most expensive investment mistake of all.*

Chapter 5
The Psychology of Conscience and Capital

Money rarely moves by logic alone. Markets may be built on models of rational actors and efficient pricing, but beneath the surface of every allocation decision lies a web of beliefs, justifications, and psychological blind spots. Nowhere is this more apparent than in the field of ethical investing. For while investors may profess a desire to align their portfolios with their values, their actual behaviour often tells a different story. The discrepancy is not simply a matter of access to information or financial literacy—it is a question of psychology. To understand why conscience so often falters in practice, one must first understand the biases and mental shortcuts that govern financial decision-making.

One of the most striking examples is the persistence of cognitive dissonance in portfolios. Many individuals who would never purchase a product from a tobacco company, for instance, continue to hold shares in firms that derive revenue from cigarettes. The same holds for fossil fuels, arms manufacturers, or companies with questionable labour practices. The contradiction is rarely intentional. Instead, it reflects the human tendency to compartmentalise—to separate what we consume as citizens from what we pursue as investors. This mental separation allows investors to maintain a sense of moral integrity in everyday life while simultaneously profiting from activities they would otherwise condemn. The dissonance is tolerated by rationalisations: *I am just one investor; the system is too complex; my responsibility is only to maximise returns.* These justifications allow the contradiction to persist unchallenged, even as portfolios become silent endorsements of industries the investor would publicly oppose.

Compounding this problem is the phenomenon of moral licensing and its financial counterpart: greenwashing. When an investor chooses a fund that excludes a handful of controversial sectors, the decision may generate a disproportionate sense of virtue. This sense of having "done one's part" can obscure the reality that the vast majority of one's capital remains invested in companies with problematic practices. Corporations exploit this psychological vulnerability. A company might publicise its commitment to renewable energy while expanding oil production elsewhere, confident that the optics of sustainability will pacify investors. Similarly, asset managers may create ESG-labelled funds that hold many of the same securities as conventional indices, relying on the halo effect of the label to attract ethically minded clients. *A token gesture becomes a shield against deeper scrutiny, and in the process, conscience is dulled rather than sharpened.*

Yet it would be a mistake to view these behaviours as evidence of hypocrisy alone. They are manifestations of broader behavioural biases that shape all investing, ethical or otherwise. Confirmation bias, for instance, leads investors to seek evidence that validates their existing choices—choosing to highlight the sustainable elements of a company while ignoring its exploitative practices. Loss aversion, the tendency to weigh potential losses more heavily than equivalent gains, can paralyse investors who fear that aligning their capital with values will sacrifice returns. Even when presented with evidence that ethical investments perform competitively, the psychological weight of a potential missed gain can outweigh the appeal of aligning principle with practice. These biases are not unique to ethical investing, but their impact is magnified here because the stakes are not only financial but moral.

Understanding these dynamics is essential because the greatest barrier to ethical investing may not be the lack of products, data, or regulatory frameworks. It is the inertia of habit. Designing ethical habits is therefore the next frontier. Just as individuals can train themselves to shop more consciously by pausing to consider the origins of what they purchase, investors can cultivate routines that ensure their capital decisions reflect their stated principles. This may involve regular audits of portfolios, deliberate reflection on whether holdings align with personal values, or committing to investment vehicles with transparent reporting. *The key is to move from occasional, symbolic acts of alignment to systematic practices that integrate conscience into the rhythm of financial life.*

The psychology of investing has long been studied in the context of speculation, bubbles, and irrational exuberance. Yet its implications for conscience are only now becoming fully visible. Ethical investing is not a simple matter of will or knowledge; it is a behavioural challenge. To navigate it successfully requires not only awareness of external risks but also honesty about internal biases. By recognising how dissonance, moral licensing, and cognitive shortcuts distort judgement, investors can begin to design strategies that resist these tendencies. The reward is more than moral consistency. It is the creation of portfolios that reflect integrity, reduce hidden risks, and contribute to the shaping of markets where values and capital are no longer in conflict but in alignment.

This chapter invites readers to confront not only the markets but themselves. It asks uncomfortable questions: *What does my portfolio say about my principles? Do my financial habits support the values I claim to hold, or do they undermine them?* In seeking answers, readers will discover that ethical investing is not solely an external discipline imposed by regulations or product offerings. It is an internal discipline, cultivated through awareness, honesty, and practice. To master it is to recognise that the psychology of capital is inseparable from the psychology of conscience—and that true wealth is built when both are brought into coherence.

Cognitive Dissonance in Portfolios

The paradox of modern investing is that people who boycott fast-fashion brands for their use of sweatshop labour, campaign against plastic waste in their communities, or carefully choose organic food in the supermarket may simultaneously own shares in corporations that embody the very practices they resist. This is not hypocrisy in the casual sense of the term, but a deeper psychological phenomenon: cognitive dissonance, the discomfort created when values and actions collide. In the context of finance, this dissonance is particularly insidious because portfolios are rarely scrutinised with the same intensity as everyday consumption. Where consumers deliberate over coffee beans or clothing, investments often sit quietly in index funds or pensions, their moral weight obscured by abstraction.

The roots of this divide are historical as much as psychological. For decades, financial orthodoxy has reinforced the notion that investing is a domain apart from daily ethics. The doctrine of shareholder primacy, popularised in the late twentieth century, suggested that the sole responsibility of investors and managers alike was to maximise returns. Within such a framework, moral concerns were dismissed as distractions or inefficiencies. This framing created permission structures for individuals to compartmentalise: to live conscientiously as citizens and consumers while embracing amoral pragmatism as investors. The portfolio became an ethical blind spot, protected by the language of fiduciary duty and efficiency. *The market, it was assumed, is a neutral mechanism, not a moral actor.*

This mental division is reinforced by a series of justifications that allow dissonance to persist. The most common is the belief in personal insignificance: *my money is too small to make a difference.* The sheer scale of global capital markets makes it easy for an individual to conclude that their choices are inconsequential, even as millions make the same calculation in parallel, producing collective outcomes of enormous consequence. Another justification is the outsourcing of responsibility: investors assume that fund managers, regulators, or other institutions are monitoring ethical risks, relieving them of the burden of scrutiny. A third rationalisation is the framing of investment returns as detached from the source of profit: money, once abstracted into dividends or price appreciation, is perceived as morally neutral, stripped of its origins in production or exploitation.

Case studies bring this dissonance into sharper relief. Consider the persistence of fossil fuel holdings in pension funds. Many beneficiaries who advocate for climate action continue to benefit financially from oil and gas companies through their retirement accounts. In the United States, university endowments have faced student-led campaigns highlighting how institutions committed to sustainability often remain invested in coal or tar sands. In the United Kingdom, surveys show that a significant proportion of individuals would prefer their pensions to exclude harmful industries, yet most do not act on this preference. The gap between stated values and actual holdings persists because portfolios are psychologically insulated from scrutiny; they are perceived as technical instruments rather than moral statements.

The psychology of dissonance does not operate in isolation. It interacts with broader behavioural biases that reinforce inertia. Status quo bias, the tendency to prefer existing arrangements over change, discourages investors from re-evaluating their holdings. Complexity aversion adds to the inertia: the sheer volume of financial products, ratings, and disclosures overwhelms many, leading to passive acceptance rather than active alignment. Even when individuals are presented with the option of switching to ethical funds, the perceived effort and risk of change often outweigh the discomfort of inconsistency. In effect, the mind resolves dissonance not by changing the portfolio, but by suppressing or reinterpreting the conflict.

This phenomenon has been studied beyond finance. In psychology, cognitive dissonance theory highlights the mental strategies people employ to reduce the tension between beliefs and actions. These include trivialisation—dismissing the importance of the issue; justification—emphasising external constraints; and denial—refusing to acknowledge the conflict altogether. In portfolios, these mechanisms translate into comments like *"ethical investing doesn't really work"* or *"returns matter more than principles."* These statements often mask not informed scepticism, but discomfort rationalised into ideology. *The cost of facing the contradiction feels higher than the cost of ignoring it.*

Yet the consequences of dissonance are not merely psychological; they are financial. By ignoring the moral character of investments, investors expose themselves to risks that are mispriced in the short term but devastating in the long term. Industries built on exploitative labour practices may face sudden regulatory changes or consumer backlash. Companies reliant on environmentally destructive activities may confront stranded assets or litigation. Investors who ignore these risks because they are shielded by rationalisations are not simply compromising values—they are compromising returns. Dissonance here is not only an ethical failure but a strategic one.

The challenge, then, is not only to expose dissonance but to provide tools to resolve it constructively. For many, the first step is recognition: mapping a portfolio against personal values and confronting discrepancies. Some investors find clarity by asking themselves simple but piercing questions: *Would I be comfortable if my investments were public knowledge? Could I defend these holdings to my children or peers?* Others turn to frameworks that integrate both ethical and financial analysis, helping to close the gap between aspiration and action. What matters is not perfection—no portfolio can be entirely free of compromise—but intentionality. *Acknowledging the dissonance is the beginning of designing coherence.*

There are also signs that this shift is accelerating. Digital platforms now allow individuals to see the social and environmental footprint of their portfolios at a glance. Campaigns by NGOs and activist investors have raised awareness about hidden holdings in controversial industries. Younger generations, less attached to the shareholder primacy orthodoxy, are demanding alignment between principles and capital. In each case, the act of exposure—making the hidden contradiction visible—forces individuals to confront the discomfort that previously remained abstract. Cognitive dissonance, once concealed, becomes a call to action.

Critics may argue that expecting perfect alignment between values and portfolios is unrealistic. After all, markets are interconnected and compromise inevitable. This is true, but the argument risks becoming a shield for inertia. The goal is not to eliminate dissonance entirely but to reduce it meaningfully. Investors can choose funds that exclude the most egregious industries, support companies with transparent sustainability practices, or engage actively as shareholders to press for change. These steps do not demand moral purity but reflect moral seriousness. The difference lies in intent: whether dissonance is passively tolerated or actively addressed.

At its core, the issue of cognitive dissonance in portfolios highlights a deeper truth: money is never morally neutral. Every pound or dollar invested sustains some vision of the world, whether acknowledged or ignored. When people continue to invest in industries they oppose, it is not merely a contradiction between conscience and capital; it is a reinforcement of the very practices they seek to resist. By recognising and resolving these contradictions, investors reclaim not only moral integrity but also financial foresight. The portfolios that withstand the future will be those that have confronted dissonance head-on, transforming discomfort into disciplined alignment.

Cognitive dissonance is often described as an internal tension, but in finance it is externalised, shaping markets and influencing corporate behaviour. Millions of small rationalisations aggregate into billions of dollars flowing towards harmful industries. Conversely, millions of small acts of alignment can redirect capital towards more sustainable, equitable futures. The challenge for investors is to recognise that their portfolios are not passive containers of wealth but active participants in shaping the world. To confront dissonance is to recognise that investing is not separate from life—it is an extension of it.

Moral Licensing and Greenwashing

There is a peculiar psychological relief that comes from doing something that feels virtuous. A person who donates a small sum to charity may feel justified in spending extravagantly on themselves afterwards; one who cycles to work may feel less guilty about a weekend flight. This dynamic—known in behavioural science as moral licensing—does not end with consumer habits. It is deeply embedded in the way people invest. Many investors, eager to see themselves as conscientious, make a symbolic allocation to a socially responsible fund or purchase a handful of "green" bonds, while leaving the overwhelming majority of their capital in conventional funds propping up industries they would never endorse in daily life. The gesture becomes a psychological cover, a way of satisfying the conscience without making substantive change. *Moral licensing allows investors to feel good while achieving little, and sometimes, while perpetuating the very problems they claim to oppose.*

The financial industry has learned to capitalise on this impulse. Asset managers, ever alert to the mood of the market, have perfected the art of packaging moral satisfaction in palatable form. This is where greenwashing enters: the deliberate presentation of investment products as environmentally or socially responsible when, under closer scrutiny, they are barely distinguishable from mainstream portfolios. Labels such as "sustainable," "green," or "ethical" are applied liberally, often on the basis of minimal exclusions or token weighting adjustments. For example, a fund might exclude only coal while maintaining significant exposure to oil and gas; another might hold a handful of renewable energy firms alongside a long list of companies with dubious labour practices. Investors, seeing the reassuring label, accept the product at face value, believing their money is aligned with their values. The market thrives on this superficial comfort.

The consequences of moral licensing and greenwashing are profound, not only for individuals but for the allocation of capital across the global economy. When investors mistake symbolic action for genuine alignment, they inadvertently reinforce the status quo. Companies with questionable environmental or social practices continue to attract funding, shielded by the illusion that capital is flowing to "better" options. Meanwhile, truly transformative enterprises—those developing new energy solutions, pioneering fair labour practices, or advancing sustainable agriculture—struggle to attract sufficient investment because the demand for depth is diluted by a flood of shallow, branded alternatives. *The very capital that could accelerate systemic change is trapped in cosmetic adjustments that protect investor conscience rather than the planet or society.*

Examples abound. In 2021, research by Morningstar found that over half of funds marketed as "sustainable" still held investments in major oil and gas firms. The controversy surrounding DWS, the asset management arm of Deutsche Bank, underscored the problem when regulators accused the firm of exaggerating the extent to which ESG criteria guided its investments. Similar scandals have emerged elsewhere, with funds claiming climate credentials while backing companies with poor emissions records. These cases highlight a troubling asymmetry: marketing promises are vivid and emotionally resonant, while disclosures are opaque, technical, and often inaccessible to the average investor. The imbalance ensures that psychological satisfaction outweighs analytical scrutiny.

Why do investors accept this? The psychology is layered. First, there is the desire to resolve cognitive dissonance without the discomfort of major change. Allocating a small portion of capital to an ESG-branded product feels sufficient to reconcile conscience and action. Second, there is the halo effect: once a fund carries the "green" label, investors assume it must be broadly aligned with sustainability, without interrogating the details. Third, there is the bias of delegation: most people assume that regulators, fund managers, or rating agencies have done the necessary diligence, freeing them from the burden of critical evaluation. These shortcuts are understandable in a complex market, but they perpetuate systemic complacency.

The dynamic is not limited to individual investors. Institutions, too, fall prey to moral licensing and greenwashing. Universities may divest from tobacco while maintaining holdings in fossil fuels. Pension funds may trumpet small allocations to renewable infrastructure while their core portfolios remain tied to high-carbon industries. Even governments participate, issuing "green bonds" that finance marginally improved projects while continuing to subsidise environmentally destructive activities. In each case, the token act of alignment provides cover for the continuation of misaligned practices on a much larger scale.

It is important to recognise that greenwashing is not always the result of deliberate deceit. Sometimes it is born of structural ambiguity. ESG metrics, as discussed elsewhere in this book, are inconsistent, allowing companies and funds to cherry-pick favourable criteria. One rating agency might award high marks for governance, offsetting poor environmental practices, while another weights environmental factors more heavily. Fund managers, facing these contradictions, highlight the favourable assessments and downplay the rest. The lack of universal standards creates fertile ground for selective interpretation, and in the gaps between metrics, the illusion of sustainability flourishes.

The risk for investors is twofold: moral and financial. On the moral side, they may believe they are contributing to positive change when they are not, perpetuating a sense of complacency that delays systemic progress. On the financial side, they expose themselves to the same risks they believe they have avoided. An investor who buys into a "green" fund with substantial fossil fuel holdings may still face the risk of stranded assets when climate policies tighten.

Similarly, those who think they are protected from reputational risks by holding "ethical" funds may discover that scandals in underlying companies erode both trust and returns. *Moral licensing may soothe the conscience, but it does not protect the portfolio.*

The challenge, then, is not merely to call out greenwashing but to cultivate discernment. Investors must ask harder questions: What exactly does this fund exclude? How does it engage with companies it holds? Are its sustainability claims independently verified? Transparency is essential, but so is investor vigilance. Just as consumers learned to distinguish genuine fair-trade products from marketing gimmicks, investors must learn to separate substantive alignment from superficial branding. This requires effort, but it is the price of integrity in capital markets.

There are encouraging signs of a cultural shift. Regulatory bodies in the European Union and the United States are tightening rules on sustainable disclosures, requiring asset managers to substantiate their claims. Activist organisations are publishing analyses of funds, exposing discrepancies between rhetoric and reality. Technology platforms are emerging to give individual investors greater visibility into the true composition of their portfolios. These developments reduce the space for greenwashing, but they cannot eliminate the temptation of moral licensing. That responsibility lies with investors themselves: to resist the comfort of tokenism and demand alignment in the majority, not the margins, of their capital.

Ultimately, the psychology of moral licensing and the practice of greenwashing illuminate a deeper truth about ethical investing: *it is easier to appear aligned than to be aligned.*

Symbolic gestures are attractive because they satisfy both marketing needs and human psychology. But systemic change requires more than gestures. It demands that investors confront the discomfort of dissonance, the complexity of transparency, and the discipline of genuine alignment. If conscience is to guide capital meaningfully, it must extend beyond a token allocation or a branded product. It must permeate the whole architecture of investment decisions, ensuring that capital is not merely a mirror of intent but a driver of transformation.

In this sense, moral licensing and greenwashing are not simply obstacles to ethical investing—they are tests of its seriousness. They force us to ask whether our actions are designed to ease our minds or to change the world. And they remind us that the line between sincerity and symbolism is thin, but the consequences of failing to cross it are immense.

Behavioural Biases in Ethical Investing

The decisions investors make are rarely governed by reason alone. Markets like to cloak themselves in the language of rationality, efficiency, and hard data, yet beneath that surface lie patterns of human psychology that shape outcomes as powerfully as balance sheets or quarterly earnings. Nowhere is this more evident than in ethical investing. When capital is meant to align with conscience, the interplay of biases intensifies, as investors juggle not only financial objectives but also moral self-image. Two of the most influential distortions—confirmation bias and loss aversion—quietly undermine the very intentions that draw people to values-based funds in the first place.

Confirmation bias, the tendency to seek information that validates pre-existing beliefs, is especially potent in the context of ethical finance. Investors who are convinced that their "green" or "socially responsible" allocation is doing good will gravitate toward articles, fund marketing, and selective statistics that confirm the moral soundness of their choice. They may ignore or downplay evidence that the fund's holdings include companies with questionable records on human rights or carbon emissions. The narrative of virtue is preserved by filtering the data that supports it. *This bias allows investors to sustain a flattering story about their portfolios, but it blinds them to hidden contradictions.* For instance, when Tesla was first added to major ESG indices, many investors celebrated it as a triumph of sustainable transport without probing its supply chain controversies, labour disputes, or reliance on emissions credits. The fact that Tesla symbolised progress was enough to silence doubt. Confirmation bias ensured that uncomfortable complexities were relegated to the background.

At the same time, loss aversion exerts a subtler but equally corrosive influence. The psychological principle, rooted in behavioural economics, states that people experience the pain of losses far more acutely than the pleasure of equivalent gains. In ethical investing, this creates a tension: investors who say they want to align their money with their values often hesitate to divest from profitable but misaligned industries for fear of missing out on returns. A pension fund trustee may acknowledge the climate risks of fossil fuel exposure yet balk at selling oil stocks that have rebounded in price. A retail investor may express outrage at exploitative labour practices but cling to a diversified index fund that includes fast-fashion giants. The spectre of short-term underperformance outweighs the long-term moral and financial rationale for change. *Loss aversion anchors investors to the very positions they claim to want to abandon.*

When confirmation bias and loss aversion intersect, the effect is a peculiar form of paralysis. Investors reassure themselves that their partial steps toward ethical alignment are adequate, while rationalising why deeper shifts must wait. They amplify evidence that suggests ESG funds can outperform while dismissing countervailing studies, and they cling to conventional holdings by convincing themselves that divestment would be reckless. In this way, portfolios become patchworks of compromise, reflecting neither pure profit-maximisation nor genuine ethical coherence. The result is not deliberate hypocrisy but the accumulation of small, biased choices that erode integrity over time.

The market provides ample reinforcement for these biases. Asset managers craft narratives that flatter investor conscience, highlighting the outperformance of select ESG funds during specific timeframes while glossing over volatility or inconsistency. Media coverage often fuels the confirmation loop, elevating stories of "green finance success" that reassure investors they are on the right path. Meanwhile, the relentless focus on quarterly reporting feeds loss aversion by framing short-term dips as catastrophic, discouraging the patience required for values-based strategies to mature. *The architecture of modern finance is not neutral; it amplifies the very biases that ethical investing seeks to overcome.*

To understand how deeply these biases can shape behaviour, consider the example of fossil fuel divestment campaigns. Universities, pension funds, and religious institutions have faced sustained pressure to withdraw capital from oil, gas, and coal. While many have eventually acted, the path has often been halting. Confirmation bias allows trustees to seize on studies suggesting that fossil fuels remain indispensable to the economy, while dismissing evidence that stranded assets pose existential risks. Loss aversion makes the prospect of underperformance intolerable, even when long-term modelling suggests the opposite. The delay in action illustrates how psychological comfort and fear of loss combine to perpetuate exposure to industries misaligned with institutional values.

The irony is that these biases can erode financial returns as much as moral credibility. Confirmation bias blinds investors to the fragility of their assumptions. Loss aversion locks them into legacy assets even as the regulatory, technological, and cultural tides shift. Both delay necessary adjustments, increasing the likelihood of being caught off guard when markets eventually reprice ethical risks. The investors who believe they are playing it safe by clinging to the familiar may, in reality, be heightening their vulnerability. *Biases that feel protective in the short term often compound risk in the long term.*

The challenge, therefore, is not simply to expose these biases but to cultivate structures and habits that counteract them. Transparency is a crucial first step: investors need better visibility into what their funds actually hold, reducing the scope for confirmation bias to flourish. Peer accountability also matters: institutions that commit to ethical principles must publish progress reports and subject themselves to scrutiny, reducing the temptation to cherry-pick data. As for loss aversion, framing is key. If divestment is presented as "giving up" a profitable sector, resistance is strong; if it is reframed as reallocating capital toward future resilience, the psychological barrier weakens. Behavioural finance teaches us that perception shapes reality as much as numbers do.

Practical measures can reinforce these shifts. Automatic divestment triggers—rules that mandate selling when companies breach specified ethical thresholds—help override individual hesitation. Long-term benchmarks, rather than quarterly comparisons, encourage patience by shifting focus away from immediate fluctuations. Advisory structures that integrate behavioural expertise alongside financial analysis can help investors recognise when their decisions are being distorted by unconscious biases. *Ethical alignment requires not only moral clarity but also psychological discipline.*

None of this eliminates the human element from investing; nor should it. The presence of biases reminds us that markets are not machines but reflections of human psychology, with all its frailties and contradictions. Yet awareness is a form of power. To understand how confirmation bias and loss aversion shape decisions is to begin the process of resisting them. Ethical investing will only achieve its potential when investors are as attentive to the architecture of their minds as to the composition of their portfolios.

Ultimately, the significance of behavioural biases in ethical investing lies in what they reveal about the limits of intention. Goodwill and aspiration are not enough; they must be matched by structures that prevent psychology from sabotaging principle. Without such discipline, the market of conscience risks devolving into a theatre of self-reassurance, where investors believe they are advancing change while merely reinforcing old patterns. By recognising and countering these distortions, investors can reclaim the possibility that values-based funds were meant to embody: not a compromise between ethics and returns, but a pathway where conscience and capital strengthen one another rather than conflict.

Designing Ethical Habits

The gap between what investors say they value and how their capital is deployed is often less a matter of cynicism than of inertia. Ethical investing does not usually fail because people reject its principles, but because aligning money with conscience requires deliberate effort sustained over years. Behavioural finance has shown that the most reliable way to overcome inertia is not by cultivating bursts of willpower, but by embedding patterns that become automatic. *To invest ethically is not merely to make a one-time choice but to design habits that persist, compound, and ultimately reshape both markets and the investor's own moral compass.*

The first and most fundamental step is clarity. Investors who are vague about their ethical priorities are far more likely to drift into compromises. A person who says they want to "do good" with their portfolio will find themselves at the mercy of fund marketing or convenient narratives. By contrast, those who articulate non-negotiables—such as a refusal to hold companies involved in fossil fuels, tobacco, or exploitative labour—create a filter that disciplines their decisions. This does not require drawing up an exhaustive manifesto, but it does demand specificity. *Vague ideals encourage rationalisation, while explicit criteria provide a framework for accountability.*

Clarity, however, is not enough without mechanisms that enforce consistency. One of the most effective is automation. Just as automatic enrolment has transformed pension savings, automatic allocation toward ethical funds can transform values-based investing. The fewer opportunities investors have to rationalise or delay, the more faithfully their stated principles will be enacted. Setting recurring contributions into screened funds or choosing default options aligned with ethical criteria removes the need to negotiate with one's own biases month after month. In this sense, automation is not a loss of freedom but a reinforcement of integrity, protecting investors from the temptations of short-termism or complacency.

Another essential habit is the practice of review—not in the sense of constantly tinkering with holdings, but of periodic reflection. Ethical criteria evolve. Social norms shift, technologies change, and new evidence emerges about corporate practices. Investors who fail to revisit their assumptions risk discovering that their "sustainable" fund has drifted into holding companies that no longer meet their standards. An annual or biennial review provides an opportunity to recalibrate, to ask whether the portfolio still mirrors the investor's moral stance, and to make adjustments without succumbing to the noise of daily market movements. *The habit of reflection ensures that ethical investing remains a living practice, not a static declaration.*

Education is another underappreciated habit. Most investors are quick to learn about tax advantages, diversification, or performance metrics, yet they rarely commit to ongoing learning about the ethical dimensions of finance. Reading fund prospectuses critically, following investigative reporting on corporate behaviour, or studying regulatory developments deepens the ability to distinguish between genuine alignment and superficial marketing. Without this discipline, investors are easy prey for greenwashing. *Sustained learning is not optional in ethical investing; it is the price of autonomy in a marketplace crowded with seductive but misleading claims.*

Practical accountability can further reinforce ethical habits. This may take the form of joining an investment club with shared values, publicly disclosing parts of one's allocation, or engaging with shareholder advocacy groups that provide collective scrutiny of corporate behaviour. The point is not to outsource conscience, but to create external reference points that counteract the human tendency toward self-justification. When decisions are visible to peers, it becomes harder to indulge in quiet compromises. Such forms of accountability also amplify individual influence, since even modest investors, when acting collectively, can exert pressure on corporate governance far beyond their own stake.

One of the most difficult habits to cultivate is patience. Ethical funds may underperform conventional indices for stretches of time, especially when markets favour extractive or unsustainable industries. Investors who have not built the expectation of volatility into their habits are prone to abandon their principles at the first sign of lagging returns. To counter this, some adopt the practice of framing performance over five or ten years rather than quarter to quarter. Others choose benchmarks that reflect values as well as returns, so that the "scorecard" itself reinforces the desired behaviour. *Patience is not simply a virtue; it is a design feature of any ethical strategy that hopes to endure.*

The final habit is engagement. Ethical investing does not end at the point of allocation; it continues through active ownership. Voting at annual meetings, submitting shareholder resolutions, and engaging with fund managers about their screening policies are all mechanisms by which investors transform passive capital into an active lever of change. Too often, investors assume that once they have chosen a "responsible" fund, their role is complete. Yet history shows that companies shift not only because capital moves away from them, but because the capital that remains demands better behaviour. *The habit of engagement ensures that ethical investing exerts pressure from within as well as from without.*

When viewed together, these habits form a kind of architecture for conscience in finance. Clarity, automation, review, education, accountability, patience, and engagement are not lofty ideals but repeatable practices. They protect investors from the biases that cloud judgement, from the fatigue that leads to compromise, and from the market's relentless pull toward the convenient over the principled. The irony is that by embedding such routines, ethical investing ceases to feel burdensome. It becomes as natural as saving for retirement or rebalancing a portfolio—an integral part of financial life rather than an occasional gesture.

The deeper significance of designing ethical habits lies in its cumulative effect. A single investor may feel that their choices are a drop in the ocean. Yet habits, by definition, are repeated. Repetition compounds. Over time, patterns of allocation redirect streams of capital, and those streams reshape industries. What begins as an individual discipline aggregates into cultural momentum, influencing asset managers, regulators, and corporations. Ethical investing, sustained by habit, thus achieves the one thing occasional virtue cannot: persistence. And persistence is what makes principles visible in balance sheets, boardrooms, and entire markets. *The alignment of conscience and capital does not hinge on heroic choices, but on ordinary habits made consistent.*

Chapter 6
Lessons from History

The idea that capital is never neutral may feel like a distinctly modern revelation, born of climate debates, corporate scandals, and the rise of ESG. Yet history reminds us that money has always carried moral weight, shaping as much as reflecting the social order of its time. Long before the vocabulary of "sustainable finance" or "impact investing" entered circulation, communities and movements were already asking: what does it mean to profit from harm? The answers they gave did not simply remain in the realm of personal conscience. They created ripples that altered industries, redirected flows of wealth, and in some cases, helped dismantle systems of oppression. *To study these episodes is not an exercise in nostalgia but an inquiry into a recurring truth: ethics may be slow to register in balance sheets, but once they do, they alter the trajectory of markets in ways that can no longer be ignored.*

Consider the transatlantic slave trade, perhaps the starkest example of profit and principle colliding. In the eighteenth century, the trade was not peripheral but central to global commerce. Ships, insurance, banks, and plantations all depended on the labour of enslaved people. Against this overwhelming tide, the decision of Quakers and early abolitionists to refuse investments linked to slavery looked financially irrational, even quixotic. Yet their stance planted the seeds of one of history's first organised divestment movements. For them, conscience could not be subordinated to returns. Over time, their refusal to treat humans as commodities helped create the moral and financial conditions that eroded the legitimacy of the slave economy. What seemed marginal at first became foundational: it revealed that *capital, when withheld, can become as powerful a lever for justice as when deployed.*

The pattern repeated two centuries later in the campaigns against apartheid South Africa. Corporations and universities faced mounting pressure from activists and citizens to withdraw capital from companies doing business with the apartheid regime. At first, the argument that divestment could influence political realities was met with scepticism. Critics argued that markets were too vast, that moral gestures could not alter entrenched power. Yet as institutions—from pension funds to municipalities—pulled their money, the cumulative effect became undeniable. Financial isolation compounded the political isolation of South Africa, hastening the collapse of apartheid. The campaign not only influenced the nation's trajectory but also set a template for later values-based movements. It demonstrated that divestment is not merely symbolic but, when sustained, can reconfigure incentives at the highest levels of power.

A more recent example lies in the global tobacco industry. For much of the twentieth century, tobacco was one of the most profitable businesses on earth. Its dominance seemed untouchable, supported by powerful lobbies and decades of advertising that blurred the link between smoking and disease. Yet the convergence of medical evidence, public health advocacy, and investor pressure began to chip away at the façade. As funds and institutions divested, they not only expressed disapproval but also redefined the calculus of risk. Tobacco companies suddenly faced rising capital costs, lawsuits, and reputational collapse. The shift did not happen overnight, but the arc was clear: what had been a lucrative sector became a pariah, squeezed not just by regulation but by the withdrawal of moral legitimacy. *Markets eventually followed where ethics had long pointed, a reminder that profitability untethered from principle is rarely sustainable.*

When viewed together, these episodes illustrate a pattern that continues to resonate. Moral clarity is often dismissed as impractical idealism, but history shows it to be a leading indicator of economic change. What is judged unsustainable in human or ethical terms eventually proves unsustainable in financial terms. The lag between the two may be years or decades, but the convergence is inescapable. This is not to say that ethics guarantee profit or that every principled stance is vindicated. But over time, industries built on exploitation, harm, or deceit reveal structural weaknesses that markets, with their focus on short-term gains, are slow to acknowledge. Investors who attune themselves to this dynamic—who recognise that *ethics are often early warnings dressed as moral imperatives*—position themselves ahead of the curve rather than behind it.

The relevance for contemporary investors is direct. Today's debates about fossil fuels, artificial intelligence, or labour practices in global supply chains are not unprecedented. They are variations on a historical theme: the contest between immediate profit and enduring principle. Just as abolitionists, divestment campaigners, and public health advocates once faced charges of naïveté, so too do advocates of ethical finance today. Yet the historical record provides both reassurance and challenge. Reassurance, in that principled action has demonstrably shifted markets before. Challenge, in that delay carries costs—not only for societies but for investors who misprice moral risk until it crystallises as financial loss.

This chapter invites the reader to examine these lessons with both humility and pragmatism. Humility, because no generation can claim to invent ethical finance anew; the struggles of the past provide the foundation on which current debates stand. Pragmatism, because the historical record underscores that aligning capital with conscience is not simply virtuous but often prescient. By tracing how money has mirrored, resisted, or reinforced ethical norms across centuries, we can better see how today's capital choices will one day be judged. The past is not just prologue; it is a map, charting the recurring ways in which principle and profit intersect, collide, and—given enough time—converge.

The Slave Trade and Early Divestment

Few episodes reveal more starkly the tension between profit and principle than the transatlantic slave trade. For centuries, it was not merely tolerated but actively integrated into the machinery of global commerce. Ships financed by European banks carried enslaved Africans across the Atlantic, their forced labour underwriting the wealth of empires. Insurance firms in London underwrote voyages, merchants in Liverpool and Bristol built fortunes, and colonial plantations produced the sugar, cotton, and tobacco that became staples of international trade. The system was vast, entrenched, and ruthlessly profitable. Against this backdrop, the decision of a small religious community to renounce all financial connection with slavery might appear inconsequential. Yet the early acts of divestment by Quakers and other abolitionists in the eighteenth century represented one of the first concerted attempts to align capital with conscience, laying intellectual and practical foundations for what we now call values-based investing.

The Society of Friends, better known as the Quakers, were among the earliest communities to grapple with the moral implications of financial entanglement with slavery. By the late seventeenth century, individual Quakers were already questioning whether participation in the trade could ever be reconciled with their spiritual commitments. This internal debate intensified through the eighteenth century, culminating in decisive action: members were prohibited not only from owning slaves but also from investing in or profiting from slavery-related enterprises. It was an unusually comprehensive stance. They recognised that complicity did not only lie in direct ownership of enslaved people but extended to financing ships, trading goods produced by forced labour, or insuring voyages. In essence, the Quakers pioneered a principle that still resonates in modern finance: *capital is never passive; where it flows, it legitimises.*

The significance of this divestment lay not just in moral symbolism but in its economic ramifications. Quakers were deeply embedded in commerce, with considerable influence in banking, manufacturing, and trade. By withdrawing their capital from slavery-linked enterprises, they introduced a fissure into the supposedly seamless logic of profit. At a time when slavery appeared indispensable to the global economy, their stance underscored that financial decisions could be moral decisions, and that profitability alone did not constitute justification. To outsiders, this may have looked like self-imposed limitation, even financial naivety. Yet history would vindicate their foresight. The moral critique of slavery, once dismissed as radical, became a political and economic reality, culminating in abolition in Britain in 1833 and in the United States three decades later.

What is striking is how closely this early movement parallels later forms of socially responsible investing. Modern investors debate fossil fuel divestment or exclusionary screens for weapons and tobacco; eighteenth-century Quakers confronted the same structural questions. Can one draw ethical boundaries around capital? How does complicity extend beyond direct involvement to secondary or tertiary exposure? Their answers were uncompromising. To profit from exploitation, even indirectly, was to endorse it. In today's language, we might call this an early articulation of supply chain responsibility and systemic risk. By refusing to separate morality from finance, they reframed investment itself as a declaration of values.

Abolitionist thinkers outside the Quaker community further amplified this stance. Campaigners such as Granville Sharp and William Wilberforce understood that moral arguments alone, however compelling, could not dismantle a system so deeply entwined with profit. They mobilised consumer boycotts—famously of sugar produced on slave plantations—as well as investor activism. This combination of capital withdrawal and public pressure demonstrated the potential of coordinated financial behaviour to reshape entire industries. By refusing to purchase goods produced by enslaved labour, ordinary citizens transformed markets into sites of resistance. The message was unambiguous: to buy, to sell, or to invest was to choose a side. *The market, far from being morally neutral, became a battlefield of conscience.*

Sceptics might argue that such gestures were negligible in economic terms. After all, the slave trade continued to flourish for decades even as Quakers and abolitionists pursued divestment and boycotts. Yet this misses the deeper point. The significance of these actions lay less in their immediate financial impact than in their capacity to delegitimise. They destabilised the moral foundations of the trade, eroding the narrative that slavery was simply an economic necessity. Once capital began to withdraw, however partially, it introduced an element of reputational risk. Merchants and investors could no longer claim ignorance; their profits were publicly linked to human suffering. Over time, this shift in perception created a political climate in which abolition became not only morally compelling but economically inevitable. The system, once treated as permanent, came to be viewed as untenable.

The parallels with contemporary debates are instructive. Today, investors in fossil fuels or surveillance technologies often argue that their withdrawal would make little difference in the grand scheme of global markets. Yet history suggests otherwise. The symbolic act of divestment, especially when taken by influential institutions, can alter narratives, shift norms, and accelerate political momentum. *Capital carries a signalling function that transcends spreadsheets; it tells societies what is tolerated and what is not.* The Quakers understood this intuitively, even before financial theory gave it formal expression.

There is also a lesson here about the lag between morality and markets. For decades, investors in slavery enjoyed extraordinary profits, seemingly immune to moral critique. Yet those profits were fragile, built on an unsustainable foundation of exploitation and violence. When abolition eventually triumphed, it did not simply end a moral crime; it also rendered vast swathes of capital obsolete. Ships, plantations, and businesses collapsed. Those who had dismissed early divestment as impractical suddenly faced total loss. Conversely, those who had already redirected their capital into industries not dependent on slavery were better positioned for the new order. *The arc from moral risk to financial risk may be long, but it is reliable.*

By examining the slave trade through the lens of early divestment, we can see how the ethics of investment are not peripheral but central to historical change. The refusal of Quakers and abolitionists to profit from slavery was not a marginal footnote but a catalyst that revealed the power of values-based finance centuries before the term existed. It reminds us that investors are not merely spectators to history but participants in shaping it. Their choices can entrench injustice or accelerate reform.

The broader lesson is as relevant now as it was then: what appears financially rational in the short term can prove ruinous when measured against the long horizon of ethics and economics combined. The slave trade, once the beating heart of global commerce, was dismantled not only by political will and human struggle but also by the withdrawal of capital that refused to legitimise it. Modern investors would do well to recall that precedent. When faced with industries built on exploitation, harm, or unsustainable practices, the question is not whether divestment matters but whether history will once again vindicate those who recognised that principle and profit are not enemies but guides to one another.

Apartheid South Africa

When investors and institutions withdrew their money from apartheid-era South Africa, they did more than register disapproval; they helped transform the political economy of a nation. The divestment movement that gathered pace from the 1970s through the 1980s remains one of the most consequential demonstrations of how finance can become an instrument of moral and political pressure. Unlike earlier boycotts and protests, this was not just about citizens refusing to buy certain goods; it was about systematically choking the flow of international capital that underpinned an unjust system. The result was not instantaneous, nor was it free from controversy, but the cumulative effect is hard to overstate: *when money left, legitimacy followed.*

The South African economy under apartheid relied heavily on foreign investment. Mining houses, banks, and manufacturing firms all depended on international capital markets to fund expansion and sustain profitability. The country's abundant mineral resources—gold, diamonds, and later platinum—attracted investors who often preferred to bracket out the political realities of racial segregation in favour of steady returns. For decades, this arrangement seemed stable. The apartheid state was repressive but resilient, bolstered by foreign loans and investments that tacitly endorsed its legitimacy. In this sense, global capital was not a bystander but an accomplice.

The divestment campaign challenged this complicity head-on. It began in universities and churches, where activists argued that investments in companies operating in South Africa were effectively underwriting racial oppression. Students demanded that endowments sell holdings in firms with South African exposure. Clergy denounced pension funds that profited from apartheid-linked industries. These efforts drew inspiration from earlier models of values-based finance, such as Quaker opposition to the slave trade, but they amplified them on a far larger, more global scale. Crucially, the campaign linked ethics with economics: to invest was to condone, but to divest was to disrupt.

By the early 1980s, the movement had gained institutional traction. Universities such as the University of California and Harvard faced mounting pressure to sell their South African holdings. Religious organisations, including the World Council of Churches, began to restructure their investment policies. Municipal governments in the United States passed resolutions banning contracts with companies doing business in South Africa. Even some corporations pre-emptively withdrew, recognising that reputational risk outweighed short-term gains. Each act of divestment, though often financially modest in isolation, contributed to a snowball effect. *The narrative shifted: apartheid was no longer just a South African issue but a global financial liability.*

Sceptics argued that divestment was symbolic at best, pointing out that shares sold by activists were quickly purchased by less scrupulous investors. Others worried that disinvestment would hurt black South Africans more than the white minority regime, as job losses and economic contraction would fall disproportionately on the oppressed. These critiques were not without substance, and they forced activists to refine their arguments. Proponents countered that the goal was not to starve ordinary South Africans but to isolate the regime, making it politically and economically untenable for the state to persist in its policies. Over time, the weight of moral consensus overwhelmed the objections.

The tipping point came in the mid-1980s when major financial institutions began to reassess their exposure. In 1985, Chase Manhattan Bank announced it would not roll over South Africa's short-term debt, triggering a crisis in the country's credit markets. Other banks followed suit. The rand collapsed, inflation soared, and South Africa was forced to declare a temporary debt standstill. The symbolism was potent: global finance had lost confidence in apartheid. Political leaders, including President P.W. Botha, were shaken not just by protests in the streets but by the retreat of the very capital that had sustained their system. *Divestment had crossed from moral gesture to material constraint.*

For investors, the South African case was a revelation. It demonstrated that capital flight could erode the foundations of an entrenched regime, especially one dependent on external financing. Unlike consumer boycotts, which could be dismissed as peripheral, divestment directly undermined the state's fiscal stability. The precedent influenced subsequent models of ethical investing, proving that the collective redirection of capital could be as forceful as sanctions or legislation. In this sense, apartheid became a template: financial activism was no longer fringe but a legitimate tool of geopolitical strategy.

The legacy of the campaign is complex. Critics note that economic sanctions and divestment alone did not dismantle apartheid; internal resistance, international diplomacy, and shifting demographics all played indispensable roles. Yet to understate the financial dimension is to misunderstand how systems of power operate. Apartheid was not only a political ideology but an economic structure that required constant infusion of capital. By disrupting that flow, divestment campaigns hastened the regime's collapse. Nelson Mandela himself later acknowledged the importance of these global financial pressures in creating the conditions for transition.

For contemporary investors, the South African experience carries several enduring lessons. First, *reputational risk can morph into financial risk faster than markets anticipate*. What once looked like a reliable investment environment was rapidly recast as toxic. Second, divestment works not by bankrupting an industry overnight but by reshaping perceptions of legitimacy. When enough institutions decide that profits are inseparable from injustice, the narrative changes, and with it, the willingness of mainstream capital to engage. Third, moral clarity is contagious. A student protest on a campus may seem insignificant, but when echoed by churches, cities, and eventually global banks, it can alter the calculus of nations.

Perhaps the most profound insight lies in how divestment redefined the purpose of investing itself. The South African campaign illustrated that shareholders are not merely neutral actors chasing returns; they are stakeholders in shaping the social and political order. Every dollar invested or withdrawn carries normative weight. To hold shares in a company complicit in apartheid was not just a financial choice but a declaration of tolerance for racial subjugation. Conversely, to divest was to refuse endorsement, to declare that profit built on injustice is neither legitimate nor sustainable.

Looking back, the divestment movement against apartheid South Africa stands as a landmark in the history of ethical finance. It showed that money can be a weapon not just of exploitation but of liberation. It revealed that capital markets, often thought of as impersonal and detached, are in fact deeply moral arenas where values are contested and enforced. And it proved that when conscience and capital converge, even the most entrenched systems of oppression can begin to unravel. The precedent set during this period continues to reverberate, informing today's debates on fossil fuels, surveillance technologies, and human rights abuses. In each of these domains, the question is not only whether divestment will work but whether investors have the courage to recognise, as their predecessors did, that the act of withdrawing capital can be one of the most powerful declarations of principle available.

Tobacco and Public Health

Few industries have been as profitable, as globally entrenched, and as devastating to human health as tobacco. For decades, cigarette manufacturers reigned over the consumer landscape, building empires on addiction while concealing or minimising the dangers of their products. Yet the story of tobacco also represents one of the most striking examples of how divestment reshaped not just public perception but the economic viability of a sector. The campaign against tobacco demonstrates that even industries once thought "too big to fail" can be weakened when investors recognise that profits are inseparable from harm. *The divestment movement did not merely punish tobacco companies; it reframed them as pariahs of capital markets.*

The scale of tobacco's impact on public health is difficult to exaggerate. By the mid-twentieth century, scientific evidence was mounting that smoking was directly linked to lung cancer, heart disease, and premature death. Governments eventually issued health warnings and launched anti-smoking campaigns, but for years the financial world largely ignored the issue. Cigarette companies continued to deliver enviable returns, paying reliable dividends and providing ballast to institutional portfolios. For pension funds and endowments, tobacco stocks were as close to a sure bet as one could imagine: demand was steady, margins were high, and global expansion promised growth even as consumption declined in wealthy countries. To many investors, ethical discomfort was an acceptable price for financial security.

This calculation began to unravel as public health campaigns gained force in the latter half of the twentieth century. The lawsuits of the 1990s in the United States marked a turning point. Documents emerged showing that tobacco companies had long known about the addictive and deadly nature of their products, yet deliberately obscured these facts. The revelation did not only damage reputations; it altered the financial outlook. Settlement agreements such as the 1998 Master Settlement Agreement imposed massive costs on the industry, while new regulations tightened marketing and sales. Suddenly, what had seemed like an unassailable profit machine was exposed as a sector facing rising liabilities and shrinking legitimacy. *The link between moral failure and financial risk became undeniable.*

Divestment campaigns gained momentum in this environment. Universities, hospitals, and public pension funds began to question the prudence of holding tobacco stocks, not only because of reputational considerations but because of the long-term risk profile. In 1982, the Harvard School of Public Health became one of the first academic institutions to divest from tobacco. Over the following decades, hundreds of institutions followed suit, from the California Public Employees' Retirement System (CalPERS) to major religious organisations. By the early 2000s, billions of dollars had been pulled out of the industry. While each individual act of divestment represented only a fraction of the global capitalisation of tobacco companies, the cumulative signal was powerful: tobacco was no longer just another consumer product; it was a financial liability disguised as an asset.

The ripple effects extended beyond investment decisions. Rating agencies and analysts began to incorporate litigation and regulatory risks into their valuations. Insurance companies raised questions about the sustainability of the business model. Corporate social responsibility frameworks increasingly excluded tobacco, often lumping it alongside armaments and pornography as a "sin stock" unsuitable for ethical portfolios. By the 2010s, many large institutional investors had written formal policies excluding tobacco, citing both ethical concerns and fiduciary duty. The stigma attached to tobacco shares meant they traded at a discount relative to other consumer goods companies, reflecting not only declining demand but also the market's recognition of their unsustainable trajectory.

Critics of divestment sometimes argued that selling shares merely transferred ownership to less ethically scrupulous investors. They contended that engagement, rather than divestment, would be more effective in changing corporate behaviour. Yet in the case of tobacco, engagement was largely futile: the very core of the business model was irredeemable. Unlike companies in energy or apparel, there was no "cleaner" or "fairer" version of the product that could align with public health. Cigarettes were lethal when used as intended. Here divestment proved particularly effective because it was not about pressuring companies to reform but about delegitimising the industry itself. *To divest was to assert that the product had no place in a civilised economy.*

The tobacco story also shows how ethics can lead markets rather than follow them. Long before regulation or litigation wiped billions from tobacco valuations, campaigners and early divestors had identified the fundamental unsustainability of the sector. Their actions anticipated financial decline by recognising a moral reality: that profiting from mass death was incompatible with long-term economic legitimacy. What began as an ethical stance became, in retrospect, a prescient investment decision. This dynamic continues to resonate in contemporary debates about fossil fuels and climate change. Just as tobacco divestment foreshadowed legal and regulatory crackdowns, so too might today's ethical campaigns signal tomorrow's financial revaluation.

Yet the impact of tobacco divestment should not be overstated as a solitary cause of decline. The fall in smoking rates in many countries was driven by public health education, taxation, advertising bans, and cultural shifts. What divestment added was moral and financial reinforcement: it removed the halo of respectability that comes from being a "blue-chip" holding. By stripping tobacco companies of institutional endorsement, divestment amplified public health efforts, making the industry a financial pariah as well as a social one. It created a feedback loop in which reduced legitimacy fuelled reduced investment, which in turn reinforced the perception of tobacco as an unsustainable enterprise.

The lessons are clear for investors today. First, *the profitability of an industry does not insulate it from moral scrutiny*. Tobacco companies once seemed untouchable, yet divestment demonstrated that capital can be withdrawn from even the most profitable sectors. Second, *ethics often predict economics*. By recognising the moral untenability of tobacco, investors anticipated the regulatory and legal costs that would eventually undermine returns. Third, *divestment is not only about moving money but about moving norms*. When enough institutions decide that a sector is incompatible with public good, they change the conversation about what counts as an acceptable investment.

In the end, tobacco divestment reshaped one of the world's most profitable industries not by bankrupting it overnight but by eroding its legitimacy, constraining its access to capital, and aligning financial markets with public health imperatives. It remains a vivid reminder that markets are not neutral mechanisms but moral arenas, where the allocation of capital carries profound social consequences. What once seemed an unshakable pillar of the global economy now stands as a cautionary tale: when an industry's core product is incompatible with human flourishing, divestment becomes not just a gesture of conscience but a rational recognition of reality.

Patterns of Change

The arc of financial history repeatedly shows that what begins as an ethical conviction often matures into an economic inevitability. Industries that once appeared untouchable—profitable, entrenched, defended by governments and consumer demand—have eventually been undermined not by sudden technological shocks but by the steady erosion of legitimacy. *Ethics, when widely embraced, tend to serve as an early-warning system for economic reality.* The challenge for investors is not simply to track short-term returns but to discern where moral energy is accumulating, because over time, these currents reshape the allocation of capital with surprising force.

Consider the campaigns against the transatlantic slave trade in the eighteenth and nineteenth centuries. At the time, slavery was not a marginal economic activity but a cornerstone of global commerce. Sugar, cotton, and tobacco—all dependent on enslaved labour—were central to the wealth of empires. Yet Quakers and other abolitionists reframed the debate: slavery was not only a social ill but a moral abomination incompatible with the values of a modern economy. At first, economic arguments dominated; defenders insisted that abolition would devastate trade and ruin livelihoods. But moral conviction proved stronger. Over time, public pressure altered legislation, and capital began to move away from industries dependent on slave labour. The economic fallout was real, but so too was the reallocation of resources toward new forms of production. *What had once seemed commercially indispensable was revealed to be ethically and financially unsustainable.*

A century later, divestment from apartheid South Africa offered another powerful demonstration. For decades, South Africa attracted foreign investment despite its segregationist policies, thanks to its mineral wealth and industrial promise. Yet as anti-apartheid movements gained international traction, investors were forced to reckon with the reputational and moral cost of association. Universities, churches, and pension funds pulled money from companies operating in South Africa. Critics derided the effort as symbolic, but the cumulative effect was substantial. The financial isolation of the apartheid regime intensified political pressure, accelerating its eventual collapse. Importantly, the divestment movement established a model for linking capital allocation to human rights outcomes—a precedent later applied to issues such as fossil fuels and arms manufacturing. The episode underscored a critical pattern: *once the ethical case becomes unignorable, capital markets adjust, often faster than political regimes.*

The story of tobacco provides perhaps the clearest example of ethics predicting economics within living memory. Cigarettes were long considered a reliable investment, their profitability underwritten by addiction and aggressive marketing. But as medical research exposed the scale of tobacco-related illness, the industry's legitimacy crumbled. Divestment campaigns stripped tobacco stocks of their blue-chip respectability. Litigation and regulation followed, imposing massive costs on firms and shrinking their market. Today, many institutional investors exclude tobacco altogether, not only on ethical grounds but because the sector's future profitability appears permanently compromised. Here again, investors who anticipated the ethical trajectory were rewarded for their foresight, while those who clung to near-term returns eventually bore the cost of denial.

From these cases a pattern emerges. Ethical concerns typically begin on the margins, voiced by activists, scholars, or communities directly affected by harm. These concerns then gain cultural traction, often through campaigns that make the issue morally visible to the wider public. Once moral legitimacy is weakened, investors face new calculations: reputational risk, regulatory shifts, and long-term sustainability. At this stage, capital begins to move, sometimes quietly at first, but in ways that erode an industry's ability to attract financing, talent, or political protection. Finally, the economic reckoning arrives. What was once considered a moral crusade becomes accepted as financial prudence. *The ethical critique precedes the market correction, and those who ignore the former are often blindsided by the latter.*

Yet patterns of change are not linear or inevitable. Resistance is fierce, and incumbents wield power. For every abolitionist campaign, there are industrialists defending their livelihoods; for every anti-apartheid protest, there are corporations arguing for "constructive engagement." Investors themselves often vacillate, torn between fiduciary responsibility narrowly defined as short-term returns and the broader recognition that markets are embedded in social systems. The delay between moral awakening and economic transformation can be long, measured in decades rather than years. This lag creates opportunities for profit but also traps for the unwary. *The lesson is not that ethics always triumph swiftly but that they gradually reshape the conditions of profitability.*

For contemporary investors, recognising these historical rhythms offers practical guidance. Climate change, labour rights in global supply chains, and the ethics of artificial intelligence are today's contested frontiers. Critics of divestment from fossil fuels often echo the arguments once made about tobacco or South Africa: that the industry is too large, too essential, too profitable to be dislodged. Yet history counsels humility. Industries have been declared indispensable before, only to be revalued when their moral cost became impossible to ignore. The question is not whether ethics will influence economics, but how long investors are willing to wait before the shift materialises.

What history reveals most clearly is that divestment and ethical investment are not merely symbolic gestures. They act as accelerants in the process of delegitimisation, amplifying the moral case and hastening economic adjustment. Investors who move early often bear accusations of idealism, but in retrospect, they appear prescient. By contrast, those who delay are left with stranded assets, reputational damage, or diminished returns. This inversion of perception—idealism reframed as foresight, complacency exposed as negligence—recurs across centuries. *Markets may be slow to price morality, but they rarely ignore it forever.*

Patterns of change remind us that finance is not a detached arena but a mirror of human values. When enough people decide that a practice is intolerable, capital eventually follows. For investors, the challenge is not only to read balance sheets but to read the cultural and ethical climate with equal acuity. To do so is not to sacrifice returns but to position capital on the right side of history, where the moral and the financial converge. Ethics do not merely predict economics—they often write its next chapter.

Chapter 7
The Instruments of Conscience

Ethical intention in finance is meaningless without vehicles that translate conviction into capital flow. For all the rhetoric surrounding values-based investment, the decisive question has always been *how*. Moral arguments shift cultural norms, and regulatory frameworks alter disclosure standards, but the mechanics of change depend on instruments—structured products, funds, and market channels—that convert principle into financial architecture. The rise of green bonds, activist shareholder campaigns, socially focused ETFs, and community lending illustrates not only the ingenuity of modern finance but also its limitations. Each instrument embodies a different theory of change: some appeal to the leverage of scale, others to the intimacy of local trust; some operate by shifting incentives within corporations, others by bypassing incumbent structures altogether. To understand the tools of conscience is to understand the evolving frontier where ethics meets capital markets.

The bond market, often considered the most staid corner of finance, has unexpectedly become a laboratory for climate action. Green bonds, first pioneered by development banks and later adopted by sovereigns and corporates, channel vast sums of debt financing toward projects deemed environmentally beneficial. They offer the promise of aligning the world's deepest pools of capital—pension funds, insurers, sovereign wealth funds—with the urgency of decarbonisation. Yet their expansion raises crucial questions: who decides what counts as "green," how risks are priced when environmental returns are uncertain, and whether such instruments truly accelerate systemic change or merely repackage traditional lending in ethical wrappers. The paradox of green bonds is that they illustrate both the power and the fragility of finance as a moral agent: they have opened a trillion-dollar market for climate-focused capital, but their credibility rests on definitions that remain contested.

If debt markets illustrate the external financing of conscience, shareholder activism embodies its internal pressure. The celebrated case of Engine No. 1 versus ExxonMobil, in which a small hedge fund compelled one of the world's largest oil companies to seat climate-conscious directors on its board, revealed that ownership rights are not passive entitlements but instruments of influence. Proxy votes, board elections, and resolution filings allow investors—whether they manage trillions or a few million—to reshape corporate priorities from within. Shareholder activism sits at the intersection of governance and strategy: it is at once a form of moral suasion and a demonstration of fiduciary risk management. When investors force companies to account for stranded assets, exploitative labour practices, or governance failures, they remind markets that morality and profitability are not parallel tracks but intertwined variables. Yet activism also reveals asymmetry: victories are rare, contested, and often symbolic, and the effectiveness of such campaigns hinges on coalition-building and sustained pressure.

Alongside direct ownership battles, a quieter revolution has unfolded through the rise of socially focused exchange-traded funds. These pooled vehicles transform ethical investing from a bespoke practice for niche investors into a scalable product for retail and institutional portfolios alike. By lowering costs and offering instant diversification, social ETFs democratise access to values-based strategies. They appeal to time-pressed investors who want impact without the burden of stock-picking or complex due diligence. At their best, these instruments aggregate individual preference into market-level demand, sending signals that capital markets cannot ignore. But they also risk diluting principle into convenience. Screening methodologies vary widely; a fund branded as "sustainable" may still include companies that many would consider ethically compromised. The strength of ETFs lies in accessibility, but accessibility can become a weakness if investors mistake a label for alignment. *The lesson is that conscience packaged for scale demands vigilant scrutiny.*

The most overlooked but perhaps most radical instruments are those rooted not in global markets but in local trust. Community investing, whether through credit unions, microfinance institutions, or social enterprises, shifts capital directly into the hands of people and projects often excluded from mainstream finance. Here, the logic of impact is tangible: funds may finance affordable housing, small business development, or renewable energy cooperatives within specific regions. While returns may be modest compared to global equities, the social dividends are clear, and default rates in many community-focused institutions are strikingly low. These vehicles remind us that not all conscience-driven finance must pass through the machinery of Wall Street or the City; sometimes the most transformative outcomes arise when investors choose proximity over abstraction. Yet local investing also poses challenges of scale, liquidity, and verification, making it less attractive to large institutional allocators.

Together, these instruments reveal the diversity of pathways by which ethics enter financial markets. Green bonds demonstrate the power of framing debt around environmental outcomes; shareholder activism illustrates the leverage embedded in ownership rights; social ETFs scale conscience into accessible products; and community finance grounds investment in tangible, local change. Each carries strengths and vulnerabilities, each reflects different philosophies of engagement. What unites them is the recognition that capital cannot remain ethically inert—that financial flows, whether global or local, inevitably carry moral weight.

This chapter examines these instruments not as static categories but as dynamic experiments, constantly evolving in response to political, cultural, and market pressures. Readers will encounter both the promise and the pitfalls: how the very tools designed to align money with values can be co-opted, diluted, or deployed with unintended consequences. Yet if history shows that ethics often predict economics, then the instruments of conscience are the levers by which that prediction is enacted. They are the bridges between principle and practice, between aspiration and allocation. To study them is to study the mechanics of moral capital itself.

Green Bonds — Explains how debt markets are harnessed for climate projects and what risks and returns they offer

The bond market, often perceived as conservative and predictable, has emerged as an unlikely stage for one of the most ambitious experiments in sustainable finance: the rise of green bonds. First issued in 2007 by the European Investment Bank and quickly followed by the World Bank, these instruments reframed an old financial technology—debt issuance—as a vehicle for climate action. At their core, green bonds operate like conventional bonds: investors provide capital to governments, corporations, or development banks in exchange for fixed income payments over time. The difference lies in the *use of proceeds*. Instead of being deployed for general balance sheet needs, the funds raised are earmarked for projects intended to deliver environmental benefits—renewable energy installations, sustainable transport systems, energy-efficient housing, or water conservation schemes. This apparently small design shift has catalysed a market that, by 2022, had surpassed US$2 trillion in cumulative issuance, signalling both a reorientation of financial capital and the growing recognition that climate change is not just a scientific or political problem, but a financial one.

The appeal of green bonds lies in their dual promise. For issuers, they provide access to new pools of capital and often come with reputational benefits, as borrowers are seen to be aligning themselves with global climate commitments. For investors, they offer the familiarity of fixed income returns combined with the satisfaction—or in some cases the fiduciary requirement—of supporting projects aligned with sustainability. *In theory, green bonds turn the world's most conservative asset class into an instrument of transformation.* Yet the very speed of their adoption raises difficult questions. Who determines what qualifies as "green"? How can investors distinguish between genuine impact and clever marketing? And what risks, both financial and ethical, lurk beneath the surface of a market designed to blend profit with principle?

One of the first challenges is definitional. The term "green" has no universal standard, and while voluntary frameworks such as the Green Bond Principles (administered by the International Capital Market Association) attempt to set guidelines, interpretation remains broad. Some issuers classify efficiency improvements in fossil fuel operations as eligible green projects, while others would exclude anything connected to hydrocarbons entirely. This ambiguity creates a fertile ground for what critics describe as "greenwashing," where bonds may be marketed as climate-friendly while supporting projects of questionable environmental merit. The problem is compounded by the global patchwork of regulatory regimes. In the European Union, the EU Taxonomy seeks to establish binding criteria for sustainable investments, but elsewhere markets remain largely self-policing. For investors committed to aligning their portfolios with principle, this lack of consistency forces a reliance on due diligence rather than trust in labels. *The green bond market is thus simultaneously a breakthrough in financial innovation and a reminder that language without verification risks undermining credibility.*

From a financial perspective, green bonds generally offer returns comparable to conventional bonds of similar credit quality and maturity. Some studies have observed a "greenium"—a slight yield discount—reflecting investor willingness to accept marginally lower returns in exchange for the non-financial value of impact. For large institutional investors under pressure from clients or regulators to demonstrate environmental responsibility, this trade-off is often acceptable. However, the existence of a greenium also raises questions about whether the environmental benefits being financed are priced fairly, and whether lower yields might limit uptake in markets where investors prioritise short-term returns. It is also worth noting that the credit risk of a green bond is tied not to the performance of the underlying project but to the issuer's overall balance sheet. A green bond issued by a corporation carries the same risk as any other debt from that corporation, regardless of whether the specific project succeeds. This structure makes green bonds more attractive to mainstream investors but potentially weakens the link between impact and accountability.

Case studies illustrate both the promise and pitfalls of the instrument. In 2014, the French utility EDF issued a €1.4 billion green bond to finance renewable energy projects, one of the largest corporate offerings of its kind at the time. The issuance attracted strong demand, demonstrating investor appetite for climate-linked products. Yet EDF continued to operate a large fleet of nuclear and fossil fuel plants, prompting critics to question whether the bond was being used as a reputational shield rather than a genuine pivot. By contrast, the issuance of sovereign green bonds by countries such as Poland, France, and more recently Egypt and Indonesia, has allowed governments to signal climate commitment while diversifying their funding base. The Polish green bond, for instance, financed clean transport and renewable energy projects, aligning directly with EU decarbonisation targets. Sovereign issues, given their scale and visibility, may hold the greatest potential for reshaping capital flows at systemic levels, but they too depend on rigorous project selection and transparent reporting.

The risk-return calculus of green bonds is not limited to yield curves and credit spreads; it also involves reputational and regulatory dimensions. For investors, the reputational risk of being exposed to a green bond later discredited as greenwashing is real and potentially damaging. For issuers, the reputational upside of being seen as sustainable is matched by the reputational liability of being accused of deception. Regulators are increasingly attuned to this dynamic. The EU's forthcoming Green Bond Standard, for example, requires alignment with the taxonomy and mandatory third-party verification of use-of-proceeds. Such frameworks may help reduce inconsistency but could also increase issuance costs, raising questions about accessibility for smaller borrowers. The future of the market may depend on balancing credibility with scalability: too lax a system risks irrelevance, too rigid a system risks exclusion.

Beyond technicalities, green bonds raise deeper philosophical questions about the role of finance in climate transition. Are they a transitional tool that nudges capital in the right direction while more ambitious reforms take shape, or are they a distraction that allows the financial sector to appear proactive while systemic change is deferred? Proponents argue that green bonds channel billions into urgently needed projects that might otherwise struggle to secure funding. Critics counter that unless they are tied to broader corporate or sovereign commitments, they risk being tokenistic. The truth likely lies in between. Green bonds will not, by themselves, close the financing gap for decarbonisation, but they represent a pragmatic step toward aligning mainstream finance with planetary boundaries.

The lesson for investors is twofold. First, *green bonds are not a homogenous product*; they require critical reading of prospectuses, project disclosures, and third-party assessments. Second, their impact cannot be measured solely in basis points or tonnes of carbon avoided, but in their ability to normalise the expectation that capital must account for environmental externalities. If the conventional bond market represents stability and predictability, the green bond market represents adaptation—an acknowledgement that even the most conservative corners of finance must evolve.

As debt markets continue to expand their role in climate finance, the story of green bonds underscores both the potential and the limits of financial engineering. They show that capital markets can be mobilised for conscience, but they also remind us that conscience without rigour risks becoming a slogan. For the thoughtful investor, the challenge is not simply to buy green-labelled debt, but to interrogate its substance: to distinguish between cosmetic alignment and authentic commitment, and to recognise that in the long run, credibility is as critical as coupon payments.

Shareholder Activism — Explores how investors pressure companies from within, citing examples like Engine No. 1 vs. Exxon

Capital markets often frame investors as passive suppliers of funding, content to accept dividends or bond coupons in exchange for their capital. Yet history shows that investors are anything but passive when sufficiently motivated. Shareholder activism—where owners of equity use their rights to challenge, direct, or reshape corporate behaviour—has become one of the most powerful instruments of conscience in modern finance. It transforms the boardroom into an arena of contest, where competing visions of a company's purpose collide: short-term returns versus long-term sustainability, narrow profit margins versus broad stakeholder responsibility. For decades, this was the domain of hedge funds seeking restructurings or break-ups for financial gain. More recently, however, a new generation of activists has begun to use the same mechanisms to push for social and environmental change. The battle over ExxonMobil in 2021, led by the little-known hedge fund Engine No. 1, epitomised this shift and demonstrated how even the most entrenched corporate strategies can be challenged from within.

The Exxon case remains striking because of the asymmetry of power. Engine No. 1 controlled just 0.02 per cent of Exxon's shares when it launched its campaign, yet within months it succeeded in placing three directors on the oil giant's board, directly challenging its climate strategy. Its argument was not framed in moral outrage but in financial logic: Exxon's failure to pivot towards low-carbon energy left it dangerously exposed to the structural decline of fossil fuels. By combining a sophisticated media campaign with alliances among large institutional investors such as BlackRock, State Street, and Vanguard, the fund reframed climate inaction as a risk to shareholder value. *The victory was a milestone: it showed that sustainability arguments could be translated into the language of fiduciary duty and win over even the most cautious investors.*

The power of shareholder activism lies in its hybridity. Unlike divestment campaigns, which remove capital as a form of protest, activism works from within, leveraging ownership rights to force change. Tactics range from filing shareholder resolutions and nominating directors to direct engagement with management or orchestrating public pressure campaigns. Activists can challenge executive pay structures, demand climate disclosure, or push for diversity on boards. While some initiatives end in compromise—companies agreeing to modest policy shifts—others result in transformative outcomes, reshaping entire industries. The campaigns that forced major American utilities to accelerate coal retirements, or that pressured global food companies to improve supply chain transparency, underscore the potential for activism to extend far beyond symbolic gestures.

Yet activism is not without its tensions. Traditionalists argue that corporate boards, elected by shareholders, already have a fiduciary obligation to act in the long-term interests of investors, and that activist campaigns risk destabilising governance or diverting resources. Moreover, the effectiveness of activism depends heavily on coalition-building. A small fund may spark a campaign, but victory usually requires the support of large institutional investors. This reliance raises questions: to what extent are the world's largest asset managers willing to exercise their power consistently, and under what conditions do they remain silent? Critics point out that the same firms that backed Engine No. 1 at Exxon have been far more cautious in supporting similar campaigns at other oil majors, suggesting that activism still faces the gravitational pull of short-term returns.

Another key issue is the metrics of success. In the world of finance, success is often measured in share price appreciation or cost reduction. But activism that seeks to align companies with ethical principles must wrestle with outcomes that unfold over decades. For example, a shareholder resolution compelling a company to disclose climate risks may not immediately affect profitability but may lay the groundwork for a more resilient strategy. Likewise, campaigns for labour rights or supply chain transparency may appear to increase costs in the short term but can protect brand value and avoid reputational crises. *The activist must therefore act as both a financial analyst and a moral strategist, articulating why ethical reforms are not a distraction from profitability but a precondition for its durability.*

The history of activism reveals cycles of scepticism and resurgence. In the 1980s, faith-based investors used resolutions to challenge companies doing business in apartheid South Africa, contributing to the broader divestment movement that eventually exerted political pressure. In the 2000s, pension funds and university endowments became prominent actors, pressing companies on issues ranging from tobacco to climate change. Each wave has broadened the scope of what counts as a legitimate shareholder concern. Where once only financial restructuring drew attention, today climate resilience, racial equity, and supply chain ethics are seen as material to long-term value. This expansion reflects a deeper shift: recognition that corporations do not operate in a vacuum but within societies and ecosystems that ultimately determine their viability.

Practical examples highlight the diverse forms activism can take. In 2018, a group of shareholders compelled Royal

Dutch Shell to strengthen its emissions targets after years of lobbying, signalling that even European oil majors could not rely on goodwill without accountability. In the United States, campaigns at McDonald's and Tyson Foods forced greater disclosure around antibiotic use in livestock, an issue with direct implications for public health. More recently, investor coalitions have pushed global banks to align their lending practices with net-zero targets, challenging the financial sector to confront its role in financing fossil fuel expansion. Each case reveals how shareholder activism is less about moral grandstanding and more about strategic negotiation—pushing corporations to recognise risks that management may prefer to defer or ignore.

The future of activism will be shaped by scale and technology. Digital platforms are making it easier for retail investors to coordinate and support resolutions, broadening participation beyond pension funds and institutional managers. At the same time, the politicisation of ESG in certain jurisdictions has created pushback, with critics accusing activists of smuggling political agendas into corporate governance. This backlash highlights a central paradox: while activism demonstrates the power of markets to internalise ethical concerns, it also reveals the contested nature of what counts as ethical. The debate is not merely about tactics but about legitimacy—who gets to decide which issues matter, and on what grounds?

For thoughtful investors, the lesson is that activism is both a tool and a test. It offers a means to exert influence on corporations whose actions affect the climate, communities, and workers far beyond their shareholder base. But it also tests whether investors themselves are willing to move beyond rhetoric into the demanding work of coalition-building, negotiation, and sustained pressure. *The Exxon episode proved that even the largest corporations are vulnerable when shareholders act with discipline and clarity of purpose.* The broader challenge is ensuring that such victories are not isolated but form part of a systematic reorientation of corporate priorities.

In this light, shareholder activism is best understood not as an optional tactic but as an essential function of ownership in an age where ethics and economics are inseparable. Investors cannot outsource conscience to labels or indexes; they must exercise it directly, recognising that the boardroom is as much a battleground for the future as parliaments or protest movements. The shareholder resolution becomes not just a procedural tool but a moral instrument, one that can recalibrate corporate behaviour and, over time, reshape the markets themselves.

The Rise of Social ETFs — Analyses how pooled vehicles make ethical investing accessible and scalable

One of the most remarkable financial innovations of the past half century has been the rise of exchange-traded funds, or ETFs. Once a niche instrument used by institutional investors to track market indices cheaply, they now account for trillions of dollars in assets globally and form the backbone of investment portfolios from pension funds to retail traders. Their appeal is straightforward: diversification, liquidity, and low cost, all packaged in a structure that can be traded as easily as a single stock. When this mechanism is applied to socially responsible and ethical investing, it produces a powerful combination—*the accessibility of pooled finance joined with the moral intentionality of values-based allocation*. The rise of social ETFs has not only expanded the reach of ethical finance but has also forced investors and regulators alike to wrestle with questions of integrity, measurement, and impact.

The earliest socially conscious funds were mutual funds, established in the 1970s and 1980s by churches, unions, and activist groups seeking to avoid industries such as tobacco, arms, or apartheid-linked businesses. These were important experiments but limited in reach: their higher costs and narrower investor base meant they remained peripheral to mainstream markets. ETFs changed the equation. By offering instant diversification at minimal fees, they democratised access to investing and made it possible for millions of small investors to align their portfolios with their principles without sacrificing performance or efficiency. The launch of the iShares MSCI KLD 400 Social ETF in 2006, one of the first mainstream products of its kind, demonstrated that ESG criteria could be applied systematically to index-based investing. From there, the growth has been exponential. Today, there are hundreds of social, ESG, or thematic ETFs globally, tracking everything from renewable energy and gender diversity to low-carbon indices.

What makes social ETFs distinctive is not only their thematic focus but their scalability. Traditional impact investments often require bespoke deals, careful due diligence, and illiquidity that limits participation to wealthy individuals or specialised funds. ETFs, by contrast, can mobilise vast sums of capital quickly by plugging into the infrastructure of public markets. When BlackRock or

Vanguard launches a sustainability-themed ETF, billions can flow in within weeks, signalling demand to corporations and shaping capital allocation across entire sectors. *Scale matters in finance because it sends a signal not only to companies but to policymakers: the more capital indexed to sustainability metrics, the harder it becomes to dismiss them as marginal concerns.*

Yet accessibility and scale come with trade-offs. One persistent critique is that many social ETFs rely on screening methodologies that are opaque or inconsistent. An investor might assume that buying a low-carbon ETF excludes fossil fuel producers entirely, only to discover that the fund still holds large oil companies deemed "best in class" under relative metrics. This tension exposes the limits of algorithmic approaches to ethics. What counts as "sustainable" can differ dramatically depending on who is doing the screening and which data are prioritised. For example, Tesla has been both included and excluded from different ESG indices, praised for its role in decarbonisation yet criticised for labour practices and governance issues. *This inconsistency reflects a broader problem: values are not easily reducible to quantitative filters, yet ETFs must rely on such filters to construct investable products.*

The success of social ETFs also raises deeper questions about what constitutes impact. Divestment removes capital from companies deemed harmful, while activism pressures firms from within. Passive ownership through ETFs sits in between: investors technically own the companies in the index but exercise little influence directly. Critics argue this dilutes the moral force of ethical investing, reducing it to a matter of optics rather than outcomes. Supporters counter that *scale itself is impact*—if billions of dollars shift towards cleaner energy or more diverse companies, corporate cost of capital is affected and incentives to reform are strengthened. The Exxon case, where large asset managers backed climate-focused shareholder campaigns, illustrates how ETF providers—though passive in allocation—can be active in governance when they choose to vote their shares.

Real-world examples reveal both the promise and pitfalls. In Europe, the Lyxor Green Bond ETF allows investors to allocate capital directly to debt instruments funding renewable projects, offering a more direct link between capital and climate outcomes. In the United States, thematic ETFs such as those focusing on clean water, solar energy, or racial equity have attracted attention for their narrative clarity and ability to resonate with retail investors. At the same time, sceptics note that many of these funds have narrow sector exposures, making them volatile and raising questions about whether they are truly diversified vehicles or simply marketing-driven bets. The boom in thematic ESG ETFs in 2020–2021, followed by sharp outflows in subsequent years, demonstrates the danger of treating moral themes as short-term fads.

Beyond performance, governance is where ETFs can demonstrate genuine influence. When the largest providers commit to voting against boards that fail on climate or diversity, the effect reverberates across markets. BlackRock, State Street, and Vanguard, who together control significant stakes in most major corporations, have made high-profile pledges to hold directors accountable on ESG issues. Yet the follow-through has been uneven, particularly as political backlash against ESG has intensified in the United States. Some providers have scaled back their activism, wary of being cast as unelected regulators. This ambivalence highlights the fragility of progress: without consistent stewardship, social ETFs risk becoming vehicles of complacency rather than conscience.

Philosophically, the rise of social ETFs embodies the central paradox of ethical finance: *how to reconcile personal conscience with collective mechanisms of capital allocation*. An individual investor may have strong convictions about fossil fuels, labour rights, or diversity, but when pooled into a fund with thousands of others, those convictions must be translated into rules and algorithms that inevitably compromise. The ETF represents a form of moral aggregation—efficient, scalable, but imperfect. The challenge for thoughtful investors is to treat ETFs not as the final word but as one layer in a broader ethical strategy, complemented by direct activism, community investment, or targeted divestment where necessary.

Looking forward, innovation is likely to refine the space. Advances in data science and AI promise more granular ESG analysis, potentially enabling ETFs to screen companies with greater nuance. Regulators, particularly in Europe, are tightening rules on disclosure to prevent greenwashing, forcing fund providers to back up their claims with evidence. Hybrid models may also emerge, blending passive allocation with active stewardship, ensuring that scale does not come at the expense of accountability. The rise of "impact ETFs" that direct capital into bonds funding specific projects, rather than broad equity indices, could offer a more tangible link between investor intention and real-world change.

The broader lesson is that social ETFs represent both progress and compromise. They have lowered barriers, brought millions into the fold of ethical investing, and signalled that conscience is no longer confined to niche corners of the market. But they also reveal the limits of standardisation in matters of principle. *Ethics, unlike indices, cannot be fully codified.* For investors who see capital not just as a means of return but as an expression of responsibility, ETFs are a useful tool—powerful in scope, imperfect in execution, and dependent on the vigilance of those who use them. The task is not to abandon them but to engage critically, ensuring that the rise of social ETFs is not merely a trend but a durable step towards aligning financial systems with the moral imperatives of our age.

Community and Local Investing – Highlights smaller, overlooked channels like credit unions and social enterprises that deliver impact with returns

In the age of trillion-dollar asset managers and algorithm-driven trading platforms, it is easy to forget that some of the most transformative forms of finance still take place at the local level. While global markets may dictate the fate of oil majors or technology giants, communities are sustained by a different kind of capital: money that circulates close to home, invested not for abstract returns but for tangible benefits that improve lives directly. *Community and local investing remind us that finance is not merely a system of numbers but a set of relationships—between saver and borrower, institution and neighbourhood, principle and practice.* These smaller, often overlooked channels—credit unions, community development financial institutions, co-operatives, and social enterprises—have proven that aligning capital with conscience does not mean sacrificing return; it means redefining what counts as valuable.

Credit unions, one of the oldest and most enduring forms of community finance, illustrate this vividly. Built on a principle of mutuality, they are owned by their members rather than external shareholders. This seemingly simple distinction alters everything: instead of maximising short-term profit, credit unions seek to balance sustainability with member wellbeing. They often lend to people overlooked by commercial banks, whether low-income households or small businesses without collateral. While their balance sheets may be smaller than those of multinational banks, the ripple effects of their lending are often more visible. A loan to a family-run bakery, for instance, sustains employment in a neighbourhood; credit extended to a first-time homeowner stabilises communities; financing for renewable installations reduces both energy costs and carbon footprints. Studies consistently show that credit unions have lower default rates and higher customer satisfaction than commercial banks. *In an era marked by distrust of finance, their cooperative model offers a rare form of legitimacy rooted in service rather than speculation.*

Beyond credit unions, community development financial institutions (CDFIs) have expanded the boundaries of what local finance can achieve. In the United States, CDFIs emerged to fill gaps left by discriminatory practices such as redlining, providing loans and services in areas neglected by mainstream finance. In the United Kingdom, community development finance institutions and building societies have played similar roles, offering credit to small enterprises, affordable housing projects, and social services. Their work is not merely charitable; it generates returns by tapping into markets often dismissed as too risky. The success of microfinance initiatives worldwide—from Grameen Bank in Bangladesh to Accion's programmes in Latin America—demonstrates the same principle: *when capital is deployed with local knowledge and trust, risk can be managed in ways large institutions often overlook.*

Social enterprises represent another crucial channel. Unlike traditional firms, their primary mission is to solve social or environmental problems, with profit serving as a means rather than an end. Investments in social enterprises can yield modest but steady returns, while simultaneously addressing pressing challenges such as healthcare access, education, or renewable energy adoption. For instance, community-owned renewable energy projects across Europe have enabled towns to reduce emissions while generating income that is reinvested locally. The RE100 initiative in Germany, where citizens own wind turbines and solar panels, demonstrates how local investment can democratise energy systems and embed sustainability into everyday life. *These enterprises prove that returns are not confined to financial margins—they can also be measured in reduced inequality, resilience, and dignity.*

Critics often dismiss community and local investing as too small-scale to matter in the face of global challenges like climate change or systemic inequality. Yet this underestimates their role. While a single credit union cannot move global oil prices, the aggregation of thousands of such institutions builds a counterweight to purely extractive finance. Moreover, the local nature of these investments ensures accountability: when investors live among the beneficiaries of their capital, failures cannot be obscured by distance or complexity. Unlike multinational corporations, which can shift operations to avoid responsibility, local institutions remain tied to their communities. *This embeddedness in place serves as both a constraint and a strength, anchoring finance to real-world consequences rather than abstractions.*

The pandemic underscored the resilience of community-focused finance. As large banks tightened credit in the face of uncertainty, credit unions, co-operatives, and CDFIs often stepped in to sustain small businesses and vulnerable households. In the United States, CDFIs played a vital role in distributing Paycheck Protection Program loans to minority-owned businesses that might otherwise have been excluded. In the UK, community banks partnered with local councils to support struggling families. These interventions did not only prevent collapse; they demonstrated that ethical alignment and financial resilience are not separate domains but intertwined. When local finance thrives, so too does the social fabric on which broader economic stability depends.

Still, challenges remain. Community and local investing must balance their mission-driven ethos with financial rigour. Poorly managed initiatives risk undermining trust and reinforcing scepticism about the viability of ethical finance. Moreover, the sector often struggles with scale: while community institutions are adept at serving specific populations, expanding their reach without losing their integrity is difficult. Partnerships with larger institutions, or the development of blended finance structures that combine public, private, and philanthropic capital, are one way to address this. For example, the UK's Big Society Capital uses dormant bank accounts and other funds to invest in social enterprises, amplifying local impact while maintaining financial discipline. Such models suggest that *the future of community finance may lie not in remaining isolated but in forming networks that preserve local responsiveness while accessing broader pools of capital.*

Philosophically, community and local investing challenge the dominant assumption that finance must be impersonal, abstract, and global. They remind us that money is not merely a medium of exchange but an instrument of trust. When individuals deposit savings into a credit union or buy shares in a local co-operative, they are not just seeking yield—they are participating in a social contract that binds their fortunes to those of their neighbours. This reframes investing from an act of personal gain to one of collective stewardship. The dividends may be smaller in absolute terms than those from speculative markets, but the sense of alignment—between values, capital, and community—offers a return not easily captured on balance sheets.

The lesson is not that all investors should abandon global markets for community-based finance, but that *ethical investing is incomplete if it ignores the local dimension*. A portfolio that includes social ETFs, green bonds, or shareholder activism may align with broad principles, but without anchoring in tangible community outcomes, it risks remaining abstract. By contrast, local investments create feedback loops of accountability, resilience, and shared prosperity. They are not an alternative to global ethical finance but a complement that grounds conscience in lived experience.

For thoughtful investors, community and local channels provide an essential reminder: impact does not always scale linearly. Sometimes the most meaningful changes are measured not in billions of dollars shifted but in a single family gaining access to credit, a neighbourhood revitalised, or a village electrified sustainably. *Ethical finance gains its fullest legitimacy not in the abstractions of indices but in the concrete realities of communities empowered by capital.* Recognising this, and integrating it into broader strategies, ensures that the instruments of conscience retain their moral centre even as they expand across global markets.

Chapter 8
The Company's Response

Corporations like to project permanence. Headquarters are built to look immovable, annual reports glow with confidence, and executives speak in the language of control. Yet few forces have unsettled boardrooms in recent decades as much as the rise of ethically driven investors. What began as a handful of shareholder resolutions from religious groups and campaigners has matured into a disciplined, data-backed challenge that is reshaping the priorities of some of the world's most powerful companies. If markets once assumed that shareholder activism was a niche irritant, they now recognise it as a structural force. Companies fear activist investors not only because they can mobilise votes, but because they can mobilise narratives—exposing contradictions between stated values and lived practices. The spectre of reputational damage, amplified by an always-on media ecosystem, transforms what might once have been dismissed as symbolic gestures into immediate financial threats.

The fear is not irrational. Campaigns once thought of as peripheral now move markets. When Engine No. 1, a previously unknown hedge fund, took on ExxonMobil in 2021, few expected its small stake to matter. Yet its carefully framed argument—that Exxon's failure to prepare for a low-carbon future was both an ethical and a financial liability—resonated with larger investors. The result was unprecedented: three new directors on Exxon's board, elected not by outsiders but by the company's own shareholders demanding strategic change. The episode sent shockwaves across the corporate world. It revealed that ethical issues could no longer be brushed aside as public relations concerns; they had migrated into the boardroom, binding questions of morality and strategy so tightly that separation became impossible. Companies now live with the knowledge that even modestly capitalised activist campaigns can catalyse a reckoning. *The shareholder register has become a stage on which ethical disputes are performed with direct financial consequence.*

This anxiety is compounded by the mounting evidence that inaction on ethical concerns carries its own financial penalty. From BP's Deepwater Horizon disaster to Volkswagen's emissions scandal, companies that underestimated the long-term risks of environmental or governance failings saw market value evaporate almost overnight. The costs were not limited to fines or settlements; they encompassed lost trust, consumer boycotts, regulatory crackdowns, and years of reputational repair. Investors increasingly read these examples not as isolated missteps but as case studies in how moral failures metastasise into balance sheet liabilities. A company that neglects human rights in its supply chain, or resists climate regulation, is now seen not only as ethically compromised but financially shortsighted. Market participants who once viewed ethics as an externality now view them as lagging indicators of future crises. *The cost of ignoring conscience is measured not in slogans but in shareholder value destroyed.*

This realisation has elevated reputation from a soft notion to a hard metric. Intangible assets now constitute the majority of corporate valuations in advanced economies.

Brands, relationships, trust, and legitimacy—once thought peripheral to financial health—are increasingly central. When Uber faced allegations of systemic workplace harassment, its valuation fell by billions even before any regulatory penalty was imposed. The erosion was driven by reputation: investors doubted the company's ability to attract talent, secure licences, or expand internationally while carrying such stigma. Similarly, when Nike faced criticism for labour conditions in the 1990s, its share price collapsed until it implemented sweeping reforms. These cases underscore that reputation is not an accessory; it is an asset class in its own right. Companies are beginning to model reputational risk with the same seriousness they once reserved for interest rates or currency fluctuations. The very language of finance has had to adapt, with intangible valuation metrics now integral to credit ratings and investment analysis.

Such shifts point towards a broader redefinition of fiduciary duty. For much of the twentieth century, fiduciary responsibility was framed narrowly: to maximise shareholder value within the boundaries of law. Ethical considerations, unless mandated by regulation, were deemed discretionary. That definition no longer holds. Courts, regulators, and institutional investors increasingly argue that boards who ignore environmental, social, or governance risks are failing in their fiduciary obligations. Climate change, labour exploitation, data privacy—these are no longer considered optional ethical extras but core financial concerns. In 2022, a coalition of pension funds filed suit against directors of an oil major, arguing that their failure to align with net-zero targets constituted a breach of duty to protect long-term shareholder interests. Even if such claims remain contested, the direction is clear: boards are being forced to expand their definition of fiduciary duty to include ethical foresight. *What was once considered activism is fast becoming orthodoxy.*

The implications are profound. Companies must now anticipate ethical critiques with the same urgency as competitive threats. Investor relations teams must speak not only the language of quarterly earnings but of carbon disclosures, human rights audits, and diversity metrics. Boards must be literate not only in balance sheets but in stakeholder expectations. The company's response to conscience-driven finance is not peripheral; it is existential. A firm that misjudges its social responsibilities risks capital flight, regulatory scrutiny, and strategic paralysis. By contrast, firms that embrace ethical alignment as integral to strategy can transform activism from a threat into a partnership. Some of the world's leading consumer brands, once lambasted for their shortcomings, now collaborate with NGOs and activist shareholders to co-design sustainability roadmaps. This does not eliminate tension, but it channels it into a productive dynamic that strengthens resilience.

The chapter that follows examines this evolving terrain with clarity and precision. It considers why corporations fear activist investors, how the cost of inaction becomes visible in market value, why reputation has moved from the margins of annual reports to the heart of valuation models, and how fiduciary duty itself is being rewritten under the pressure of conscience. The purpose is not merely descriptive but diagnostic: to show that the company's response to ethical finance is not optional but unavoidable, and that the way in which firms engage with these pressures will shape their future. For the thoughtful reader—whether investor, executive, or citizen—the lesson is stark yet empowering. *Ethics is no longer an external debate imposed on companies from without; it is an internal calculus of survival, woven into the DNA of corporate decision-making.*

Why Corporations Fear Activist Investors

Few words unsettle a chief executive more than "shareholder resolution." Not because the proposals themselves always pass—in fact, many do not—but because the process makes visible the one thing companies work tirelessly to control: the story told about them. Activist investors do not need to own a majority of shares to alter a firm's direction; they need only enough influence to frame a question that captures the attention of larger institutional holders and the media. Once that happens, the corporate agenda can shift overnight, away from the metrics executives are comfortable presenting and towards the ethical and strategic dilemmas they would prefer remain hidden. *The fear is not about losing a vote; it is about losing the narrative.*

At its core, shareholder activism exploits a paradox: companies are both private enterprises and public institutions. While management teams insist on the primacy of their business judgement, listed firms are accountable to a diffuse set of owners whose values may not align neatly with short-term profits. For decades, this tension remained largely theoretical; resolutions on social or environmental issues were filed but rarely supported by more than a handful of investors. Yet over the past two decades, a dramatic shift has occurred. Pension funds, sovereign wealth funds, and asset managers managing trillions of dollars have begun to see activism not as an eccentricity but as a legitimate tool for safeguarding long-term value. What once seemed fringe has become mainstream, and this mainstreaming terrifies corporations.

The ExxonMobil battle of 2021 illustrates the new calculus. Engine No. 1, a relatively obscure hedge fund with just 0.02 per cent of the company's shares, launched a campaign arguing that Exxon's refusal to address climate transition risks imperilled its future. On the surface, the odds of success were negligible. Yet by framing the issue as a matter of fiduciary responsibility rather than ideology, Engine No. 1 persuaded major asset managers like BlackRock, Vanguard, and State Street to support its nominees. The result was historic: three dissident directors elected to Exxon's board, effectively forcing the company to take energy transition strategy seriously. What corporations fear in episodes like this is not simply embarrassment, but exposure to the reality that power no longer rests solely with entrenched executives. *A tiny, well-prepared actor can marshal alliances that challenge the largest companies in the world.*

The anxiety is amplified by the asymmetry of reputational risk. Corporations spend heavily to curate their public image, investing in marketing, sponsorships, and philanthropic initiatives designed to maintain goodwill. Activist investors, by contrast, can puncture these efforts with a single well-documented resolution. Consider when shareholders at Amazon pressed for greater disclosure of workplace injury rates in warehouses. The resolution itself was non-binding, yet the media coverage ensured the issue became part of the company's public identity. Similarly, shareholder proposals on human rights policies at technology firms have repeatedly surfaced uncomfortable questions about surveillance, censorship, and supply chains. Even when defeated at the ballot, such proposals reframe how a company is perceived. From a corporate perspective, this is existential: *losing control of the narrative can inflict damage more lasting than losing a single vote.*

Another dimension of fear stems from the potential for activism to set precedents. Corporations know that once a resolution garners meaningful support, even if not adopted, it can trigger a cascade. Regulators take note of shareholder sentiment, journalists treat it as a barometer of public expectation, and employees find validation in voicing concerns internally. The pressure multiplies across constituencies. When a resolution on racial equity audits gained significant backing at several U.S. banks, it not only forced boards to commission new studies but also signalled to the broader financial sector that scrutiny on this front was intensifying. What terrifies corporate leadership is not just the immediate outcome but the precedent: *a single resolution can alter the governance landscape across an entire industry.*

Yet fear is not distributed evenly. Companies with transparent governance structures and credible sustainability strategies often engage with activist investors more confidently, seeing resolutions as opportunities for dialogue. By contrast, firms with opaque reporting, entrenched boards, or misaligned incentive structures are far more vulnerable. They recognise that activism exposes weaknesses that competitors or regulators can exploit. The asymmetry here is telling: it is not activism itself that threatens corporations, but the possibility that activism will reveal truths management has failed—or refused—to confront.

The philosophical dimension of this fear lies in the redefinition of shareholder rights. For much of the twentieth century, corporations treated shareholders as providers of capital entitled to dividends but little else. Governance reforms, global capital flows, and rising public consciousness have altered this equation. Shareholders are now seen as stakeholders in corporate ethics, not just corporate profits. The recognition that a pension fund investing on behalf of teachers or healthcare workers has an interest in environmental justice or labour rights fundamentally reshapes the dialogue. Companies fear activist investors precisely because they embody this shift: they collapse the distinction between ownership and accountability, reminding management that capital itself can be conscientious.

From another perspective, the fear is rational. Shareholder activism complicates strategic planning, disrupts managerial autonomy, and exposes corporations to volatility. Critics argue that activism can be superficial, pushing symbolic gestures without driving substantive change. Some resolutions are indeed performative, attracting headlines but offering little in the way of actionable strategy. Executives worry about resource diversion—time and capital spent addressing activist demands rather than core operations. Yet even here, fear reveals something deeper: that corporations know the moral and strategic critiques will not simply vanish. They must be engaged with, whether or not management believes them justified. *The unease lies less in the demands themselves than in the recognition that avoidance is no longer an option.*

Perhaps the most telling aspect of corporate fear is its connection to legitimacy. In a world where intangible assets dominate valuations, legitimacy is a scarce and fragile currency. Activist investors, by forcing votes on ethical questions, threaten to expose gaps between what companies say and what they do. This exposure undermines legitimacy in ways that cannot easily be repaired by advertising or lobbying. Companies fear activist investors not because they misunderstand them, but because they understand them all too well: they are agents of accountability in a system that long resisted it. The campaigns and resolutions may be modest in scope, but the signal they send is immense: that conscience has entered the balance sheet, and companies that fail to adapt may find themselves not merely criticised, but restructured from within.

The Cost of Inaction

Markets are often described as forward-looking, but history is littered with examples of companies punished not for what they did, but for what they failed to do. Ethical blind spots—whether in environmental stewardship, labour rights, or governance practices—rarely remain invisible forever. When exposed, they metastasise into financial crises, reputational collapse, and lost market capitalisation. *The cost of inaction is not abstract morality; it is shareholder value left on the table, sometimes wiped away in a matter of weeks.* What makes these stories striking is that the warnings were rarely absent. They were ignored, deferred, or rationalised away until it was too late.

Volkswagen's 2015 emissions scandal, perhaps the most infamous corporate debacle of the decade, demonstrates the price of deferring accountability. For years, critics questioned whether the company's diesel claims were too good to be true. Internal engineers had raised concerns, but management opted for concealment, installing defeat devices to pass regulatory tests. When the deception became public, Volkswagen lost nearly a third of its market value in days, faced over €30 billion in fines and settlements, and watched its brand collapse from aspirational to tarnished. More telling, though, was what the scandal revealed about the opportunity costs of inaction: Volkswagen could have invested in genuine clean technologies earlier, positioning itself as an electric vehicle leader. Instead, it squandered capital, reputation, and time—all to postpone an ethical reckoning that was inevitable. *The lesson is clear: ethical shortcuts create debt that compounds, and markets collect the bill with interest.*

If Volkswagen was a parable of environmental evasion, Rana Plaza in 2013 was one of human neglect. The collapse of the garment factory in Bangladesh, killing over 1,100 workers, cast a harsh light on global fashion brands whose supply chains were built on cost-cutting at the expense of safety. In the weeks following, companies named in investigative reports saw consumer boycotts, reputational damage, and pressured stock prices. Investors realised that the apparent efficiency of fast fashion concealed systemic risks: weak oversight, exploitative conditions, and a brittle supply chain vulnerable to scandal. Several brands were forced into expensive rehabilitation efforts, including costly safety audits and participation in the Accord on Fire and Building Safety. Here again, the cost of inaction was not limited to the humanitarian disaster but extended to shareholder value. Companies that had dismissed earlier warnings from NGOs and labour groups discovered too late that *ignoring ethics in supply chains was not a form of neutrality but a material risk mispriced on their balance sheets.*

Closer to the financial sector, Wells Fargo's fake accounts scandal in 2016 epitomises governance failure as a liability. For years, reports of aggressive sales tactics and whistleblower complaints circulated, but leadership brushed them aside. When regulators revealed that employees had created millions of unauthorised accounts to meet sales quotas, the bank lost $25 billion in market value within weeks, faced billions in fines, and suffered long-term reputational damage that eroded customer trust. The irony is that Wells Fargo's aggressive pursuit of short-term cross-selling revenues undermined the very foundation of its business: credibility. Ethical negligence was not a peripheral concern—it was the catalyst for a sustained erosion of profitability and investor confidence.

The oil and gas industry provides perhaps the most striking illustration of the financial consequences of ignoring slow-burn ethical issues. For decades, major fossil fuel companies dismissed climate science, lobbying against regulation while continuing to expand reserves. Investors who raised questions about "stranded assets"—fossil fuel reserves that could never be burned if climate goals were met—were dismissed as alarmist. Yet over the past decade, trillions of dollars in value have been erased as renewable energy gained traction, climate litigation intensified, and policy shifted. The Norwegian sovereign wealth fund, one of the world's largest investors, divested from several oil and gas companies not out of ideology but because it concluded the business model was unsustainable. Companies like Peabody Energy, once the world's largest private-sector coal company, filed for bankruptcy. *The cost of inaction in this case was not a scandal or a single fine, but an entire sector watching its valuations contract as it ignored moral imperatives tied directly to planetary survival.*

Ethical inaction is not always spectacular or sudden; sometimes it erodes value quietly, through missed opportunities. Kodak serves as an instructive case, not because it was unethical in a traditional sense, but because it failed to act on a responsibility to adapt. When its engineers pioneered digital photography, leadership shelved the technology for fear of cannibalising film profits. The ethical failure here lay in a deeper corporate complacency: prioritising short-term margins over stewardship of innovation that could redefine the industry. The result was bankruptcy and the loss of its place as a household name. The lesson transfers directly to sustainability and social governance: *failing to prepare for the future, even when the signals are clear, is an ethical abdication that markets punish.*

These examples also challenge the belief that markets are ruthlessly efficient. In each case, information about the risks was available well before collapse. Reports, whistleblowers, civil society campaigns, and even internal data highlighted the problems. What failed was not information flow but corporate will. This dynamic reveals a paradox investors must confront: *markets can misprice morality for years, but when the adjustment comes, it is swift, brutal, and often irreversible.* The deferred costs of inaction accumulate invisibly until they suddenly crystallise into financial reality.

One could argue that the fear of overreach—of responding too aggressively to ethical concerns that may not be material—justifies caution. Yet history shows that overreaction is rare compared to the far more common pattern of underreaction. Companies are structurally biased towards denial: executives are rewarded for short-term performance, boards are slow to acknowledge systemic risks, and investors too often assume someone else will act. The cost of inaction, therefore, reflects not just poor ethics but poor governance.

What unites Volkswagen, Rana Plaza, Wells Fargo, fossil fuel firms, and Kodak is not simply their ethical missteps but their failure to see that ethics and economics are intertwined. A diesel engine, a garment supply chain, a cross-selling strategy, an oil reserve, a film roll—all seemed profitable until their ethical liabilities were revealed. Once exposed, those liabilities converted directly into financial losses. This is why the cost of inaction matters: not as a moral abstraction but as a market imperative. For modern investors and corporate leaders alike, the message is unavoidable—*waiting to address ethical concerns is not risk-neutral; it is risk compounding.*

Reputation as a Balance Sheet Item

The most valuable asset a corporation owns rarely appears on its balance sheet. Factories, patents, and cash reserves can all be quantified, depreciated, and audited, but reputation defies neat accounting. Yet when crises erupt, it becomes clear that reputation is not a vague abstraction but a tangible driver of valuation, influencing market capitalisation, borrowing costs, recruitment, customer loyalty, and the ability to expand into new markets. *Reputation, though intangible, behaves like equity capital:*

painstakingly accumulated over years, easily destroyed in days, and indispensable for long-term resilience.

Investors have long understood that markets operate not just on hard numbers but on trust. When Arthur Andersen collapsed in the aftermath of the Enron scandal, its legal liabilities were vast but survivable. What killed the firm was reputational contagion. Clients fled, staff resigned, and the company's capacity to generate future revenue evaporated. It went from being one of the world's "Big Five" accounting firms to non-existence in less than a year. The lesson was unambiguous: without reputation, no amount of technical expertise or historical success can preserve enterprise value.

This truth has become more pronounced in a digital age defined by instantaneous information flows. Social media, activist campaigns, and investigative journalism ensure that reputational damage is no longer localised or slow-moving. A single scandal can trigger global boycotts, investor withdrawals, and regulatory scrutiny within hours. Consider the case of Uber in its early years: allegations of toxic culture, lax safety policies, and aggressive regulatory evasion did not prevent user growth initially, but they did erode investor confidence, culminating in the ousting of its founder and billions shaved off its potential IPO valuation. *The company's difficulties were not simply operational but reputational, demonstrating how intangible trust functions as a form of financial leverage.*

One way to understand reputation is as an invisible asset that acts like a risk buffer. Firms with strong reputational capital can survive mistakes that would cripple weaker peers. Johnson & Johnson's handling of the Tylenol poisoning crisis in 1982 remains a case study in this principle. By responding quickly, recalling products at enormous cost, and demonstrating transparency, the company reinforced trust rather than losing it. The brand recovered swiftly, and the episode became a benchmark for crisis management. The financial cost of the recall was significant, but the reputational dividend preserved future earnings power. The paradox here is that reputation, unlike traditional assets, can grow through ethical sacrifice; companies that prioritise principle in difficult moments often emerge with stronger valuations.

Contrast this with BP's response to the Deepwater Horizon oil spill in 2010. The scale of environmental destruction was vast, but the financial damage was magnified by perceptions of evasion, downplaying, and inadequate safety culture. BP lost half its market value in months, paid over $65 billion in penalties and claims, and became synonymous with corporate irresponsibility. What investors punished was not just the spill itself, but a failure of governance and culture that made the event appear predictable rather than accidental. *Where Johnson & Johnson's reputation cushioned its crisis, BP's reputation acted as a liability multiplier.*

Markets have begun to systematise this intuition. Credit rating agencies now factor reputational risks into ratings, particularly where environmental, social, and governance (ESG) metrics are concerned. Banks adjust lending rates based on perceived ethical reliability. Insurers set premiums higher for firms with weak safety records or histories of governance failure. In effect, reputation has become *financialised*: though it resists line-item reporting, it influences the cost of capital just as directly as interest rates or tax obligations.

There is a temptation to see reputation as a soft concern for marketers and public relations professionals. But its financial consequences are increasingly quantifiable. Studies by Oxford University and others show companies with strong reputational standing—measured through consumer trust, employee satisfaction, and sustainability scores—enjoy lower volatility and superior returns over the long term. Reputation thus operates both as a shield and as a growth engine. A trusted brand attracts loyal customers, top-tier employees, and favourable regulation. An untrusted one finds itself constantly firefighting crises, haemorrhaging value even when financial statements appear robust.

This recognition has driven a shift in corporate reporting. Integrated reporting frameworks now encourage firms to disclose non-financial indicators that shape reputation: diversity statistics, carbon emissions, labour practices. Investors are no longer satisfied with glossy sustainability brochures; they demand auditable data. The rationale is clear: *if reputation drives valuation, then the inputs that shape reputation must be visible and accountable.* Transparency becomes not a moral nicety but a financial necessity.

Critics may argue that markets still overreact to reputational concerns—that temporary boycotts or viral scandals exaggerate real risks. Yet the counterpoint is that reputation determines a company's "licence to operate." A food company that loses consumer trust, a bank tainted by fraud, a social media platform accused of spreading misinformation—all may survive operationally, but they suffer constricted growth potential. Investors discount future earnings not because of moral outrage per se but because reputation erosion changes the probabilities of regulation, lawsuits, and customer attrition. The financial market's logic is ruthless: reputation is priced not as sentiment but as risk-adjusted cash flow.

The intangible nature of reputation also creates a paradox for boards and executives. Unlike machinery or real estate, reputation cannot be insured in the traditional sense, nor can it be easily restored once destroyed. It must be cultivated continuously, often through decisions that seem costly in the short term. Investing in ethical supply chains, robust compliance systems, or transparent reporting rarely boosts quarterly earnings. But it accumulates reputational capital that becomes decisive when shocks occur. *The real financial return of reputation lies in its asymmetry: it is slow to build, but when tested, it can prevent catastrophic loss.*

Modern investors would do well to think of reputation not as a public relations concern but as an asset class in its own right. It is the connective tissue between ethics and economics, the mechanism through which moral choices are translated into market valuations. The companies that understand this are those that treat reputation not as an afterthought but as a strategic resource—one requiring governance, investment, and accountability. The companies that ignore it learn, often too late, that in the balance sheet of modern capitalism, *the most decisive numbers are those that cannot be counted.*

The New Fiduciary Duty

For much of modern corporate history, fiduciary duty was defined in narrow financial terms: boards were expected to maximise shareholder returns, often at the expense of broader concerns. The prevailing orthodoxy, cemented by

Milton Friedman's doctrine in the 1970s, was that "the business of business is business." Ethical considerations—environmental stewardship, labour rights, community welfare—were relegated to the sphere of philanthropy, divorced from the boardroom's central mandate. Yet the contours of fiduciary responsibility are shifting, driven by systemic risks, investor expectations, and the growing recognition that ignoring ethical factors exposes companies to direct financial harm. *Boards can no longer plead neutrality on questions of conscience; these have become inseparable from their duty of care to shareholders.*

The catalyst for this transformation is the changing nature of risk. Climate change provides the most vivid example. Rising global temperatures, increasingly volatile weather patterns, and tightening regulatory regimes all pose material threats to assets, supply chains, and insurance costs. A board that fails to account for climate liability is not demonstrating principled neutrality but practising negligence. This has been underscored by regulatory interventions: in 2021, the US Securities and Exchange Commission (SEC) signalled that climate-related disclosures would become a requirement, while in the UK, listed companies have been pressed to align with the Task Force on Climate-related Financial Disclosures (TCFD). What was once seen as optional transparency is now a compliance necessity. Ethical negligence has thus been recast as financial malpractice.

The same logic applies to social issues. Consider supply chain exploitation. For years, multinational apparel brands outsourced production to factories with weak labour protections. The collapse of Rana Plaza in Bangladesh in 2013 killed more than 1,100 garment workers and exposed systemic abuses. The financial consequences for global retailers were severe: consumer boycotts, investor pressure, and long-term reputational damage. In hindsight, the failure of boards to scrutinise supply chain ethics was not just a moral oversight but a breach of fiduciary duty, leaving shareholder value vulnerable to predictable catastrophe. *The lesson is clear: social risks translate into financial liabilities when ignored.*

Shareholder activism has accelerated this redefinition. Pension funds, sovereign wealth funds, and institutional investors increasingly demand that boards integrate environmental, social, and governance (ESG) metrics into corporate strategy. BlackRock's Larry Fink has repeatedly written in his annual letters that climate risk is investment risk, urging companies to articulate how they will operate in a net-zero economy. While critics dismiss some of this rhetoric as performative, the capital markets have responded decisively: companies seen as lagging on ESG performance face higher costs of capital, while those aligning with sustainable strategies often enjoy valuation premiums. The shift in fiduciary logic is therefore not ideological but empirical: capital markets now price ethics as risk-adjusted returns.

The courts, too, are beginning to test this redefinition. In 2019, a group of Australian pension fund members brought a lawsuit against their superannuation fund for failing to disclose climate risks in its portfolio. The case, settled with the fund agreeing to disclose and integrate climate considerations, signalled a new legal precedent: fiduciary duty includes consideration of systemic ethical risks. Similar litigation has been launched in Europe and North America, raising the prospect that boards could one day face legal liability for failing to integrate sustainability into governance. *The boundaries of fiduciary duty are being rewritten not by philosophy but by law.*

Sceptics argue that expanding fiduciary duty risks diluting its clarity. If boards must balance financial returns with a broad set of ethical imperatives, how can they avoid paralysis or subjectivity? Yet this objection overlooks the practical reality: boards are not asked to become moral philosophers but risk managers. When regulatory fines, consumer boycotts, and stranded assets arise from ethical neglect, boards cannot credibly claim that these were outside their remit. Integrating ethics into fiduciary duty is not about diluting financial discipline but about *redefining materiality.* Materiality once meant quarterly earnings and cost efficiencies; now it encompasses carbon liabilities, reputational capital, and workforce welfare because these factors demonstrably affect financial outcomes.

The case of Volkswagen's emissions scandal illustrates the point. When the company was exposed in 2015 for installing defeat devices to cheat emissions tests, the immediate financial penalties exceeded €30 billion. But the greater cost was reputational, with long-term damage to brand equity and investor confidence. A board that had treated regulatory compliance and environmental responsibility as core fiduciary concerns might have avoided the crisis altogether. Instead, ethical shortcuts were rationalised as competitive necessity, leading to a breach of fiduciary responsibility in its most basic sense: protecting shareholder value. The scandal was not about moral grandstanding; it was about governance failure.

Conversely, boards that anticipate ethical risks often generate durable competitive advantage. Unilever, under the leadership of Paul Polman, pursued a long-term strategy centred on sustainability, reducing short-term profit guidance to focus on structural resilience. While some investors grumbled, the strategy positioned the company as a leader in ESG, attracting patient capital and insulating it from many reputational shocks faced by peers. Here, ethical integration was not a distraction but a fiduciary recalibration—recognising that in an era of heightened scrutiny, doing good and doing well converge. *The redefined fiduciary duty does not erode shareholder primacy; it secures it against new categories of risk.*

There is also a generational dimension to this shift. Millennial and Gen Z investors place higher weight on sustainability, diversity, and social impact in their investment choices. As they inherit trillions in assets, boards that ignore these priorities will find themselves misaligned with capital inflows. Fiduciary duty, then, is not only about mitigating downside risk but about capturing future capital flows. Companies that integrate ethics today position themselves for resilience in tomorrow's investment landscape, while those clinging to an outdated model risk exclusion from capital markets altogether.

This transformation invites boards to ask harder questions of themselves. Does fiduciary duty require actively divesting from harmful industries? Does it oblige boards to prioritise long-term planetary health over short-term profit maximisation? The answers are contested, but the trajectory is unmistakable: fiduciary duty is no longer a minimalist doctrine of maximising quarterly returns. It is evolving into a more complex, but more realistic, responsibility: to ensure that corporations can generate sustainable value in a world where ethics and economics are fused. Boards that fail to adapt will not only court moral criticism but breach their fundamental obligation to safeguard shareholder value.

The new fiduciary duty is, therefore, less about altruism than realism. It acknowledges that ethics have become financially material, that conscience now shapes cash flows, and that neglecting these forces is tantamount to dereliction of duty. The boardroom is being redefined not by abstract principle but by empirical necessity: *to fulfil their mandate, directors must treat ethical risks as financial risks, and ethical opportunities as financial opportunities.* Anything less is not just outdated governance—it is a failure of fiduciary care.

Chapter 9
Building Your Ethical Framework

Every investor, no matter how disciplined, carries an invisible framework into the markets: a set of preferences, instincts, and compromises that shape financial decisions. Yet few stop to examine whether those decisions reflect their professed values or whether, more subtly, they reveal a disconnect between principle and practice. In the age of conscience-driven capital, this gap cannot remain unexamined. Money is no longer just a vehicle for personal wealth—it is also a mirror of what we endorse, ignore, or resist. To invest without an ethical framework is to drift between contradictions, pulled by the tides of markets and marketing, rather than guided by conviction. The purpose of this chapter is to help bring clarity where confusion so often reigns: how to identify one's principles, prioritise them, translate them into action, and recognise the trade-offs that no ethical investor can entirely escape.

The need for such a framework becomes apparent when one considers the complexity of the modern investment landscape. There is no shortage of funds that brand themselves as "sustainable," "green," or "impactful," yet behind the labels lies a web of exclusions, inclusions, and thresholds that may or may not align with the investor's own moral compass. A fund that excludes tobacco might still hold oil majors. Another that champions gender diversity might remain silent on arms manufacturing. Without a personal structure to interpret these nuances, investors risk outsourcing their conscience to fund managers whose priorities may diverge from their own. *Clarity begins not with the marketplace but with the self.*

The first step is recognising that values are plural, not singular. For some, climate change is the paramount concern, overshadowing all else. For others, labour rights or animal welfare take precedence. Many will find themselves balancing overlapping principles—environmental stewardship, social justice, corporate transparency—that resist neat alignment. The act of investing, then, is not only financial but philosophical: it forces us to ask which values matter most when they cannot all be served simultaneously. This is why a personal values audit is indispensable. Just as a balance sheet clarifies assets and liabilities, such an audit surfaces the convictions that truly define one's investment identity, distinguishing them from preferences that, while important, may be negotiable.

From this recognition emerges the necessity of hierarchy. Without prioritisation, ethical investing risks paralysis. Consider the investor who wishes to avoid fossil fuels, support clean energy, reject exploitative labour, and insist on gender equity in leadership. These are all legitimate principles, but the universe of investable assets that satisfies every one of them simultaneously may be vanishingly small. A hierarchy of non-negotiables allows the investor to move forward with conviction rather than stall in indecision. It also prevents unconscious compromises from slipping into the portfolio under the guise of pragmatism. *To invest ethically is to choose, and to choose is to rank.*

Yet even the most carefully ranked principles remain abstractions until they are translated into operational screens. The discipline of ethical investing lies in building filters that align practice with principle: exclusions of certain industries, positive screens for desired characteristics, or weighting methodologies that reward better performers within a sector. This translation is both technical and moral. Technical, because it requires understanding financial instruments and data sources. Moral, because it forces investors to confront the imperfections of available metrics. Carbon disclosure, for example, may be incomplete; gender diversity measures may mask tokenism. The screen is not a perfect mirror of values, but a pragmatic approximation—an expression of intent refined over time.

No framework, however rigorous, can erase the inevitability of trade-offs. Ethical investors often find themselves navigating dilemmas where no option is pure. Investing in renewable energy might entail exposure to rare-earth mining with its own environmental harms. Supporting microfinance might raise concerns about high interest rates charged to vulnerable borrowers. Even divestment itself carries complexities: selling shares in a polluting company may cleanse the portfolio, but it does not directly change the company's behaviour, whereas shareholder activism might. *The choice is not between purity and compromise, but between conscious trade-offs and unconscious contradictions.* To accept this is not to dilute one's ethics but to practise them with maturity.

History shows that those who articulate and adhere to an ethical framework are better positioned not only to preserve their integrity but also to anticipate the direction of markets. The abolitionist investors of the eighteenth century, who refused to finance the slave trade, stood on what seemed then to be marginal moral ground. Over time, their ethical stance anticipated economic reality, as slavery's abolition reshaped global commerce. The same applies today: those who align capital with principle may face short-term limitations but often find themselves on the right side of history, as values gradually crystallise into regulation and market consensus. *An ethical framework is therefore not only a moral compass but a form of foresight.*

Building such a framework requires patience and honesty. It is not a checklist to complete once, but an evolving discipline that adapts as both personal convictions and the external world change. Ethical awareness grows with exposure to new evidence, debates, and lived experience. What felt negotiable yesterday may feel non-negotiable tomorrow. Conversely, principles once treated as absolute may be reinterpreted in light of new realities. A well-designed framework is not rigid but resilient—it anchors the investor in conviction while allowing room for reflection and recalibration.

In the chapters that follow, the tools of ethical investing—values audits, hierarchies, screens, and trade-offs—will be examined not as abstract concepts but as practical disciplines. The aim is not to impose a universal code but to equip each reader with the means to construct their own, in full awareness of both its strengths and limitations. Ethical investing is not about arriving at a final state of purity, but about engaging with markets consciously, with eyes open to the consequences of one's choices. *To invest without such a framework is to drift; to build one is to navigate.* This chapter is an invitation to the latter.

Personal Values Audit – Guides readers in clarifying which ethical principles matter most for their portfolio decisions

Every investment decision, no matter how detached it may appear, is also a moral decision. When capital flows into fossil fuel exploration, arms production, or exploitative labour systems, it sustains those industries as surely as a direct purchase of their products would. Conversely, when funds are directed toward renewable energy, affordable housing, or inclusive enterprises, they strengthen the scaffolding of a different economic future. Yet most investors, even those who consider themselves ethically minded, rarely pause to articulate what principles they want their money to embody. The absence of deliberate reflection is not benign—it leads to portfolios that silently contradict their owners' stated convictions. The task of a personal values audit is therefore not a philosophical indulgence but a practical necessity, a way to anchor investment decisions in clarity rather than drift.

The exercise begins with recognising that values are plural and often conflicting. Unlike financial goals, which can usually be reduced to numbers, values resist neat quantification. An individual may place high importance on environmental stewardship but also want to support domestic manufacturing jobs. A fund that screens out overseas sweatshops might inadvertently exclude companies that lead in decarbonisation. To invest without a clear understanding of personal priorities is to risk being pulled into such contradictions unconsciously. *A values audit provides the first discipline of ethical investing: it forces investors to name what they truly stand for and to distinguish principle from preference.*

History demonstrates that those who took the time to clarify their values often shaped the markets themselves. Quakers in the eighteenth century not only refused to profit from the slave trade but also influenced broader patterns of divestment and commerce. More recently, faith-based investors catalysed the first wave of socially responsible investing by explicitly stating which activities their money should not touch. These examples reveal that what begins as private conviction can, when systematically applied, set new norms. The investor who conducts a values audit is therefore not only clarifying a personal stance but potentially contributing to larger shifts in capital markets.

The method of such an audit need not be elaborate, but it must be honest. It requires asking questions that go beyond surface-level sentiment: Do I believe certain industries—such as tobacco, fossil fuels, or weapons manufacturing—are so fundamentally harmful that I cannot profit from them under any circumstances? Do I prioritise climate impact over social justice, or do I view them as inseparable? Am I willing to tolerate imperfect companies if they show credible commitment to transition, or do I insist on immediate purity of practice? These questions matter because they establish boundaries and hierarchies that can later be translated into portfolio screens. Without this groundwork, investors risk being seduced by superficial labels or greenwashed marketing.

One of the most powerful insights that arises from a values audit is the recognition that ethical consistency is more difficult than it appears. Many individuals voice opposition to environmental destruction while maintaining pensions heavily invested in oil and gas majors. Others decry inequality yet profit from firms that pay starvation wages in their global supply chains. This is not necessarily hypocrisy but rather the consequence of never subjecting one's portfolio to the same scrutiny applied to one's consumption choices. The audit forces alignment: it closes the gap between the values proclaimed at the dinner table and the values enacted in financial markets.

Yet the process is not without discomfort. A rigorous audit will often surface tensions that cannot be neatly resolved. For example, an investor might discover that their desire to exclude all companies associated with animal testing collides with their interest in biotechnology firms pioneering life-saving treatments. Or they may face the trade-off between maximising diversification for risk management and narrowing their investable universe to align with stringent ethical criteria. *The act of confronting these dilemmas is itself a moral education: it teaches the investor that conscience in markets is rarely a matter of absolutes but of carefully weighted choices.*

Real-world examples illustrate the stakes. Consider the rise of green bonds: some investors treat any such instrument as ethically sound, while others, upon closer reflection, reject those tied to projects they deem inadequate or superficial. A values audit clarifies whether one's standard is *relative improvement*—supporting better practices even if imperfect—or *absolute exclusion,* drawing hard lines regardless of context. Similarly, in shareholder activism, some investors see engagement with fossil fuel companies as a way to accelerate transition, while others regard ownership itself as complicity. A values audit does not dictate which stance is correct, but it ensures that whichever stance is taken reflects conscious deliberation rather than passive drift.

The process also compels investors to separate emotional impulse from enduring conviction. It is easy to be swayed by the moral urgency of the moment—by headlines about climate disasters or scandals in tech supply chains. While such stimuli can sharpen awareness, they should not alone dictate an investor's ethical framework. A disciplined audit distinguishes between temporary outrage and sustained values, between reaction and principle. *The goal is not to mirror the news cycle but to articulate a stable compass that guides decisions through changing contexts.*

Critics may argue that personal values audits are too subjective to be useful, that investment decisions must remain grounded in financial metrics alone. Yet this perspective underestimates the growing integration of environmental, social, and governance factors into financial analysis. When values are ignored, investors still make ethical decisions—they simply do so by default, allowing the prevailing structure of markets to decide for them. An explicit audit is not the abandonment of financial rationality but its enrichment. It acknowledges that risk and return are increasingly tied to societal expectations and reputational pressures. To clarify one's values is, therefore, to anticipate the direction in which markets themselves are moving.

The discipline of a values audit also strengthens accountability. When investors state clearly which principles they seek to uphold, they create a benchmark against which their portfolios can be assessed. This prevents the erosion of standards over time through rationalisation or convenience. A fund that slips in exposure to industries once deemed unacceptable can be identified and reconsidered. In this sense, the audit functions not only as a declaration of intent but as an ongoing monitoring tool. *Clarity at the beginning guards against compromise in the end.*

Finally, a values audit cultivates coherence between the financial and the personal. In a world where many feel alienated from the consequences of their capital, it reconnects investing with identity. The act of aligning money with principles, however imperfectly, can restore a sense of integrity and purpose to financial life. It transforms investing from a purely transactional exercise into an expression of what one believes ought to thrive in the world. For individuals and institutions alike, this coherence is not merely morally satisfying but strategically advantageous: it builds resilience in the face of growing demands for transparency and accountability.

The personal values audit, then, is the foundation upon which all ethical investing rests. Without it, the investor risks incoherence, contradiction, and susceptibility to superficial marketing. With it, they gain clarity, discipline, and the ability to navigate complex trade-offs consciously. More than a checklist, it is a process of moral articulation, one that equips the investor to act not only as a participant in markets but as a custodian of conscience within them.

Hierarchy of Non-Negotiables – Encourages ranking principles to avoid paralysis when conflicts arise

Ethical investing is not defeated by a lack of conviction but by too much of it, all pulling in different directions. The modern investor, faced with a cascade of possible screens and exclusions, often discovers that their conscience is less a compass pointing due north than a cluster of needles tugging at different magnetic fields. Climate change, labour rights, animal welfare, gender equity, indigenous sovereignty, digital privacy—each is a principle with legitimate moral gravity. But when they clash, as they inevitably do, paralysis can set in. An investor who refuses to rank their priorities risks a portfolio that is either impossibly narrow or incoherently broad. The practice of constructing a hierarchy of non-negotiables is not an exercise in abandoning values but in disciplining them into a workable order.

The first step is to acknowledge that all values are not equal in weight. To pretend otherwise is to create the illusion of consistency while masking contradictions. A pension fund, for example, may declare commitment to both maximising worker welfare and pursuing decarbonisation. Yet what happens when a renewable energy company is found guilty of union-busting? Without an explicit ranking, decision-makers are left to muddle through, often privileging expediency over principle. *A hierarchy clarifies in advance which principles are core, which are secondary, and which may be traded off under specific circumstances.*

Historical precedent shows the importance of this kind of moral triage. Abolitionist investors in the eighteenth and nineteenth centuries were unequivocal in placing the fight against slavery above other economic concerns. They did not allow their opposition to war or gambling—issues they also debated—to distract from the central non-negotiable. Their clarity gave coherence to campaigns that reshaped global trade. More recently, anti-apartheid divestment campaigns made racial justice the primary principle, even as companies targeted by activists sometimes had better records on other social issues. By establishing a clear hierarchy, campaigners avoided the dilution of their efforts and mobilised coalitions around a focused demand.

In contemporary markets, the need for this hierarchy is even more acute. ESG ratings often aggregate dozens of metrics into single scores, concealing trade-offs that investors must eventually confront. A technology company may receive high marks for carbon efficiency while simultaneously facing criticism for data privacy abuses or exploitative supply chains. Which matters more? Without a prior sense of hierarchy, investors risk being seduced by aggregate ratings that hide the underlying moral choices. *Ranking principles restores transparency, reminding investors that conscience cannot be outsourced to algorithms.*

The process of defining non-negotiables requires intellectual honesty. Investors must move beyond generic aspirations—"I care about the environment" or "I want companies to treat people well"—toward sharper articulation. For one individual, the absolute exclusion of fossil fuels may sit at the top of the hierarchy. For another, the guarantee of fair labour practices may override environmental compromises. Neither is wrong; what matters is that the hierarchy reflects deliberate choice rather than ad hoc reaction. In the absence of such clarity, investors risk being captured by narratives of convenience, shifting principles according to market conditions rather than moral conviction.

One striking example is the debate over nuclear energy. For decades, many ethical funds excluded nuclear on safety and waste grounds. Yet as climate urgency has grown, some argue that nuclear must be embraced as a transitional technology. Investors who have placed *climate impact* as their paramount principle may now reconsider exclusion, while those whose non-negotiable is *safety and intergenerational justice* will continue to refuse it. Both stances can be defended, but only a clearly articulated hierarchy prevents confusion or rationalisation.

The discipline of ranking principles also inoculates investors against the paralysis of moral perfectionism. Many individuals hesitate to act because they fear inconsistency—what if supporting a sustainable food company inadvertently channels profits to a parent conglomerate with dubious practices? A hierarchy allows for action even amidst imperfection. By prioritising the most critical values and treating others as aspirational but flexible, investors avoid the trap of all-or-nothing thinking. *The pursuit of coherence should not become an excuse for inertia.*

Philosophically, the hierarchy acknowledges the reality of moral pluralism. Human life is structured around competing goods, and investing is no exception. The idea that one can create a "pure" portfolio untouched by compromise is a mirage, particularly in globalised markets where supply chains and ownership structures entangle nearly every industry. A hierarchy provides a framework for navigating this pluralism with intentionality rather than illusion. It is a recognition that integrity is not about achieving perfection but about being able to explain, with clarity and consistency, why certain trade-offs were made.

Practically, the hierarchy of non-negotiables functions as a decision-making tool. When faced with two investment opportunities, investors can quickly reference their ranked principles to determine alignment. This reduces decision fatigue and streamlines portfolio construction. It also improves communication with advisors and fund managers, ensuring that instructions are understood not merely as vague preferences but as structured commitments. Over time, the discipline of applying a hierarchy fosters consistency, reducing the risk of portfolios drifting away from stated ethical intentions.

There are risks, of course. A rigid hierarchy may blind investors to emerging issues or prevent them from seeing the interconnectedness of values. Climate, labour, health, and equity are not discrete silos but deeply interwoven dynamics. Too narrow a focus on one principle can lead to blind spots. The challenge is to design a hierarchy that is firm enough to guide decisions but flexible enough to adapt to new evidence and evolving contexts. This requires periodic review: what seemed peripheral a decade ago—such as digital privacy—may now rank higher as awareness grows of its societal implications. *A hierarchy of non-negotiables should not be static dogma but a living framework, tested and refined over time.*

Corporate boards, too, are increasingly compelled to establish their own hierarchies as part of governance.

Fiduciary duty no longer allows directors to treat ethical issues as peripheral. Whether it is climate risk, diversity, or data governance, companies must now decide which principles are non-negotiable in their operations. Investors who have clarified their own hierarchies are better positioned to interrogate corporate priorities, to ask whether stated commitments reflect substantive ranking or merely public relations. The dialogue between investor and corporation becomes sharper, more grounded, and less vulnerable to spin.

The hierarchy of non-negotiables ultimately represents a shift from vague aspiration to disciplined conscience. It challenges investors to grapple with moral conflict directly rather than sidestep it. In doing so, it transforms ethical investing from a loose cluster of sentiments into a structured practice capable of navigating complexity without paralysis. By ranking principles, investors gain the clarity to act decisively, the resilience to defend their choices, and the coherence to sustain their strategies over time. *In markets where every pound or dollar cast is a vote for the world we want, a hierarchy of non-negotiables ensures that those votes are cast with conviction rather than confusion.*

Translating Values into Screens — Shows how to move from abstract principles to portfolio filters

Every investor who sets out to align money with conscience eventually encounters the same barrier: values are written in language, but portfolios are constructed in numbers. The statement "I care about human rights" has clarity as an ethical position, but it is too abstract to guide an allocation decision without translation into metrics, thresholds, and exclusions. The bridge between principle and practice lies in the design of screens—the criteria that filter investment universes, shaping what is considered investable and what is ruled out. *Screens are where conscience becomes operational.*

The very idea of screening has deep historical roots. In the nineteenth century, religious groups such as the Quakers excluded "sin stocks" like alcohol, weapons, and gambling from their holdings, using simple categorical bans as their screen. These were blunt tools, but they established the precedent that portfolios could be structured around moral limits. Today, the sophistication of data and the complexity of global markets demand far more nuanced approaches. Instead of simply excluding industries outright, investors may now screen within industries, differentiate between leaders and laggards, or apply positive screens that tilt portfolios toward companies exhibiting strong performance on selected values. The challenge is not the availability of tools but the precision with which they are applied.

A crucial step in translation is specificity. To say one values "sustainability" is to invite confusion: does that mean prioritising carbon emissions, biodiversity protection, water usage, or all of the above? Without precision, screens risk becoming cosmetic—statements that sound virtuous but fail to direct capital in measurable ways. *Clarity demands that each value be expressed in terms that can be tested against available data.* For climate-conscious investors, this might mean setting explicit thresholds, such as excluding companies with more than 30 per cent of revenues from coal or including only those with validated net-zero transition plans. For those concerned with labour rights, it might involve screening companies based on supply chain audits, union recognition, or rates of workplace accidents.

The translation process is rarely straightforward. Take human rights, for instance. While it is easy to condemn violations in principle, quantifying compliance is fraught with difficulty. Multinationals may have immaculate headquarters policies but rely on opaque subcontractors in regions with weak enforcement. Here, screens often turn to proxy indicators such as membership in international compacts, transparency in reporting, or frequency of third-party controversies. None of these is a perfect measure, but together they create a mosaic that approximates alignment with stated principles. Investors must be candid about the imperfections of such measures while still using them as a disciplined guide.

One of the paradoxes of translating values into screens is that it can expose conflicts between principles that seemed harmonious in the abstract. An investor committed to both animal welfare and climate action might discover that plant-based food companies, while lowering emissions relative to meat producers, rely heavily on monoculture soy that drives deforestation and biodiversity loss. How should this be screened? Does climate trump biodiversity, or vice versa? The process forces investors to confront trade-offs head-on, rather than cloaking them in rhetoric. *A screen is not merely a technical tool but a mirror that reflects the hierarchy of one's priorities.*

Screens can be negative, positive, or thematic. Negative screens exclude industries or behaviours—tobacco, weapons, fossil fuels. Positive screens tilt portfolios towards best-in-class performers, rewarding leaders in areas such as renewable energy adoption or gender diversity. Thematic screens go further, selecting only companies explicitly engaged in solutions, such as clean water, affordable housing, or sustainable agriculture. The choice among these approaches reflects not just technical preference but philosophical stance: is the goal to avoid harm, encourage better practice, or actively fund solutions? Translating values into screens requires answering this question with conviction.

Case studies show how impactful well-designed screens can be. When major university endowments adopted fossil fuel exclusion screens, they did not merely rebalance their portfolios—they signalled to markets and policymakers that carbon-heavy assets carried reputational and financial risk. Over time, these screens contributed to the broader perception of stranded asset risk in the fossil sector. Conversely, poorly designed screens can backfire. Funds that exclude "controversial weapons" may still hold defence contractors if their revenues from banned categories fall below a set threshold. This creates the impression of ethical purity while leaving exposure largely intact. *Screens are only as effective as the rigour with which they are defined.*

Technology has expanded the toolkit. ESG data providers track thousands of companies across hundreds of metrics, enabling highly granular screens. Artificial intelligence promises to further refine analysis by scanning news flows, litigation records, and social media for real-time signals of alignment or misconduct. Yet this abundance introduces new risks: metrics can be inconsistent across providers, methodologies opaque, and scores vulnerable to manipulation. The act of translating values into screens therefore requires critical engagement with data quality. Investors must ask not only what is being measured but how, and whether the measurement genuinely captures the ethical dimension they intend to prioritise.

There is also the question of materiality. Should screens be applied universally or weighted by relevance? For example, carbon emissions are material for an energy company but far less so for a software provider. Labour rights may be paramount in apparel manufacturing but peripheral in asset-light businesses. Some investors apply values screens uniformly, treating principles as non-negotiable across contexts. Others apply sector-adjusted screens, recognising that the most meaningful improvements may lie in addressing the highest risks specific to each industry. Both approaches have merit, but the choice must be deliberate rather than accidental.

The process of screen design also raises issues of transparency and accountability. Investors must be able to explain their screens clearly to stakeholders—clients, beneficiaries, or members. Vague references to "sustainability criteria" or "social responsibility" do little to inspire trust. By contrast, a transparent articulation of screening thresholds, data sources, and rationale strengthens credibility and makes portfolios more defensible against accusations of greenwashing. *The discipline of explaining screens publicly is itself a safeguard against ethical drift.*

Importantly, screens should not be mistaken for static instruments. Ethical priorities evolve, data improves, and new risks emerge. A decade ago, few investors screened for digital privacy or artificial intelligence ethics; today these are pressing concerns. The discipline of translating values into screens must therefore be iterative, with periodic reviews to ensure alignment with both evolving conscience and emerging evidence. *A portfolio aligned with yesterday's ethics is no more defensible than one aligned with yesterday's technologies.*

At its best, the process of translation deepens rather than dilutes ethical conviction. It forces values out of the realm of comfortable abstraction and into the domain of accountability. To build a portfolio is to decide, concretely, what one is willing to tolerate and what one refuses to finance. Screens provide the grammar of that decision-making. They may be imperfect, but without them the connection between belief and action remains vague. By committing values to the discipline of filters, investors transform conscience from aspiration into architecture—visible, testable, and capable of guiding capital with clarity.

Accepting Trade-Offs — Prepares readers to make conscious compromises rather than unconscious contradictions

Every ethical investor eventually collides with the uncomfortable reality that values are rarely absolute in practice. A portfolio cannot exist in a realm of purity; it exists in markets, which are messy, contradictory, and governed by trade-offs. To pretend otherwise is to risk paralysis or self-deception. The discipline of ethical investing is not about eradicating compromise but about making it visible, deliberate, and conscious. *Clarity lies not in escaping trade-offs but in acknowledging and navigating them with integrity.*

Consider the dilemma of renewable energy. Wind farms, solar installations, and battery production are celebrated as central pillars of the climate transition. Yet their supply chains are entangled with resource extraction that carries its own ethical costs: lithium mining linked to water depletion in South America, cobalt extraction in the Democratic Republic of Congo often associated with unsafe labour conditions, or the displacement of communities for large-scale solar projects. To divest entirely from these technologies in the name of human rights would be to undermine decarbonisation goals. To ignore the ethical concerns altogether would be to perpetuate injustice under a green banner. The investor is therefore called to hold both truths simultaneously and decide what balance of harm reduction and progress they can accept.

Trade-offs are not confined to environmental issues. Social principles, too, frequently clash. A pension fund might prioritise gender diversity in leadership, only to discover that some of the firms with strong female representation are also implicated in aggressive tax avoidance strategies that undermine public revenues. An endowment might value community regeneration, investing in local property projects, but face criticism that such developments accelerate gentrification and displace vulnerable tenants. *Ethical consistency across all dimensions is an aspiration; in practice, prioritisation is unavoidable.*

The greatest risk is not compromise itself but unconscious contradiction—the comfortable belief that one's investments are wholly aligned with stated values when, in reality, they contain dissonance hidden beneath vague labels. For example, investors in ESG funds may assume their money avoids fossil fuels, only to find exposure to natural gas companies classified as "transition assets." Others may believe they support "sustainable agriculture" without recognising that the term can cover both regenerative farms and monoculture plantations certified through lenient standards. Conscious trade-offs demand transparency, vigilance, and a willingness to admit imperfection rather than clinging to illusions.

One way to approach these dilemmas is to distinguish between principles that are non-negotiable and those that can be flexed in context. For some, absolute exclusion of tobacco or controversial weapons may serve as firm lines. Beyond those red lines, however, degrees of tolerance must often be introduced. Investors may accept holdings in an industrial company that produces carbon-intensive materials if it demonstrates a credible transition plan and significant capital expenditure on cleaner technologies. Others may allow a company with imperfect labour practices but strong commitments to reform, viewing investment as a lever for positive pressure rather than endorsement. *Compromise becomes most defensible when paired with evidence of directionality—progress towards better alignment, not stasis in contradiction.*

Historical perspective reveals that trade-offs often reflect the temporal lag between ethics and economics. Abolitionist investors in the eighteenth century who sought to avoid slave-linked industries faced immense difficulty: sugar, cotton, and shipping were all entangled with the trade. Total purity was impossible; what mattered was the deliberate stance to minimise complicity and channel capital towards less exploitative enterprises. Similarly, modern investors may not be able to eliminate exposure to fossil fuels overnight without destabilising portfolios, but they can phase reductions in ways that reflect both conscience and prudence. *Trade-offs, when transparent, can serve as bridges across historical transitions.*

The act of accepting trade-offs is also an act of humility. It recognises the limitations of both investors and markets. No single individual can dismantle systemic injustice through portfolio selection alone. However, by choosing consciously where to compromise, investors can signal priorities, exert incremental influence, and avoid the hypocrisy of claiming alignment while masking contradiction. This humility does not weaken the ethical stance; it strengthens it by anchoring it in reality rather than idealised abstraction.

Practical methods can help. Some investors adopt tiered frameworks, grading companies not only on current performance but also on trajectory of improvement. This allows for investment in firms that are imperfect but reforming, while excluding those that remain stagnant. Others employ "impact offsets," balancing necessary exposure to controversial sectors with targeted allocations to solution-oriented assets. For example, an investor who accepts holdings in resource-intensive technology firms might deliberately counterbalance with investments in biodiversity restoration or circular economy ventures. *Such strategies transform trade-offs from passive contradictions into active choices embedded in broader purpose.*

Yet not all compromises should be entertained. The discipline lies in recognising when a trade-off has slipped into rationalisation. For instance, continuing to invest heavily in coal on the grounds of short-term returns, while making token gestures towards renewables, is not a principled trade-off but a disguised abdication of responsibility. The boundary between compromise and capitulation is delicate, and investors must guard against ethical drift by regularly interrogating the rationale behind their decisions.

Communication plays a decisive role. Trade-offs are easier to justify internally than to explain to stakeholders, yet the discipline of articulation is essential. Beneficiaries of pension funds, clients of asset managers, and members of cooperatives deserve to know not only what screens and policies are in place but also where compromises exist and why they were accepted. Far from undermining trust, such candour can enhance it, showing that decisions are thoughtful, honest, and responsive to complexity. *Silence breeds suspicion; transparency, even about imperfection, builds credibility.*

The psychological burden of compromise should not be underestimated. Investors, especially those deeply committed to moral causes, may feel guilt or frustration when confronted with inescapable contradictions. But reframing trade-offs as conscious, disciplined choices rather than failures can alleviate this strain. In this sense, the work of ethical investing is not only financial but also philosophical, demanding comfort with nuance and imperfection in pursuit of progress.

Ultimately, accepting trade-offs is not an admission of defeat but a recognition of maturity. The world is too interconnected for pure investment to exist, but that does not absolve investors of responsibility. Instead, it calls for an ethic of discernment: to identify, rank, and consciously navigate the inevitable conflicts that arise when values meet markets. By doing so, investors prevent unconscious contradictions from hollowing out their principles and instead embody a practice of alignment that is honest, transparent, and adaptable. *Ethical investing is not about achieving purity but about practising integrity within complexity.*

Chapter 10
Designing the Ethical Portfolio

Every investor eventually reaches the moment where ideals meet arithmetic. Principles, however clearly defined, must be expressed through instruments and allocations that can weather markets, meet personal financial objectives, and remain consistent with ethical commitments. Designing an ethical portfolio is therefore not a matter of aspiration alone but of architecture: an intricate balance of exclusion, inclusion, diversification, liquidity, and practicality. It is here that philosophy meets spreadsheets, and conscience collides with covariance matrices. The exercise is less about perfection and more about coherence—ensuring that the structures of capital reflect the structures of belief.

The debate often begins with the tension between exclusion and inclusion. Exclusion has deep historical roots, from abolitionists avoiding slave-linked enterprises to modern funds barring investments in tobacco, weapons, or fossil fuels. It offers a sense of moral clarity, drawing firm boundaries around what an investor refuses to endorse. Yet exclusion alone risks leaving a hollowed-out portfolio, defined more by what it avoids than what it supports. Inclusion, by contrast, shifts the focus towards identifying enterprises actively generating social or environmental value: renewable energy innovators, affordable housing projects, or healthcare providers serving underserved populations. The most robust ethical portfolios often weave these approaches together, recognising that *virtue lies not only in refusing harm but also in fostering benefit*. The challenge is to calibrate how much weight one places on each side of the scale.

This calibration leads naturally to the question of diversification with conscience. Ethical investors are sometimes accused of narrowing their horizons to such a degree that portfolios become dangerously concentrated. Excluding entire sectors can amplify exposure to others, creating vulnerabilities that undermine both financial and ethical objectives. For instance, heavy reliance on clean technology stocks might tie the fate of the portfolio too closely to government subsidies or volatile commodity markets. Conversely, ignoring diversification altogether risks the financial sustainability of the ethical project itself. The task is to expand the investable universe creatively, drawing upon a broader range of sectors and geographies without diluting principles. Credit unions, green bonds, social enterprises, and carefully screened multinationals can all play a role in constructing a mosaic that is both principled and resilient. *The true test of conscience-led diversification is whether an investor can spread risk without scattering values.*

Liquidity, too, demands scrutiny. Many ethical assets promise compelling long-term impact but lock up capital in illiquid structures: community housing funds, private equity in sustainable agriculture, or infrastructure projects for renewable energy. While these investments can deliver profound impact, they also restrict flexibility, leaving investors exposed in times of financial stress. Publicly traded ESG funds, by contrast, provide daily liquidity but may compromise on depth of impact. The portfolio designer must therefore ask: how much liquidity is truly needed, and at what cost to principle? A family office with intergenerational horizons may afford to tie up capital for decades, while a young professional saving for a home deposit cannot. *Liquidity is not merely a technical detail; it is the pivot where ethical ambition meets the realities of life circumstances.*

Against this backdrop emerges the need for practical allocation models. Abstractions about values must eventually be translated into percentages, benchmarks, and asset classes. Conservative investors may prefer ethical bonds, screened equity indices, and a modest allocation to impact funds, balancing conscience with stability. More risk-tolerant investors might pursue aggressive allocations towards climate technology, frontier-market microfinance, or venture capital in social enterprises, accepting volatility in pursuit of transformative outcomes. Between these poles lies a spectrum of possibilities, each shaped by the interplay of values, risk appetite, and financial goals. Here, theory becomes practice: asset allocation ceases to be a sterile exercise in optimisation and becomes instead an expression of moral identity.

The deeper lesson of designing an ethical portfolio is that it is not a static event but an evolving practice. Industries once considered untouchable may reform; others once celebrated may reveal hidden harms. An ethical framework must therefore be dynamic, revisited regularly to ensure that screens, allocations, and liquidity decisions remain aligned with both evolving values and changing markets. Portfolios, like the societies they reflect, are works in progress. To design them ethically is to accept responsibility not only for today's allocations but for tomorrow's adaptations.

What the reader gains in approaching this chapter is not a blueprint to be followed blindly but a set of guiding principles and tested strategies for reconciling conscience with capital. Exclusion versus inclusion, diversification with conscience, the liquidity question, and practical allocation models are not mere technicalities—they are the essential scaffolding through which values take tangible financial form. Designing an ethical portfolio is not about constructing a fortress of moral purity but about building a resilient vessel capable of navigating markets without losing sight of purpose. *It is here, perhaps more than anywhere else, that the claim of investing as a moral act is either validated or exposed as hollow.*

Exclusion vs. Inclusion

The heart of ethical investing lies not only in financial performance but in the act of selection. Every portfolio tells a story: of what its owner refuses to support, and of what they actively choose to cultivate. This duality—between exclusion and inclusion—frames one of the most significant strategic questions for the ethically minded investor. While exclusion draws boundaries by eliminating harmful industries, inclusion goes further, redirecting capital towards enterprises that generate positive impact. Both approaches share a common impulse—aligning money with values—but they diverge in practice, in psychological resonance, and in long-term effect on markets.

Exclusion is often the first instinct, and for good reason. It is clear, decisive, and rooted in a history of moral refusals. When the Quakers barred investments in the transatlantic slave trade, or when campaigners pressed for divestment from apartheid South Africa, the logic was simple: to profit from certain industries is to endorse their practices. In the modern context, exclusion lists might ban companies engaged in tobacco, fossil fuels, weapons manufacturing, or exploitative labour practices. The appeal is straightforward: *to exclude is to withhold complicity.* Investors draw a moral perimeter around what is unacceptable, using the tools of finance to enforce boundaries once reserved for law or religion.

Yet exclusion, while powerful, has its limits. A portfolio built solely on avoidance risks becoming more a catalogue of prohibitions than a vision of possibility. The absence of harmful industries does not automatically ensure the presence of virtuous ones. A fund that excludes oil and tobacco may still be heavily weighted towards technology giants whose record on data privacy, labour rights, or tax practices remains contested. Here lies the central critique: exclusion may cleanse a portfolio of obvious harms but does not necessarily advance the causes investors wish to promote. This gap leads naturally to inclusion.

Inclusion shifts the focus from abstention to intention. Rather than asking only *what must be avoided,* the inclusive investor asks *what deserves amplification*. This is the logic behind the growth of impact funds, green bonds, and sustainability-focused indices. By deliberately seeking out renewable energy firms, affordable housing developers, healthcare innovators, or companies with exemplary governance standards, investors are not merely neutralising harm—they are financing solutions. The distinction is subtle but profound: exclusion speaks the language of restraint, inclusion the language of construction. One is defensive, the other aspirational.

The market implications of these approaches differ. Exclusionary strategies can deliver symbolic and financial impact when broadly adopted: widespread divestment depresses valuations, raises capital costs, and signals reputational risk for targeted industries. Yet inclusion has the potential to reshape economies more actively by directing fresh capital into underfunded sectors. For example, while fossil fuel divestment movements have tarnished oil's long-term prospects, it is the parallel growth in renewable energy investment that has built the infrastructure of a low-carbon economy. *Exclusion punishes; inclusion empowers.* Effective ethical portfolios often combine both, applying exclusion as a guardrail and inclusion as an engine of progress.

There is, however, a conceptual tension at play. Exclusion feels morally pure but financially blunt; inclusion feels innovative but financially complex. Exclusion can be implemented through relatively simple screens, often with low cost. Inclusion demands deeper due diligence, nuanced metrics, and often a tolerance for higher volatility. Investors must wrestle with these trade-offs. A pension fund with fiduciary obligations may lean heavily on exclusion to satisfy ethical mandates without sacrificing returns. A mission-driven foundation may embrace inclusion more aggressively, accepting that financing early-stage social enterprises carries both greater impact and greater risk.

Philosophically, exclusion and inclusion reflect two different ways of thinking about responsibility. Exclusion is about *not doing harm,* an ethic rooted in restraint. Inclusion is about *doing good,* an ethic rooted in active agency. Both are legitimate moral positions, but they appeal to different sensibilities. For some investors, the peace of mind that comes with avoiding complicity is sufficient. For others, only proactive engagement in solutions can satisfy the imperative of conscience. In practice, most serious ethical investors will navigate between the two, acknowledging that *moral clarity often arises from holding both principles in tension.*

Consider how this plays out in modern markets. Fossil fuel exclusion lists have grown rapidly, with universities, cities, and even sovereign wealth funds pulling billions from carbon-intensive industries. At the same time, green bond issuance has surged, financing renewable energy, clean transport, and climate adaptation projects worldwide. The two movements operate in parallel but complementary fashion: one eroding the foundations of unsustainable industries, the other building scaffolding for sustainable ones. Their combined effect is far greater than either could achieve alone.

The question for individual and institutional investors is not whether to choose exclusion or inclusion, but how to balance them in light of objectives, resources, and convictions. Exclusion may offer clarity in avoiding reputational pitfalls; inclusion may offer credibility in demonstrating a proactive stance. Exclusion signals *what you stand against*; inclusion signals *what you stand for*. When aligned thoughtfully, the two create a portfolio that is both shield and beacon: protected from complicity in harm, and oriented towards the creation of value consistent with principle.

In the final analysis, the divide between exclusion and inclusion is less a binary than a spectrum. An ethical portfolio can lean towards one pole or the other, but to ignore either is to leave an ethical gap. The challenge is to resist the temptation of easy purity on the one hand or uncritical optimism on the other. Exclusion without inclusion risks becoming sterile; inclusion without exclusion risks becoming naive. The art of ethical investing lies in recognising that the integrity of a portfolio depends not on choosing one approach but on weaving both into a coherent strategy. Investors who master this balance find themselves not only avoiding harm and seeking virtue but embodying a more sophisticated understanding: that conscience in markets is strongest when it operates with both boundaries and aspirations.

Diversification with Conscience

One of the central paradoxes of ethical investing is that the very principles that sharpen clarity of purpose can also narrow the field of available opportunities. A portfolio guided by exclusionary screens or focused on impact-led sectors risks clustering into a handful of industries or geographies, raising concentration risk precisely at the moment when the investor seeks stability. The challenge is not merely technical but philosophical: how to honour convictions without succumbing to fragility. Diversification, long considered the most reliable defence against uncertainty, must itself be reimagined when applied through the lens of conscience.

Traditional finance treats diversification as almost axiomatic. Spreading investments across asset classes, sectors, and regions reduces exposure to any single failure, thereby stabilising returns. Harry Markowitz's modern portfolio theory, with its notion of the "efficient frontier," made diversification not only intuitive but mathematically compelling. Yet ethical portfolios face constraints that conventional models do not. Screening out fossil fuels, arms, or fast fashion, for instance, narrows the investable universe. Actively favouring renewable energy, social housing, or fair-trade supply chains can tilt a portfolio heavily toward emergent or niche markets. The risk is not only underperformance but volatility—a renewable-heavy portfolio in 2015 looked very different by 2020, and again by 2022. *The disciplined ethical investor must balance the rigour of principle with the humility of probability.*

This tension has created a persistent debate within sustainable finance. Critics argue that ethical portfolios cannot achieve genuine diversification, that their commitment to values inevitably compromises resilience. Supporters counter that the assumption of limitation is outdated: the rapid expansion of green bonds, social ETFs, and ESG-integrated funds provides breadth that rivals conventional universes. Moreover, ethical portfolios may in fact achieve *superior* diversification in the long run by steering away from industries vulnerable to regulatory crackdowns, litigation, and reputational collapse. Fossil fuels, once considered an essential anchor in any diversified portfolio, have increasingly become a liability. Tobacco, once lauded for its defensive qualities, now faces structural decline. Here lies the inversion: ethical exclusion does not merely reduce diversification, it may *enhance* it by pre-empting stranded assets.

Still, diversification with conscience is not achieved through theory alone; it requires design. Investors must move beyond simple sectoral substitution and ask deeper questions. If fossil fuels are excluded, what provides the hedge against energy price shocks? If consumer staples are filtered for labour rights, what ensures exposure to defensive growth? Creative solutions emerge when ethical priorities are matched with structural needs. Renewable infrastructure projects, for example, can play a stabilising role akin to traditional utilities. Green bonds can substitute for sovereign debt in providing steady income. Social housing funds, while more illiquid, can offer counter-cyclical qualities in downturns. *The key is not to abandon the principles of diversification but to reinterpret them through ethical constraints.*

Practical examples highlight this balance. The Norwegian Government Pension Fund Global, one of the largest sovereign wealth funds, excludes entire sectors such as coal and controversial weapons, yet maintains one of the most diversified portfolios in the world. It does so by reinvesting across a wide spectrum of equities, fixed income, and real estate, while constantly recalibrating to avoid overexposure to the green technology boom or the volatility of emerging markets. Similarly, university endowments that adopted fossil fuel divestment often faced fears of reduced diversification. Many discovered, however, that reinvestment in broader indices—minus the offending sectors—delivered comparable or even superior risk-adjusted returns. Diversification with conscience, then, is less a limitation than a discipline of careful substitution and imaginative allocation.

The psychological dimension is equally important. Investors can become so focused on the purity of alignment that they unconsciously accept concentration risk as a badge of integrity. Yet the very purpose of ethical investing is not martyrdom but impact. A concentrated portfolio vulnerable to collapse serves neither the investor's financial needs nor the ethical causes it aims to support. *Conscience without durability risks irrelevance.* By contrast, a well-diversified ethical portfolio demonstrates that values and resilience can coexist—that one can reject exploitative industries while still participating robustly in the dynamics of global markets.

There are, however, trade-offs. Ethical portfolios often rely on emerging sectors where liquidity is thinner and valuations more volatile. Solar power manufacturers or microfinance institutions, while promising, cannot offer the same stability as consumer staples or large-cap pharmaceuticals. To manage this, some investors adopt a "core-satellite" approach: a diversified ethical core built on broad ESG-screened indices, supplemented by satellites of higher-impact but riskier assets. This structure ensures breadth while still honouring depth of conviction. Another method is thematic layering: spreading investments across multiple ethical themes—climate, healthcare, gender equality, financial inclusion—rather than concentrating heavily in one. Each theme carries its own risks, but collectively they approximate the balance of traditional diversification.

The broader philosophical lesson is that ethical investing does not release one from the ordinary laws of finance. Convictions cannot eliminate volatility, nor can screens guarantee safety. What they can do is create a new map of possibilities, one where resilience is measured not just in financial stability but in alignment with a plausible future. If a portfolio is diversified across industries that are likely to grow under stricter environmental regulations, or across companies prepared for social and governance scrutiny, then its resilience extends beyond short-term risk management into long-term viability. Diversification with conscience thus becomes not merely a defensive tactic but a forward-looking strategy: a way of ensuring that capital remains relevant in a world where ethics and economics converge.

Ultimately, diversification with conscience is less about sacrificing choice than about refining it. It requires creativity, discipline, and a willingness to question both conventional wisdom and ethical rigidity. A purely mechanical approach—screening out harm without rebalancing—invites fragility. A purely idealistic approach—loading up on virtuous but volatile assets—invites disappointment. The intelligent investor seeks the middle ground: a portfolio that avoids complicity, advances positive change, and remains resilient across cycles. *Ethical integrity and financial prudence are not mutually exclusive; they are mutually reinforcing when diversification is applied with imagination and care.*

The Liquidity Question

Every financial strategy is ultimately tested in moments of stress. It is easy to hold a position when markets are rising and confidence abounds, but the true measure of an investment is revealed when liquidity is scarce, prices fall rapidly, and the need for flexibility becomes urgent. Ethical investing is no exception. Indeed, it raises a sharper question: do values-based investments hold up under pressure, or do the very constraints that give them purpose also reduce their ability to weather crises? The liquidity question lies at the heart of whether ethical portfolios are practical strategies or aspirational ideals.

Liquidity, at its simplest, refers to the ease with which an asset can be bought or sold without causing a significant shift in its price. Listed equities in large companies tend to be highly liquid; shares can be traded almost instantaneously with minimal price impact. Private equity stakes in social enterprises or loans to community housing projects, by contrast, may take months or years to unwind. Ethical investing often gravitates towards the latter: illiquid instruments that channel capital into projects with tangible social or environmental outcomes but limited secondary markets. *This tension between impact and liquidity defines one of the central trade-offs of conscience-driven capital allocation.*

The global financial crisis of 2008 offers an early lens on this issue. Ethical funds were still a niche sector, yet the crisis revealed the vulnerabilities of illiquid holdings across the financial system. Investors trapped in private real estate vehicles or structured credit found themselves unable to redeem, even as values plummeted. Ethical funds with heavy allocations to community finance or private green infrastructure faced similar challenges. While their underlying projects often retained intrinsic value—the housing built, the wind farms constructed—investors discovered that their ability to exit was constrained just when liquidity was most prized.

More recently, the COVID-19 market shock of March 2020 provided a more nuanced test. Exchange-traded funds (ETFs) with ESG mandates proved remarkably resilient, benefitting from the liquidity of their structure and the broad diversification they offered. Flows into sustainable funds held steady, even as conventional funds experienced withdrawals. By contrast, investors in niche ethical vehicles—such as impact-first private equity funds or community development finance institutions—were reminded that liquidity was not guaranteed. Yet here lies the complexity: while public market ESG funds offered liquidity, they sometimes did so at the cost of depth, their ethical criteria diluted to accommodate tradability. Private funds, though less liquid, remained truer to their mission. *The ethical investor must ask whether liquidity is a virtue if it is achieved at the expense of integrity.*

Liquidity is not merely a technical consideration but a philosophical one. To demand instant access to capital may be at odds with the nature of ethical impact. Social housing cannot be flipped like a stock. Reforestation projects cannot be liquidated overnight. Some of the most meaningful ethical investments require patience and a willingness to tie up capital for years. In this sense, illiquidity is not a flaw but a feature—a reflection of long-term commitment rather than speculative trading. However, *the risk is in over-concentration*: an investor whose portfolio is dominated by illiquid assets may face paralysis during crises, unable to rebalance or meet urgent financial needs.

The response has been innovation. Green bonds, for instance, were partly designed to reconcile impact with liquidity. By structuring climate-related projects through the bond market, issuers offer investors a tradable security that supports long-term environmental goals while still allowing exit through secondary markets. Similarly, social ETFs have provided retail and institutional investors alike with liquid exposure to ethical themes. Yet these instruments carry their own risks: the liquidity of a green bond depends on market demand, which can vanish in times of stress; ETFs, while liquid in form, may suffer from thin underlying markets that reveal fragility under pressure. The liquidity mirage is a danger even for conscience-led vehicles.

Case studies illuminate both sides. During the oil price collapse of 2014–2016, funds heavily weighted toward fossil fuels struggled with both performance and liquidity. By contrast, renewable energy infrastructure funds—though less liquid—retained steady income streams and rebounded more quickly. In 2020, when airline and hospitality equities collapsed, ethical portfolios underweight in these sectors suffered less liquidity strain. Yet, in the same year, investors in microfinance institutions reported delays in withdrawals, as loan repayment schedules could not be accelerated without harming vulnerable borrowers. These examples reveal that *ethical alignment can sometimes enhance liquidity resilience by avoiding fragile sectors, but it can also constrain flexibility when capital is tied to socially embedded obligations.*

The liquidity question thus becomes a test of intentionality. For institutional investors with long horizons—pension funds, endowments, sovereign wealth funds—the illiquidity of certain ethical assets may be acceptable, even desirable, as it matches their time frame and provides stability against short-term speculation. For individual investors or entities with pressing liquidity needs, a different balance must be struck: blending liquid ESG funds with a smaller allocation to illiquid impact projects, ensuring flexibility while preserving principle. *Liquidity management is, in essence, values management: a discipline of aligning the time horizon of conscience with the time horizon of financial obligations.*

Critics argue that ethical investing cannot claim equivalence to conventional strategies until it solves the liquidity dilemma at scale. Proponents respond that conventional investing suffers its own illusions of liquidity—witness the "flash crashes" in equities or the temporary freezes in bond markets during crises. Liquidity, they suggest, is never absolute but contingent on market confidence. In this light, ethical portfolios are not uniquely fragile but merely more transparent about the trade-offs they embody. What matters is whether investors enter them with eyes open, conscious of the compromises they accept.

The future of ethical investing will hinge on how this balance is managed. As impact measurement becomes more sophisticated and secondary markets for ethical assets develop, the liquidity gap may narrow. Tokenisation of assets, digital exchanges for social bonds, and innovative fund structures promise to bridge the divide between patient capital and flexible capital. Yet it would be naïve to imagine a perfect reconciliation. Ethical impact often requires capital to stay put. The investor's task is not to eliminate illiquidity but to design around it—to hold liquid instruments for flexibility, and illiquid ones for impact, with a clear-eyed understanding of what each contributes.

The liquidity question is therefore not a peripheral detail but a central axis of ethical portfolio design. It forces investors to confront uncomfortable but essential questions: How much liquidity do you truly need? What trade-offs are you willing to make between access and impact? And at what point does the pursuit of liquidity undermine the very principles that led you to ethical investing in the first place? The answers will differ by individual, institution, and context. What matters is that they are answered deliberately, not by default. *For in the end, liquidity is not just about markets, but about the clarity with which we balance our conscience against our constraints.*

Practical Allocation Models

The central challenge of ethical investing is not deciding whether values should matter but determining how they can be translated into a coherent portfolio. Principles are essential, yet without practical structures they risk remaining abstract. Asset allocation is where values meet the hard discipline of finance: a set of choices about risk, return, liquidity, and diversification that must be made with both conscience and realism. The task is to design models that allow investors to embody their ethical convictions while still navigating the unforgiving realities of markets. *A well-constructed allocation model is not simply a technical framework but a moral architecture, balancing ideals with pragmatism.*

At the most basic level, asset allocation reflects an investor's risk tolerance and time horizon. Conventional financial theory divides portfolios into categories—conservative, balanced, aggressive—each with different weights in equities, bonds, alternatives, and cash. Ethical investing must adapt these familiar models by substituting, excluding, or re-weighting asset classes based on values. The complexity arises because ethical constraints do not always align with diversification benefits. Excluding fossil fuels, for instance, removes a historically significant sector of global equity markets, while prioritising community finance channels capital into illiquid instruments. Each adjustment reshapes both the ethical profile and the financial dynamics of the portfolio.

Consider a conservative ethical portfolio. A traditional conservative allocation might place 60 per cent in bonds, 30 per cent in equities, and 10 per cent in cash. Its ethical counterpart could employ green bonds and social bonds to replace conventional fixed income, thereby aligning stability with impact. Equities would focus on companies with high ESG ratings or funds explicitly excluding harmful industries. Cash could be placed with ethical banks or credit unions rather than conventional institutions. This model prioritises capital preservation and predictable income while ensuring that every allocation has a conscience filter. The challenge lies in the relative scarcity of long-duration, high-quality ethical bonds, which may require investors to accept slightly lower yields or explore innovative debt structures such as sustainability-linked bonds.

A balanced ethical portfolio might distribute capital across 50 per cent equities, 40 per cent bonds, and 10 per cent alternatives. Here the equity portion could include a blend of ESG-screened global equities and thematic funds focusing on renewable energy, healthcare innovation, or gender diversity. Bonds would again lean toward green and social issuance, with some exposure to sovereign green bonds for diversification. Alternatives could incorporate renewable infrastructure projects, private equity in social enterprises, or real estate aligned with sustainable urban development. *The balanced model illustrates how ethical investors can combine liquidity with targeted impact, accepting moderate risk while ensuring that diversification does not dilute values beyond recognition.*

Aggressive ethical portfolios demand a different orientation. With 70 to 80 per cent in equities, such allocations must grapple with the limitations of ESG indices, which often mirror broad markets but exclude only the worst offenders. The aggressive ethical investor may therefore need to embrace active management or thematic concentration: allocating heavily to renewable technologies, sustainable agriculture, or circular economy innovation. Private equity becomes more significant, as does venture capital in mission-driven start-ups. Alternatives may include impact-first funds in areas such as microfinance or affordable housing. The risk profile here is undeniable—returns depend heavily on sectors exposed to policy shifts and technological disruption—but so too is the potential for transformative impact. *Aggressive ethical allocation reveals the tension between financial ambition and ethical clarity: the higher the stakes, the more deeply values influence outcomes.*

Within each of these archetypes lies the question of value systems. A climate-first investor might weight green bonds and renewable equities more heavily, even at the expense of sectoral diversification. An investor focused on social justice could tilt towards microfinance, community development funds, or companies with strong labour practices. Faith-based investors might exclude industries such as alcohol, gambling, or defence, regardless of their financial contribution. *The same risk profile can yield vastly different portfolios once ethical hierarchies are applied.* The essential discipline is recognising that values dictate constraints and opportunities, and then building the allocation model to reflect them with coherence rather than contradiction.

Case studies demonstrate how this can function in practice. A European pension fund committed to net-zero allocations by 2050 has restructured its portfolio gradually, increasing its weighting to renewable infrastructure while divesting from coal, oil, and gas. The allocation still resembles a traditional institutional mix—equities, bonds, alternatives—but the exclusions and inclusions are guided by a carbon reduction pathway. In contrast, a North American university endowment prioritising social equity has allocated a significant portion to local community investment funds, accepting reduced liquidity but strengthening its mission alignment. The financial structures differ, but both demonstrate that ethical allocation can be integrated systematically rather than treated as an overlay.

The liquidity question inevitably intersects with allocation. A portfolio overly tilted to illiquid impact assets risks impairing flexibility. Models must therefore ensure that enough capital remains in liquid instruments—ESG equities, green bond ETFs, sustainable index funds—to allow rebalancing, redemptions, and tactical adjustments. Practical models often adopt a "core-satellite" structure: a core of liquid, values-aligned public securities complemented by satellite allocations to illiquid, high-impact projects. This approach permits both responsiveness and depth, reducing the danger of paralysis while preserving the integrity of the ethical mission.

One of the most contentious debates is whether ethical portfolios should aim to mirror the performance of conventional benchmarks or consciously diverge. Some models prioritise tracking error minimisation, adjusting allocations only enough to meet basic exclusions. Others embrace active divergence, seeking to overweight virtuous industries and underweight harmful ones. Both approaches have merit. Minimisation models appeal to cautious investors who fear underperformance; divergence models suit those who believe ethics will outperform over time. The key is transparency: investors must know whether their allocation is designed to shadow conventional markets or deliberately depart from them.

Another dimension is geographical allocation. Global diversification is a cornerstone of conventional portfolios, yet ethical screens can alter this dramatically. Emerging markets, for example, often present ethical dilemmas: exposure to coal, governance weaknesses, or labour concerns. Yet they also offer some of the most compelling opportunities for social and environmental impact. A practical model might therefore maintain emerging market exposure but route it through carefully selected vehicles—sustainable sovereign bonds or funds focusing on companies with demonstrable ESG progress. *Exclusion without nuance risks missing opportunities where capital can achieve both returns and transformation.*

Risk management within ethical portfolios must also evolve. Concentration risk can arise when investors overweight "safe" ethical sectors such as technology or healthcare, inadvertently reducing diversification. Practical models must guard against such clustering by ensuring exposure to multiple industries, even within ethical parameters. Stress testing against ethical shocks—such as regulatory changes in carbon pricing or supply chain scandals in ostensibly virtuous companies—adds another layer of prudence. Allocation models are not static templates but living systems that must adapt to both markets and values as they evolve.

The ultimate measure of a practical allocation model is not whether it conforms to a theoretical blueprint but whether it enables an investor to live consistently with their principles while meeting their financial needs. Portfolios are not abstract exercises; they embody choices about what matters and how much compromise is acceptable. A conservative ethical investor may sleep well knowing their wealth is financing green bonds rather than arms manufacturers, even if their yield is lower. An aggressive ethical investor may take pride in backing renewable start-ups, accepting volatility in exchange for the possibility of systemic change. Both models are valid because both are deliberate.

Ethical asset allocation is not about creating the perfect formula but about building a framework that integrates conscience, risk, and return in proportions suited to the individual or institution. Models must be practical, but they must also be principled. They require clarity of intention, transparency of trade-offs, and resilience under stress. In the end, *the most effective allocation models are those that serve not just the investor's portfolio, but their integrity.*

Chapter 11
The Investor's Dilemmas

Ethical investing is often described as a way of aligning money with values, but the simplicity of that phrase belies the complexity beneath it. To treat capital as an expression of conscience is to accept that it will constantly collide with competing priorities. The investor who attempts to make every pound or dollar serve a higher purpose is not simply choosing between funds, indices, or instruments; they are navigating a series of profound moral trade-offs that expose the limits of both markets and ideals. These dilemmas are not abstract—they surface at the very moments of decision when one investment opportunity must be embraced and another must be set aside. They are the crossroads where principles and pragmatism are forced into negotiation.

Perhaps the most uncomfortable of these crossroads is the tension between profit and purity. An investor may encounter a company whose operations align perfectly with their ethical convictions—say, a renewable energy provider serving marginalised communities—but whose financial performance is volatile, with modest returns compared to the index. Another option may be a company making incremental sustainability improvements yet offering robust, predictable profits. Which is preferable: absolute adherence to principle even if it jeopardises financial goals, or a compromise that sustains wealth while supporting partial progress? This tension goes to the heart of what it means to be a conscientious investor. *A decision framed as financial is often, at its core, a question of moral patience: should one prioritise short-term returns or the long-term fulfilment of values?*

The scale of investment presents another dilemma, equally demanding. A local credit union might transform lives in its community, offering fair lending and keeping capital circulating close to home. Yet the total reach of such investments is limited; the same capital placed in a global renewable energy fund might drive systemic decarbonisation on a scale no local project could match. Investors must ask themselves whether impact is measured in depth or breadth—whether a smaller, more intimate intervention is preferable to contributing to a vast, impersonal movement of capital. Neither choice is inherently superior, but the act of choosing defines the kind of ethical footprint the investor wishes to leave. *Local intimacy and global reach are not merely different scales of impact; they embody different philosophies of responsibility.*

Even when deciding on scale, another ambiguity complicates matters: the imperfection of companies. Few businesses are paragons of virtue. The majority fall somewhere along a continuum of progress, where improvements are genuine yet incomplete. For instance, a consumer goods company may have committed to eliminating deforestation from its supply chains but still source palm oil from regions where enforcement is weak. Should investors support such a company, believing that capital encouragement will accelerate reform? Or should they withdraw until promises are met, denying support to entities that remain entangled in harm? This is not a matter of neat classifications but of moral calibration. *To invest in imperfection is to accept that change is iterative; to withhold support is to insist that virtue must precede capital, not follow it.* Both positions carry weight, and both demand courage.

A final dilemma—the exit question—tests an investor's resolve when faced with companies that resist reform. Divestment is a powerful moral signal, depriving firms of legitimacy and, in some cases, capital. Yet walking away also means surrendering influence. Remaining invested, by contrast, allows shareholders to vote, lobby, and pressure management from within, as activist investors have done with oil majors and technology giants. The decision is rarely straightforward: exit too soon and one forfeits the chance to influence change; stay too long and one risks complicity in practices that values cannot condone. The exit question, then, is not about whether to leave but about when—and that "when" demands both strategic timing and ethical clarity.

What unites these dilemmas is the fact that they resist formulaic resolution. They are not solved by applying a single screen, following a checklist, or trusting a rating agency. They require investors to exercise judgement, to weigh competing goods against one another, and to accept that any path taken leaves another untrodden. In this sense, ethical investing is not merely about aligning portfolios with pre-set values but about developing the capacity to think critically, act consistently, and live with imperfection. *The dilemmas of the conscientious investor are not flaws in the system but features of what it means to invest in a world where values are contested and capital is never neutral.*

This chapter examines these tensions in detail—not to offer easy answers but to provide frameworks for grappling with them. Readers will encounter the sharp trade-offs of profit versus purity, the philosophical divide between local and global impact, the ambiguity of imperfect companies, and the strategic challenge of knowing when to exit. Each dilemma is explored not as an obstacle but as an opportunity: an invitation to engage more deeply with the responsibilities that accompany wealth. For in the end, the dilemmas of ethical investing are not problems to be eliminated but disciplines to be practised—tests of integrity that ensure conscience remains not just an aspiration but a lived reality in the markets where money speaks.

Profit vs. Purity

Few decisions reveal the true character of an investor more clearly than those that pit immediate profit against moral conviction. In theory, the conscientious investor wishes to achieve both: strong returns and alignment with values. In practice, the most ethical option often proves to be the least profitable—at least in the short term. Choosing between them forces a reckoning with priorities. It tests whether ethics are a marketing accessory, to be worn when convenient, or a genuine compass capable of guiding choices even when they carry a financial cost. *The conflict between profit and purity is not a flaw of ethical investing; it is its crucible, the place where principles prove their durability.*

Consider the early years of renewable energy investment. In the late 1990s and early 2000s, solar and wind companies were often unprofitable, propped up by subsidies and plagued with volatility. Many investors dismissed them as niche, risky bets compared to the steady dividends of fossil fuel majors. Yet those who persisted, motivated not only by anticipated returns but by a belief in decarbonisation, eventually saw vindication. Today, clean energy is one of the fastest-growing sectors globally, and oil and gas firms face structural decline. The pattern is clear: *short-term financial sacrifice can be the price of long-term alignment with reality.* Ethics, in this light, are not a constraint but an early warning system, pointing investors toward industries whose long-term prospects are stronger precisely because they accord with social and environmental imperatives.

Still, the moral arc is not always so predictable. Not every virtuous investment matures into profitability within a timeframe tolerable to investors. Social housing projects, for instance, generate stable but modest yields, far below the double-digit expectations of private equity. Microfinance in emerging markets has often been lauded for expanding access to credit, yet it can expose investors to currency risks and political instability. These examples remind us that not all ethical investments will outperform simply because they are ethical. Believing otherwise is to replace sober analysis with wishful thinking. *The serious investor must distinguish between principled patience and naive optimism.*

What complicates matters further is the human tendency to rationalise compromises. Faced with a choice between the virtuous but unprofitable option and the lucrative but ethically compromised one, investors often persuade themselves that their money can do more good if it grows quickly, even if it means tolerating questionable practices in the interim. The logic is seductive: profits today can be reinvested into worthier projects tomorrow. But this postponement of virtue risks becoming permanent. When financial performance becomes the overriding metric, ethics are quietly relegated to a secondary role. This is why many ethical funds explicitly set out non-negotiable exclusions—

to prevent investors from drifting into moral incoherence under the pressure of returns.

The question then arises: should an investor accept lower returns for the sake of purity? One school of thought insists yes, arguing that capital is a moral force and to compromise on principles is to dilute one's integrity. Another perspective warns against idealism, noting that without returns, funds lose relevance, scale, and ultimately the ability to exert influence. Both views have merit. The disciplined investor recognises that the right answer is contextual, shaped by risk appetite, time horizon, and the ethical weight of the issue at stake. For example, refusing to invest in tobacco even when it remains profitable may reflect a categorical moral judgement: some harms are intolerable regardless of returns. But when evaluating imperfect companies making incremental progress on climate or labour issues, the calculus may be different: engagement, rather than exclusion, could yield both financial and ethical gains over time.

An instructive case lies in the divestment campaigns against fossil fuels. Universities, pension funds, and foundations faced criticism for holding oil and gas stocks long after evidence of climate harm was undeniable. Defenders argued that these stocks were still profitable and provided diversification benefits. Critics countered that clinging to them compromised institutional values and lent legitimacy to an industry driving existential risks. Many institutions eventually chose purity, divesting despite fears of underperformance. Yet studies later revealed that divested portfolios did not necessarily lag behind; in some cases, they outperformed due to the declining fortunes of fossil fuels. The lesson is not that purity always pays, but that financial orthodoxy often underestimates the hidden risks of unethical industries. *Ethical clarity can reveal risks that traditional metrics obscure.*

The debate extends to individual investors. A pension saver choosing between a mainstream fund and a stricter ethical alternative confronts the same dilemma, but in a more personal form. Accepting slightly lower projected returns may mean retiring with less wealth, but it may also mean peace of mind, knowing their savings have not financed practices they oppose. Here, the value of purity cannot be captured on a balance sheet. It speaks to identity, to coherence between one's financial life and one's moral commitments. For some, this coherence is worth more than an incremental percentage point of return. For others, the sacrifice is too high. Neither position is inherently right or wrong, but both demand honesty. *The real danger lies in evasion—pretending that no trade-off exists, when in truth it does.*

Profit versus purity is, in essence, a question about time and conviction. Are investors willing to endure short-term underperformance for the possibility of long-term vindication, both financial and moral? Or do they demand immediate returns, even at the cost of undermining the very values they profess? The disciplined path does not promise comfort. It demands patience, courage, and sometimes loss. Yet it also offers integrity, a quality as rare in finance as it is necessary. When the most ethical option proves the least profitable, the investor's choice is not only about money but about meaning. And in that choice, wealth becomes more than capital: it becomes a mirror of conscience.

Local Impact vs. Global Scale

Every investor committed to ethics confronts a deceptively simple question: should capital flow into local initiatives where the effects are visible and immediate, or into global funds capable of addressing challenges on a systemic level? The tension between proximity and scale is not merely a technical matter of portfolio allocation; it is a philosophical dilemma about the nature of responsibility and the reach of finance. *To prioritise the local is to embrace intimacy, community, and trust; to prioritise the global is to embrace leverage, breadth, and efficiency. Both paths hold promise, but each carries limitations that become sharper the closer one looks.*

Take the example of a community-owned solar cooperative in a small British town. Investors who contribute can see panels installed on local schools and businesses, meet the people whose energy bills are reduced, and measure the environmental benefits in their own postcode. The impact is direct and emotionally resonant. Yet the scale of such projects is modest: a few hundred households benefit, carbon savings are incremental, and financial returns tend to be modest. Contrast this with a large renewable energy exchange-traded fund (ETF) that pools billions to back solar farms across multiple continents. Here the impact is vast in aggregate—gigawatts of clean power added to the grid, entire industries nudged toward transformation—but diffuse. No single investor can easily connect their capital to a tangible story. *Local investing delivers clarity of cause-and-effect; global investing delivers magnitude.*

The trade-off is further complicated by risk and resilience. Local investments, such as credit unions or community development financial institutions, often prove less correlated with global market swings. Their returns may be modest, but they can provide a cushion during crises, as they are rooted in the real economy rather than abstract market sentiment. Yet they can also be fragile, dependent on local politics, volunteer governance, or limited customer bases. Global funds, by contrast, diversify risk across regions and sectors, offering liquidity and scalability. But in times of financial panic, they are subject to the same rapid sell-offs that destabilise broader markets. The choice is not only ethical but strategic: *does one seek stability in the tangible or efficiency in the vast?*

Historical examples illuminate the stakes. The rise of microfinance in the 1990s promised to empower local communities in developing countries. By offering small loans to entrepreneurs excluded from traditional banking, it aimed to tackle poverty at its roots. For early investors, the appeal was clear: measurable social good combined with financial return. Yet microfinance struggled to expand beyond a certain scale, and in some regions, over-indebtedness and exploitation tarnished its reputation. Meanwhile, large global development funds, backed by multilateral institutions, have channelled capital into infrastructure, healthcare, and education at enormous scale—but often at the cost of responsiveness to local context. The lesson is sobering: local impact may lack scale, while global scale may lack sensitivity.

There is also a psychological dimension. Investors drawn to ethical finance often seek a sense of agency, a feeling that their money is not vanishing into an anonymous pool but making a discernible difference. Local investments satisfy this desire, offering stories that can be told at the dinner table or boardroom. Global funds, while powerful in aggregate, rarely provide that intimacy. This gap matters because ethical investing is not only about outcomes but about sustaining the will to act. *Without a sense of connection, ethical conviction can wither into abstraction.*

Yet the dichotomy is not absolute. Hybrid models are emerging that attempt to marry local responsiveness with global resources. For instance, place-based impact funds pool capital from global institutions but direct it into carefully chosen local initiatives, blending professional management with community engagement. Similarly, some global funds now dedicate sleeves of capital to support grassroots enterprises within their broader portfolio. These innovations suggest that the choice need not always be binary, but they also highlight the complexity of aligning investor expectations with diverse outcomes.

One cannot ignore the ethical asymmetry embedded in this debate. Local investments tend to privilege those geographically close to the investor, often reflecting a subtle bias toward familiar communities. Global funds, by contrast, distribute resources across borders, reaching those who may never otherwise encounter the benefits of international capital. The tension echoes an old moral question: do we owe more to those near us, whom we can see and touch, or to those far away, whose needs may be greater but whose faces remain unseen? Philosophers from Adam Smith to Peter Singer have wrestled with this dilemma. Ethical investors must do the same, recognising that their portfolios inevitably express a hierarchy of concern.

Practicality also shapes the decision. An investor with limited resources may find that directing capital locally delivers a sense of efficacy and accountability otherwise unavailable. For large institutions—pension funds, endowments, sovereign wealth funds—the scale of assets under management often necessitates global vehicles, as local projects cannot absorb such vast sums efficiently. In this sense, the size of one's capital constrains the form of one's ethics. *The moral purity of localism may be most viable for individuals and small funds, while systemic change often requires the brute force of global scale.*

Ultimately, the question is not which approach is objectively superior, but which best aligns with an investor's purpose and constraints. Those who value tangible narratives and community cohesion may prioritise local projects, accepting their modest scale. Those who prize systemic transformation may gravitate toward global funds, tolerating their impersonality. The wisest recognise that portfolios can combine both, balancing the intimacy of localism with the reach of globalism. Such integration reflects a broader truth: ethical investing is not about absolutes, but about navigating tensions with clarity.

The debate between local impact and global scale is a reminder that finance is never value-neutral. Every allocation decision privileges certain communities, geographies, and time horizons over others. To weigh local versus global is to grapple with the geometry of responsibility, deciding whether conscience is best expressed through the visible neighbour or the unseen stranger. The conscientious investor must accept that no choice is perfect, but each choice is revealing. It discloses not only what they believe about money, but what they believe about justice, belonging, and the reach of their responsibility in a connected world.

Imperfect Companies

Few investors would dispute that no company is flawless. Even the most celebrated champions of sustainability and social responsibility carry blemishes—be it in their supply chains, labour practices, tax arrangements, or political lobbying. Yet the ethical investor is confronted with a practical dilemma: should capital be withheld until perfection is achieved, or is partial progress worthy of support? *To demand purity risks paralysis; to tolerate imperfection risks complicity.* The answer lies not in absolutes, but in a careful weighing of trajectories, commitments, and credibility.

The tension is well illustrated by the technology sector. Take Apple, a company lauded for its advances in renewable energy and supply-chain transparency. It has invested billions in clean energy projects, pledged to become carbon neutral across its entire value chain by 2030, and pushed suppliers to follow suit. Yet critics point to labour rights abuses in its Asian supply chain and environmental costs associated with device disposal and resource extraction. The investor faces a dilemma: is Apple's forward momentum toward sustainability sufficient to justify support, or do its unresolved issues undermine its credibility? Here, the investor must decide whether *direction of travel* matters more than the unfinished distance.

The fossil fuel industry presents an even sharper example. Consider BP, which has branded itself as moving "Beyond Petroleum" for more than two decades, investing heavily in renewables while continuing to extract and profit from oil and gas. Activists argue that such companies use token green investments to mask ongoing environmental damage.

Yet others counter that if major energy firms, with their capital reserves and technical expertise, are excluded from investment, the transition to clean energy may slow rather than accelerate. *The question is not simply whether a company is ethically imperfect, but whether its imperfections are being offset by credible, measurable steps toward improvement.*

This logic is reflected in the emergence of ESG integration strategies that differentiate between leaders and laggards within sectors. For instance, rather than excluding the entire automotive industry due to its historic reliance on internal combustion engines, investors may favour companies such as Tesla or even Volkswagen, which, despite past scandals, has committed hundreds of billions of euros to electrification. The imperfect company in this case becomes a vehicle for transformation. The investor is not condoning past or present shortcomings, but is betting on a trajectory that aligns with broader societal goals. *Perfection, in this frame, is less important than momentum.*

The challenge, however, lies in distinguishing genuine evolution from opportunistic marketing. Greenwashing remains pervasive, with corporations adopting the language of responsibility while avoiding meaningful structural change. Investors must scrutinise not only what companies say but how they allocate capital, structure incentives, and disclose progress. A firm that announces lofty net-zero goals but continues to lobby against climate regulation or rewards executives for fossil fuel expansion cannot reasonably be deemed on a credible path. The ethical investor's task is therefore not merely to tolerate imperfection, but to discern *which imperfections are symptoms of transition and which are signs of evasion.*

Philosophically, the dilemma echoes debates in moral theory. Utilitarian thinkers argue that supporting imperfect companies can maximise overall good if it accelerates systemic change. Deontological perspectives caution against endorsing harmful practices, even if progress is underway, because complicity erodes principle. The investor thus operates in a space of moral pluralism, where neither extreme offers a fully satisfactory answer. The practical question becomes: how much imperfection is acceptable, and under what conditions does tolerance become complicity?

Case studies from recent years show the consequences of misjudgement. Volkswagen's diesel emissions scandal revealed how investors, regulators, and customers can be blindsided by corporate dishonesty. Despite its subsequent investments in electric vehicles, many investors remain wary, viewing the company's past deceit as evidence of cultural rot. In contrast, Unilever, though not without flaws, has managed to position itself as a credible leader in sustainable business, in part because it integrates ethical considerations into core strategy rather than treating them as public relations exercises. The market has often rewarded Unilever with resilience and trust, suggesting that *imperfect companies can retain investor support when their commitments appear integrated, consistent, and authentic.*

There is also a practical point about market influence. If ethical investors universally excluded imperfect companies, capital would simply flow from less discriminating investors, often with fewer concerns about externalities. This raises a strategic question: does divestment starve a company of influence, or does it surrender influence to others who may push it in the opposite direction? Many activist investors argue that engagement—using ownership stakes to press for change—is often more effective than exclusion. The imperfect company becomes not a liability, but a stage for active dialogue. The case of Engine No. 1's campaign at ExxonMobil exemplifies this. By taking a small but strategic stake, the activist fund was able to secure board seats and force the oil giant to take climate risk more seriously. Here, imperfection became the arena for transformation.

None of this is to suggest that tolerance should be limitless. There are companies whose practices are so egregious—be it in human rights abuses, environmental destruction, or corruption—that any support amounts to endorsement. For such firms, exclusion remains not only justifiable but necessary. The task for the ethical investor is to differentiate between companies that are unwilling to change and those that are imperfect but reforming. *The former represent entrenched harm; the latter represent potential progress.*

Investors must also guard against their own biases. It is tempting to excuse imperfections in companies that deliver strong financial returns or are culturally admired, while punishing others more harshly. Such inconsistency risks undermining credibility and turning ethical investing into selective rationalisation. The discipline of ethical investing demands transparency, consistency, and a willingness to acknowledge the messy reality of compromise.

Ultimately, the question of imperfect companies reveals that ethical investing is not about drawing hard lines but about cultivating judgement. It requires a willingness to tolerate ambiguity, to engage with complexity, and to recognise that progress is often incremental. The conscientious investor must learn to differentiate between companies that are stumbling forward and those that are deliberately standing still. Support for imperfection, when carefully judged, can be a lever for systemic change. But support without scrutiny becomes complicity.

The decision to back imperfect companies therefore reflects not only financial strategy but ethical philosophy. It forces investors to articulate their thresholds, to defend their rationale, and to accept that their capital has consequences beyond balance sheets. *In tolerating imperfection, investors reveal what kind of progress they believe in: progress that is messy, halting, and human, but potentially transformative if guided with rigour and resolve.*

The Exit Question

Few decisions in ethical investing generate as much debate as the choice between staying invested to influence change or withdrawing capital in protest. *The exit question* is not simply financial but profoundly strategic and moral: is an investor's leverage greater as an owner demanding reform, or as a dissenter whose withdrawal signals rejection? At stake is the practical balance between influence and integrity, between the hope of transformation and the statement of refusal.

Staying invested rests on the premise that ownership confers a voice. Shareholders can file resolutions, vote on board appointments, question executives, and exert pressure in ways that outsiders cannot. This argument is not abstract. Consider the campaign led by the activist hedge fund Engine No. 1 against ExxonMobil in 2021. With just a 0.02% stake, the fund successfully rallied large institutional investors to install three new board members with climate expertise, forcing the oil giant to reckon with its carbon strategy. Had Engine No. 1 divested instead, its protest would have been silent; by remaining invested, it turned capital into leverage. *Engagement, when well-organised, can convert even a minority stake into outsized influence.*

Divestment, by contrast, functions as a form of economic sanction. When enough investors withdraw, the cost of capital rises, the share price weakens, and management faces pressure to reform or lose market relevance. The fossil fuel divestment movement exemplifies this approach. University endowments, pension funds, and sovereign wealth funds have withdrawn trillions of dollars from coal, oil, and gas. While divestment alone has not bankrupted the sector, it has reshaped public discourse, stigmatised investment in fossil fuels, and influenced the long-term strategic calculations of energy companies. *Divestment, therefore, acts less as a scalpel than as a megaphone: it sends a signal to markets and society, even if it offers little direct influence on corporate governance.*

The choice between engagement and divestment is not binary but contextual. A company's openness to dialogue matters. If management is responsive, transparent, and willing to adapt, engagement can be effective. If leadership resists, obfuscates, or doubles down on harmful practices, remaining invested may legitimise behaviour rather than challenge it. The South African apartheid divestment campaigns of the 1980s illustrate this point. Shareholder engagement initially failed to persuade companies operating in South Africa to change. It was the wave of divestments—combined with political activism—that eventually forced a rethink. Here, exit carried more weight than voice.

For many investors, the exit question is also about *thresholds of tolerance*. No company is perfect, but investors must decide what constitutes unacceptable harm. Child labour, systemic corruption, or severe environmental destruction may represent red lines beyond which engagement loses legitimacy. By contrast, less entrenched issues—such as supply-chain transparency or gender diversity on boards—may be fertile ground for ongoing pressure and gradual improvement. *Engagement requires hope that a company can change; divestment declares that it will not.*

The scale of investment further shapes the calculus. Large institutional investors, such as BlackRock or Norges Bank, hold stakes across the economy. For them, divestment from entire sectors may be impractical, undermining diversification. They are therefore more inclined to pursue stewardship through engagement. Smaller, values-driven funds or individual investors, however, may prefer divestment as a clearer statement of principle, particularly when their withdrawal contributes to broader reputational pressure. The asymmetry of influence means that what is viable for one type of investor may be ineffective for another.

Timing complicates the dilemma. Divesting early can position an investor as a moral leader, even at the cost of short-term returns, while delaying may allow for greater leverage during a company's transition. Yet there is also the danger of *holding on too long*—mistaking token gestures for genuine reform and thereby enabling delay. Investors must ask not only "Can this company change?" but also "Is it changing fast enough given the urgency of the issue?" Climate change, human rights abuses, and data privacy risks are not problems that tolerate indefinite patience.

Philosophically, the debate echoes a larger tension between consequentialist and deontological reasoning. Consequentialists argue that staying invested maximises the chance of better outcomes, even if it means temporary complicity. Deontologists argue that withdrawal is necessary when principle is at stake, regardless of practical outcomes, because participation itself is a moral compromise. Neither framework alone suffices. Ethical investors must combine pragmatism with principle, calibrating their strategy to context rather than ideology.

Examples abound where the choice was consequential. When Nike faced scrutiny over sweatshop labour in the 1990s, many investors stayed engaged, pushing for transparency and standards. Nike's subsequent reforms—though imperfect—helped reshape global supply-chain accountability. Conversely, in the case of tobacco, widespread divestment campaigns effectively stigmatised the industry, making it increasingly unpalatable for mainstream portfolios and limiting its political influence. Both outcomes were significant, but they were achieved through opposite strategies. *The lesson is that engagement and divestment are not competing dogmas but complementary tools.*

Ultimately, the exit question forces investors to confront their own priorities. Is the aim to purify one's portfolio, signalling moral clarity even if little change occurs at the company? Or is the aim to drive transformation from within, even at the cost of reputational association with flawed firms? Neither choice is inherently superior; each carries risks of hypocrisy, ineffectiveness, or moral compromise. What matters is that the choice is conscious, reasoned, and transparent.

Investors should resist simplistic answers. Divestment without engagement risks forfeiting influence. Engagement without the credible threat of divestment risks toothlessness. The most effective strategy may combine both: engage as long as progress is genuine and measurable, but exit decisively when dialogue becomes a fig leaf for inaction. In this way, investors can balance principle and pragmatism, using both voice and exit to shape markets in line with values. *The true power of ethical investing lies not in avoiding dilemmas but in meeting them with clarity, courage, and consistency.*

Chapter 12
The Future of Ethical Capital

The question of what finance is for is no longer confined to ethics seminars or activist circles; it is being asked in boardrooms, trading floors, and sovereign wealth funds. Capital, once justified solely by its ability to generate return, is being reframed as a force that must account for the world it shapes. The future of ethical capital is not a niche or a trend but a defining challenge to the very structure of markets. What lies ahead is not simply a debate about whether investors should consider conscience, but how deeply conscience will be embedded in the machinery of capital allocation, risk pricing, and wealth creation.

The most pressing crucible for this shift is climate. No issue better illustrates the collision between long-term survival and short-term profit, nor the inadequacy of financial models that externalise systemic costs. Climate change is not just a line item under environmental, social, and governance frameworks; it is *the* stress test for values-based investing. Rising sea levels, stranded assets, disrupted supply chains, and unprecedented insurance risks are forcing capital markets to reckon with physical and transition risks on a scale that dwarfs most other ethical dilemmas. Already, we see entire sectors revalued not on quarterly earnings but on their ability—or refusal—to adapt to a decarbonising economy. Investors are learning that ignoring climate is not neutral; it is an active bet against resilience, and one increasingly mispriced. If ethical capital is to prove its worth, climate will be the proving ground.

Yet climate is only one axis of transformation. Technology is redrawing the boundaries of what can be known, measured, and verified. Artificial intelligence is turning ESG disclosures into analyzable data at a speed unimaginable a decade ago, surfacing inconsistencies between rhetoric and action. Blockchain promises immutable records of supply-chain practices, from conflict minerals to carbon offsets, offering investors unprecedented transparency in tracing corporate claims. Big data, once the preserve of marketing departments, is being harnessed to assess social and environmental performance in real time, shifting ESG from retrospective reporting to predictive analytics. The promise of this technological revolution is radical: *trust is no longer assumed; it is verifiable.* But with transparency comes complexity, and the risk of drowning in signals without clarity. The challenge for ethical capital will be to harness technology not as a gimmick but as a guardrail against greenwashing and as a compass for credibility.

Another powerful current reshaping the landscape is cultural. Wealth is transferring from one generation to the next, and with it, values. Younger investors—millennials and Gen Z in particular—are not treating ethical finance as optional but as a baseline expectation. Surveys consistently reveal that these cohorts prefer investments aligned with climate action, diversity, human rights, and social impact, even at the expense of marginal returns. The scale of this generational wealth shift—trillions of dollars over the next two decades—means that markets will be reshaped not by regulation alone but by demand. Asset managers are already adapting, racing to design products that speak to this values-driven capital. What distinguishes this shift is not mere consumer preference but the embedding of moral accountability into the grammar of finance itself. *For the next generation, ethical investing is not an alternative strategy; it is the default lens.*

Out of these forces emerges what might be called the conscience economy. This is not about philanthropic carve-outs or optional ESG labels but about the embedding of ethical accountability into the infrastructure of capital markets. Credit ratings may increasingly incorporate sustainability scores. Stock exchanges could require verified ESG disclosures as a condition of listing. Fiduciary duty, long defined narrowly as maximising shareholder return, is being expanded to encompass stewardship of environmental and social systems. In such an economy, the line between financial prudence and ethical responsibility begins to blur: companies that mistreat workers or degrade ecosystems are not only morally compromised but financially hazardous. The conscience economy is thus not a moral overlay on capital—it is capital redefined by moral accountability.

The significance of this future is not that investors will be forced to choose between ethics and returns but that the very definition of returns will evolve. A portfolio that ignores climate resilience, governance integrity, or social legitimacy may deliver profits in the short term but is increasingly vulnerable to long-term collapse. Conversely, portfolios aligned with ethical principles are not acts of charity; they are acts of foresight. As climate shocks, technological scrutiny, cultural shifts, and systemic accountability converge, ethical capital will move from the margins to the mainstream, from the optional to the essential.

This chapter does not offer predictions in the style of futurism but a framework for understanding how these forces interact. Climate will set the stakes, technology will shape the tools, culture will drive demand, and markets themselves will absorb conscience into their structure. The future of ethical capital is not simply about where money flows but about how the architecture of finance itself is redesigned to account for the world it inhabits and influences. For investors, policymakers, and citizens alike, the question is no longer whether capital can afford to be ethical, but whether capital can afford not to be.

Climate as the Defining Test

For decades, financial markets treated the atmosphere as a limitless dumping ground, a place where emissions could be externalised without consequence. That illusion has collapsed. Today, climate change is not a distant ethical cause but the single most material risk facing capital markets in the coming decade. Wildfires that obliterate supply chains, floods that devastate infrastructure, droughts that cripple agriculture, and policies that render entire fossil-fuel reserves unburnable have demonstrated that climate risk is not confined to environmentalists' manifestos—it is balance-sheet reality. *If ethical investing is to prove its credibility, climate will be the defining test of whether values-based capital can both protect returns and reshape the world it finances.*

The uniqueness of climate risk lies in its scope. Traditional financial risks—whether credit defaults, currency swings, or geopolitical shocks—are localised and cyclical. Climate risk is systemic and compounding. It operates on multiple time horizons simultaneously: immediate physical damage from extreme weather, medium-term transition risks from regulatory shifts, and long-term existential threats to economic stability itself. No industry is exempt. From banking to real estate, insurance to consumer goods, the very assumptions underpinning valuation models—discount rates, growth projections, asset lifespans—are destabilised when climate volatility is factored in. The cost of inaction, once externalised, now surfaces in stranded assets, escalating premiums, litigation, and collapsing consumer trust.

Investors are already seeing how climate risk translates into financial loss. Consider the case of Pacific Gas and Electric (PG&E), once a stable utility in California, which filed for bankruptcy in 2019 after wildfires linked to its equipment led to liabilities exceeding $30 billion. The company's collapse was not simply a failure of corporate governance but a stark demonstration of how climate-exacerbated events can annihilate shareholder value. In another sphere, the fossil-fuel divestment movement, initially dismissed as symbolic, has accelerated the devaluation of coal producers, whose market capitalisation has plummeted as capital flees stranded carbon assets. These are not moral punishments imposed by activists but financial recalibrations forced by reality: *business models that ignore climate are becoming uninvestable.*

And yet, climate is not only a threat but also the largest investment opportunity of our era. The transition to a low-carbon economy is spawning entire industries—renewable energy, battery storage, sustainable agriculture, green hydrogen, carbon capture—that demand trillions in capital. Those who dismiss ethical investing as sacrificing returns miss the larger picture: the companies positioned to solve climate challenges are the ones poised to dominate twenty-first-century markets. Tesla, despite its controversies, exemplifies how climate-aligned innovation can attract extraordinary capital flows, while Ørsted, once a fossil-fuel-dependent utility, transformed itself into a global leader in offshore wind, with its share price rising accordingly. Climate is, paradoxically, both the greatest risk and the greatest driver of wealth creation, and investors who fail to recognise this duality will be left behind.

Yet the crucible of climate investing is not merely technical; it is philosophical. Investors are forced to confront questions of intergenerational equity. Climate impacts unfold over decades, but markets are trained to prize quarterly results. To integrate climate into finance is to reject the tyranny of the short term. It requires acknowledging that fiduciary duty extends not only to immediate shareholders but to future stakeholders—retirees whose pensions depend on sustainable growth, communities whose tax bases fund public services, and children whose economic futures are tied to the stability of the planet. *Climate forces us to redefine prudence itself, not as maximising near-term return but as safeguarding enduring value.*

The pushback, of course, is significant. Critics argue that markets are not moral actors and that their task is efficiency, not conscience. They warn of politicising capital allocation or of greenwashing, where firms cloak themselves in sustainability rhetoric while continuing harmful practices. These objections cannot be ignored. There is a real danger that ESG funds over-promise impact while under-delivering, and that climate-conscious capital becomes another marketing tool. The antidote is rigour: insisting on credible metrics, demanding verifiable disclosures, and recognising that imperfect progress is better than paralysis. Markets must become literate in distinguishing authentic transition from superficial branding.

The policy landscape intensifies the stakes. Governments worldwide are tightening climate regulations, from the European Union's taxonomy for sustainable activities to the United States' Inflation Reduction Act, which channels subsidies into clean energy. Carbon pricing schemes, once theoretical, are proliferating, with over sixty jurisdictions now imposing a cost on emissions. For investors, this means climate is not optional; it is embedded in law. To ignore it is not neutrality but negligence. Boards that fail to integrate climate into strategy risk shareholder lawsuits, regulatory penalties, and reputational collapse. Climate is no longer a footnote in corporate reports—it is becoming the architecture of financial disclosure itself.

The most profound test climate presents is psychological. For the first time, capital markets must reckon with planetary boundaries. Infinite growth on a finite planet is no longer an abstraction but an arithmetic impossibility. Ethical investing, when measured against climate, is not about polishing reputations but about survival. *The question is no longer whether markets will adapt to climate constraints but whether they will do so in time to avert systemic breakdown.* Here lies the crucible: investors are being asked not simply to express values but to confront the structural limits of the system from which those values are derived.

This reframing places extraordinary responsibility on institutional investors—pension funds, sovereign wealth funds, asset managers—whose scale allows them to tilt the system. BlackRock's annual letters may not resolve climate change, but when the world's largest asset manager signals that climate risk is investment risk, the implications cascade across markets. The choices of such institutions—whether to divest, engage, or demand transition plans—will determine whether climate-aligned investing remains marginal or becomes mainstream. For individual investors, the question is equally pressing: are their portfolios complicit in delay, or are they aligned with resilience?

Ultimately, climate as the defining test of ethical capital is about credibility. If values-based investing cannot grapple with the most urgent, systemic, and measurable risk of our time, then its legitimacy collapses. Conversely, if it can, it will prove not only its ethical seriousness but its financial acumen. Climate is thus the proving ground on which the future of finance is being forged. *The test is not whether we can afford to integrate climate into investing but whether we can afford not to.*

Technology and Transparency

The credibility of ethical investing rests on trust, yet trust has become its most fragile commodity. Investors are told that ESG-labelled funds align with sustainability, but the metrics behind those labels remain opaque, inconsistent, and often riddled with conflicts of interest. One index may award a technology giant high marks for carbon efficiency while ignoring its labour practices, while another may penalise it for data privacy scandals yet praise its governance. This fractured landscape erodes investor confidence and fuels scepticism that ESG is more branding exercise than substantive shift. The promise of technology—artificial intelligence, blockchain, and big data—is to cut through this opacity, replacing inconsistent narratives with verifiable evidence. *The decisive question is whether technology can do more than refine disclosure: can it fundamentally reshape how markets measure, verify, and trust claims of responsibility?*

Artificial intelligence has already begun to alter the ESG landscape by sifting through data that human analysts could never process at scale. Satellite imagery can now estimate methane leaks from oil fields in real time, cross-checking corporate emissions reports with observable reality. Natural language processing can scan thousands of annual reports, press releases, and even court filings to detect inconsistencies between what companies say and what they do. Algorithms are increasingly used to identify "greenwashing"—the gap between stated commitments and measurable outcomes. For instance, firms claiming alignment with the Paris Agreement can be tested against AI models projecting whether their current emissions trajectory aligns with a 1.5°C pathway. By automating scrutiny, artificial intelligence reduces reliance on voluntary self-disclosure, which has too often been selective and self-serving. Yet AI also raises a philosophical challenge: if ethical evaluation is outsourced to opaque algorithms, do we risk creating new blind spots, embedding bias at scale while believing we are achieving objectivity?

Blockchain, in contrast, offers transparency not by interpretation but by design. Its distributed ledger technology creates immutable records, allowing every stage of a supply chain to be traced and verified. A diamond tagged on a blockchain cannot be laundered from conflict zones without leaving a digital footprint; a coffee bean certified as fair trade can be traced from farm to cup. For ESG investors, this offers the possibility of trust that does not depend on intermediaries. Rather than relying on rating agencies or corporate auditors, investors could verify for themselves whether a company's claims hold true. Projects like Provenance and IBM's Food Trust are early demonstrations of how blockchain can anchor sustainability in verifiable data. Yet scalability remains a barrier: the energy demands of some blockchain systems risk undermining the very sustainability they seek to guarantee, while the cost and complexity of adoption mean only a fraction of companies currently integrate blockchain traceability into their disclosures. The test will be whether this technology matures into infrastructure rather than remain a boutique innovation.

Big data provides the connective tissue between AI and blockchain, expanding the scope of ESG measurement to include signals once considered irrelevant to finance. Social media sentiment, employee reviews, NGO reports, and even geospatial patterns of deforestation can now be aggregated into real-time reputational risk scores. This granularity makes it harder for companies to control the narrative: reputational failures surface faster, and market reactions are swifter. Consider how consumer boycotts against fashion brands accused of forced labour now gather momentum within hours on digital platforms, impacting stock valuations before official investigations conclude. Big data thus accelerates accountability by collapsing the time lag between misconduct and consequence. But it also risks overwhelming investors with noise. Not every critical tweet signals systemic malpractice, and not every NGO report carries equal weight. The art lies in distinguishing signal from distraction—a task that demands both technological sophistication and ethical judgement.

The convergence of these technologies forces a rethinking of what "trust" means in finance. For centuries, investors trusted intermediaries—auditors, rating agencies, regulators—to validate corporate claims. That trust has eroded under scandals from Enron to Wirecard, where oversight failed to prevent catastrophic deception. With AI, blockchain, and big data, the locus of trust shifts from institutions to systems. Trust becomes less about personal credibility and more about the integrity of data architectures. *The implication is profound: markets may evolve towards a model where transparency is engineered, not merely promised.* This shift, however, demands careful stewardship, for technologies themselves are not inherently ethical. Algorithms can be gamed, blockchains can entrench inequalities of access, and data can be manipulated. Technology expands the possibility of trust but does not guarantee it; governance and oversight remain indispensable.

The commercial implications are immense. Asset managers who harness these tools effectively can differentiate themselves by offering ESG products that are not just aspirational but demonstrably robust. Imagine funds where every holding is accompanied by blockchain-verified supply chain records, AI-validated emissions trajectories, and big-data analysis of stakeholder sentiment. Such funds would be more than labels—they would be auditable ecosystems. This could mark a decisive break from the present, where investors rely on ESG scores that vary wildly across providers, sometimes with correlations no stronger than chance. Technology has the potential to transform ESG from a narrative-driven market to a data-driven discipline.

And yet, transparency is not simply about data; it is about meaning. Information without context can confuse as easily as it can clarify. Investors will still need frameworks for deciding what matters: is a company's carbon footprint more significant than its labour practices, or vice versa? Should AI models weight water usage in arid regions more heavily than in temperate ones? Should blockchain traceability prioritise human rights in supply chains over carbon efficiency? These are not technical questions but normative ones, reminding us that technology can illuminate but not resolve the ethical debates at the heart of responsible investing. *Transparency makes hidden facts visible; it does not dictate how we weigh them.*

The danger, ironically, is that greater transparency could produce paralysis. Investors inundated with conflicting datasets may find it harder, not easier, to act. Already, some institutions complain of "ESG fatigue," overwhelmed by the proliferation of standards, metrics, and disclosure regimes. The promise of technology is to simplify complexity, not amplify it. The challenge is designing systems that prioritise clarity without flattening nuance, providing investors with tools to act decisively without disguising the ethical ambiguities that cannot be quantified.

What is clear is that the future of ESG will not be decided in boardrooms alone but in data infrastructures that define how accountability is measured. AI, blockchain, and big data are not peripheral tools; they are becoming the scaffolding of twenty-first-century finance. Their adoption will determine whether ethical investing matures into a discipline with rigour equal to traditional financial analysis, or whether it remains vulnerable to charges of inconsistency and greenwashing. *The legitimacy of ethical capital will increasingly depend not on promises but on proof—and technology is the crucible through which proof must pass.*

Cultural Shifts in Generational Wealth

The transfer of wealth from older to younger generations is one of the most significant economic shifts of the twenty-first century, yet its importance cannot be measured by capital alone. What distinguishes this transition is the values attached to money as it changes hands. Surveys consistently show that younger investors—particularly millennials and members of Generation Z—prioritise social and environmental responsibility in ways their parents and grandparents often did not. They do not simply view investing as a means of preserving or growing wealth; they see it as a form of participation in shaping the world. *Conscience, once a secondary consideration in financial decision-making, is being embedded into the very mechanics of capital allocation.*

This generational divergence is not a matter of rhetoric but of practice. Consider the rapid growth of ESG-focused funds, which despite facing criticism for inconsistency still attract billions in inflows, particularly from younger investors. These cohorts express less tolerance for investments in fossil fuels, weapons, or exploitative labour practices, and greater enthusiasm for sectors such as renewable energy, health technology, and inclusive finance. Platforms that allow fractional investing and thematic ETFs have flourished because they cater to this demand, enabling younger investors to channel capital directly towards causes that reflect their ethical priorities. This is not merely symbolic. When sustained at scale, such preferences shift the cost of capital: companies aligned with sustainability can access funding more cheaply, while those perceived as irresponsible face higher barriers. The cultural shift becomes a market force.

Unlike earlier generations, for whom investment choices were often mediated through financial advisers and pension funds, younger investors are digital natives accustomed to making decisions with immediacy and autonomy. The democratisation of finance through apps like Robinhood, Wealthsimple, and sustainable investment platforms has accelerated their ability to express values in markets. Transparency is not a bonus feature but a baseline expectation. They demand to know not only the return on their money but also the social and environmental consequences of where it is placed. In this sense, *trust is no longer about assurance from institutions but about direct access to verifiable information.* Companies that fail to disclose in sufficient detail risk exclusion not just from niche portfolios but from mainstream capital flows.

The influence of generational wealth is particularly striking in the context of inheritance. Studies suggest that trillions of dollars are poised to transfer to younger generations in the coming decades, particularly in North America and Europe. The recipients of this wealth are not only more diverse in background but also more politically and socially engaged, with higher expectations of corporations. Where older investors may have tolerated a trade-off between returns and responsibility, younger heirs increasingly see no contradiction: they measure success in both financial and moral terms. Wealth managers, long accustomed to a formulaic approach, are being forced to adjust. Advisers who cannot speak fluently about sustainability, impact metrics, and the broader purpose of wealth will find themselves obsolete.

The cultural shift is not without tension. Critics argue that younger investors are sometimes guided more by ideals than by pragmatism, risking exposure to volatility if they avoid entire sectors of the economy. Fossil fuels, for example, still dominate global energy production, and complete divestment can mean foregoing returns during commodity upswings. Yet the counterpoint is that younger investors adopt a longer time horizon, less concerned with quarterly performance than with systemic resilience. They ask not only "What will deliver returns this year?" but also "What will still be viable in thirty years?" That perspective aligns their values with risk management in ways that traditional analysis often neglects. Climate risk, for instance, is both an ethical concern and a material financial one. By embedding conscience into investment strategy, younger investors may prove not to be idealists but realists of a different order.

This reorientation also has geopolitical implications. In Asia, the Middle East, and Africa, younger investors are increasingly shaping investment cultures historically dominated by family businesses and state-driven capital. A rising generation of entrepreneurs and philanthropists is fusing commercial ambition with social purpose, particularly in technology, healthcare, and infrastructure. Whereas Western debates often focus on exclusion—avoiding harmful industries—emerging markets illustrate the inclusionary side of ethical investing, where capital actively seeks to build positive outcomes. Whether funding solar microgrids in rural India, fintech platforms enabling access to banking in Nigeria, or clean water technologies in Latin America, younger investors are demonstrating that local impact and global responsibility need not be opposed.

Philosophically, what defines this generational shift is a reconceptualisation of wealth itself. For much of modern capitalism, wealth was understood as private accumulation; its legitimacy rested on the right of individuals to deploy it as they wished. Younger investors challenge that assumption by treating wealth as a form of stewardship. The question is not simply "What do I want to gain?" but "What kind of world do I help create?" This reframing moves finance closer to moral philosophy, acknowledging that money is never neutral—it always carries consequences. *Capital, in this view, is not just an economic resource but a civic responsibility.*

The challenge for institutions is to adapt without diluting the seriousness of these expectations. Financial firms have been quick to market "sustainable" products, but many have been exposed for shallow commitments. Younger investors are acutely sensitive to this, often quicker than regulators to spot inconsistencies. Social media amplifies these perceptions, meaning that reputational missteps can undo years of carefully cultivated branding. For asset managers and companies alike, it is not enough to appear ethical; they must substantiate every claim with evidence that can withstand scrutiny. In this sense, younger investors are not only embedding conscience into finance but also raising the bar for accountability across the entire system.

The durability of this cultural shift will be tested by economic downturns. History shows that in times of crisis, investors often prioritise survival over ideals. Yet early evidence suggests younger investors maintain their commitment to values-based finance even under stress. During the market turbulence of the pandemic, for instance, ESG funds not only saw strong inflows but often outperformed conventional funds, driven in part by resilience in sectors like technology and healthcare. The lesson is that values and returns need not be mutually exclusive. Indeed, the alignment of conscience with resilience may prove to be the defining insight of generational wealth.

What is emerging is not a niche preference but a mainstream realignment. The cultural shift driven by younger investors is reshaping the conversation from the margins to the centre of finance. Ethical considerations are no longer treated as optional screens applied after the fact but as integral to the construction of portfolios, the governance of companies, and the strategies of asset managers. *Generational wealth is not just redistributing capital—it is redefining the very terms by which capital is legitimised.* That transformation may be gradual, uneven, and contested, but its trajectory is unmistakable: the conscience of the younger generation is embedding itself into the architecture of finance, and with it, into the future of capitalism itself.

The Conscience Economy

For much of the twentieth century, capital markets operated under a narrow assumption: their sole purpose was to allocate resources towards the most financially efficient ends. Moral questions were considered external, the domain of governments, activists, or civil society. That separation is collapsing. Today, markets themselves are beginning to embed ethical accountability into their mechanics, reshaping the incentives that guide corporate behaviour. *Profit remains central, but profit unmoored from conscience is no longer seen as sufficient legitimacy.* This quiet but profound transformation is what can be called the emergence of the conscience economy.

The most visible signs of this shift lie in the rise of environmental, social, and governance (ESG) frameworks. Despite their inconsistencies, ESG metrics have forced boards, investors, and asset managers to confront questions of sustainability, labour practices, and governance not as peripheral issues but as core determinants of long-term viability. Where once disclosure of carbon emissions or supply chain conditions was voluntary, it is increasingly mandated by regulators and demanded by investors. The European Union's Sustainable Finance Disclosure Regulation, for example, now requires asset managers to detail the environmental and social impact of their funds. In the United States, the Securities and Exchange Commission has signalled greater scrutiny of climate risk disclosures. What these developments represent is not merely policy evolution but a fundamental market recalibration: access to capital is becoming contingent on the capacity to demonstrate ethical responsibility.

The mechanism is subtle yet powerful. Companies that fall short on ethical performance often face higher costs of borrowing, reduced equity valuations, and increased reputational risks. Those that excel enjoy preferential access to funding, more resilient investor bases, and reputational capital that translates into competitive advantage. For instance, firms such as Ørsted, once a fossil fuel-dependent utility, saw dramatic revaluation when it transitioned aggressively towards renewables, becoming a global leader in offshore wind. The transformation was not only moral in framing but financial in outcome: the company's creditworthiness improved, its investor base diversified, and its market capitalisation surged. *The conscience economy is not simply about exclusion—it is about rewarding transformation with tangible valuation benefits.*

The shift is also driven by the rise of collective investor activism. Pension funds, sovereign wealth funds, and large asset managers—once perceived as passive allocators—now use their voting power to influence corporate direction. Campaigns by groups such as Climate Action 100+ illustrate how coordinated shareholder pressure can compel companies to adopt emission reduction targets or overhaul governance structures. This is not moral persuasion in the abstract; it is moral persuasion backed by trillions in assets. When BlackRock, the world's largest asset manager, declares climate risk as investment risk, the signal reverberates across boardrooms globally. Even sceptics must respond, not necessarily out of conviction but because capital increasingly flows in line with these new expectations.

Critics argue that markets are ill-suited to bear moral weight, noting that the pursuit of financial returns and ethical integrity often diverge. They highlight the inconsistencies in ESG ratings, the prevalence of greenwashing, and the difficulty of quantifying moral impact. These criticisms are valid, yet they overlook a deeper point: *markets evolve precisely through contestation and imperfection.* What matters is the direction of travel. Fifty years ago, ethical accountability was virtually absent from mainstream capital flows; today, it is a growing baseline.

The conscience economy does not imply that markets have suddenly become paragons of virtue, but that markets are now structurally unable to ignore conscience without cost.

The rise of the conscience economy can also be traced to technological transparency. Data analytics, blockchain, and artificial intelligence are enabling unprecedented visibility into corporate behaviour. Supply chains once opaque can now be mapped, monitored, and audited in near real time. Algorithms can identify patterns of labour exploitation or environmental harm more quickly than traditional oversight mechanisms. This transparency erodes the ability of firms to externalise costs unnoticed. In a market where information asymmetry once shielded misconduct, the conscience economy thrives on exposure: *ethical lapses are no longer hidden liabilities but immediate market risks.*

Yet the conscience economy is not driven by institutional change alone. Cultural shifts in generational wealth are accelerating it. Younger investors, as discussed elsewhere, are embedding values into their financial choices in ways that older generations often did not. They treat capital allocation as a form of civic participation, demanding that portfolios reflect both financial performance and moral coherence. As trillions in wealth transfer to these cohorts, the conscience economy will cease to be a niche concern. It will become the expectation against which all capital flows are judged. Companies that cling to the assumption that markets will forgive ethical failure so long as profits remain strong are likely to find themselves out of alignment with the dominant currents of capital.

Importantly, the conscience economy reframes the definition of fiduciary duty. Traditional finance equated fiduciary responsibility with maximising short-term financial returns. In the emerging landscape, fiduciary duty includes protecting beneficiaries against systemic risks such as climate change, social instability, or reputational collapse. Trustees and asset managers are compelled to consider not only the direct returns of an investment but its broader capacity to preserve long-term value in a world of interconnected risks. Far from diluting fiduciary duty, the conscience economy expands it—placing ethical considerations at the heart of prudent financial management.

The implications extend beyond individual companies or funds. Capital markets, as aggregators of vast social expectations, are becoming instruments of governance in their own right. They cannot replace democratic institutions or public regulation, but they increasingly act as parallel mechanisms of accountability. When investors demand net-zero commitments, board diversity, or human rights compliance, they enforce standards that may outpace political consensus. This raises profound philosophical questions: should markets wield such influence over moral questions? Does the conscience economy risk substituting democratic deliberation with financial coercion? These are unresolved tensions, yet they highlight the depth of the shift underway. The question is no longer whether markets will incorporate conscience, but how they will do so, and under whose authority.

Perhaps the most striking feature of the conscience economy is its self-reinforcing nature. Ethical accountability is no longer a matter of corporate goodwill but of systemic expectation. Firms that resist face exclusion from indices, disqualification from contracts, and reputational damage amplified by digital media. Those that embrace conscience can attract loyal investors, talent, and customers. Over time, this creates a feedback loop: ethical accountability is rewarded, unethical behaviour is penalised, and the norm gradually shifts. What began as an aspirational fringe becomes an embedded baseline.

The conscience economy does not mark the end of capitalism, but it does suggest a transformation of its rules. Markets still allocate capital, but the criteria by which they do so are broadening to include moral legitimacy as well as financial efficiency. This evolution is uneven, contested, and at times contradictory. Yet the trajectory is unmistakable. *Capital markets are becoming arenas where conscience is not an optional virtue but a structural necessity.* Those who grasp this shift early will shape not only their own fortunes but the moral architecture of finance in the decades ahead.

Chapter 13
Compounding with Conscience

The true genius of investing has never been in sudden windfalls or clever speculation, but in the quiet, almost invisible process of compounding. Over time, small, consistent gains accumulate into extraordinary outcomes, not because of brilliance in any single moment but because of the discipline to persist. Ethical investing demands precisely the same temperament. The impact of aligning capital with conscience is rarely immediate; it unfolds across years, even decades, in ways that mirror the mathematics of compounding itself. What begins as a marginal sacrifice—a foregone opportunity in a high-yield but harmful industry, a slower initial return on a green technology still scaling—gradually accumulates into resilient wealth and durable social value. In the long horizon of finance, patience is not only a virtue but a form of strategy, and conscience is not a drag on returns but a reinvested dividend.

The test of ethical portfolios has often been their ability to endure crises. Here the evidence is striking. Studies conducted during the financial meltdown of 2008 and again during the COVID-19 pandemic revealed that funds with robust ESG criteria tended to decline less sharply and recover more swiftly than their conventional peers. Their resilience was not accidental but structural. Companies with stronger governance were less likely to be over-leveraged; those attentive to employee welfare maintained loyalty and productivity under strain; firms attuned to environmental risks were less exposed to regulatory shocks or reputational collapses. In essence, *portfolios built on principle displayed a form of anti-fragility*: they did not merely withstand turbulence but often emerged stronger for having weathered it. By contrast, strategies designed purely around short-term profit found their weaknesses ruthlessly exposed when the conditions of the market shifted. The lesson is that resilience, not raw return, is the truer measure of wealth designed to last.

Yet the integration of conscience into investment cannot remain a loose ideal. For it to function as a serious discipline, investors need a mental model—a framework that reconciles the apparent tension between profit and principle. This requires rejecting the false binary in which one must choose between moral satisfaction and financial prudence. Instead, one must understand how values and returns can reinforce each other. For example, the decision to support renewable energy is not merely about reducing carbon emissions but about positioning capital in industries that will define the next half-century of growth. Similarly, choosing to back firms that practise diversity and equitable governance is not only an ethical stance but a recognition that such organisations attract better talent, innovate more effectively, and face fewer litigation risks. *The overlap between what is right and what is profitable is larger than sceptics admit—but it reveals itself only when viewed through a lens of patience, systems thinking, and long-term perspective.*

The act of investing in this way ultimately reshapes the role of the investor. To compound with conscience is to acknowledge that one is not a spectator of markets but an architect of future realities. Every allocation of capital is a signal: it rewards certain behaviours and penalises others. The aggregated choices of investors shape which industries thrive, which fade, and which adapt. This power is often underestimated, diluted by the perception that individual investors are too small to matter. Yet collective flows are built from individual choices, and the redirection of even marginal capital away from harmful enterprises and towards sustainable innovation creates ripples that accumulate—like compounding itself—into systemic change. To embrace this role is to move beyond viewing investments solely as instruments of personal gain and instead as tools for constructing a world in which financial prosperity and ethical responsibility are not opposing goals but mutually reinforcing outcomes.

This chapter sets out to explore that idea with precision and depth. It examines why ethical investing cannot be judged on quarterly reports alone but must be understood through the lens of decades; it considers how portfolios aligned with conscience demonstrate structural resilience in the face of crises; it develops a mental model in which values and profit strengthen one another rather than collide; and it reframes the investor as a participant in shaping not just markets but society itself. The argument is not that ethical investing is easy or that it guarantees unbroken financial outperformance. It is that, like compounding, its value lies in persistence, patience, and the willingness to see beyond the immediate to the enduring. To compound with conscience is, ultimately, to accept that wealth is never neutral: it either contributes to the erosion of the future or to its repair. The responsibility, and the opportunity, rests with those who hold the capital.

The Long Horizon

The most powerful force in finance is not leverage, arbitrage, or even innovation—it is time. Compounding, which Einstein reputedly described as the eighth wonder of the world, relies less on the brilliance of strategy than on the discipline to stay the course. Ethical investing magnifies this truth. Aligning capital with conscience often produces slower, steadier gains at the outset, making it tempting to abandon principle for speed. Yet over the long horizon, patience becomes the decisive factor that allows both values and value to reinforce one another. To understand why ethical investing demands a lengthened time frame is to recognise how structural shifts in markets unfold, how reputational dividends accumulate, and how risk management based on values pays off not in weeks but in decades.

Investors accustomed to quarterly earnings cycles face a tension when they seek to embed ethics into their portfolio construction. The very companies that excel in governance, sustainability, and employee welfare may appear more conservative in the short term. A firm that invests heavily in clean energy infrastructure, for example, may initially report narrower margins than a peer that externalises its costs onto the environment. To the impatient observer, this difference can look like underperformance. To the disciplined investor, it is the price of building resilience. *The long horizon reframes temporary opportunity costs as investments in durability.* If the purpose of capital is not merely to chase returns but to sustain them across generations, then ethical allocation becomes less an indulgence and more a necessity.

Historical case studies illustrate this point. In the 1980s and 1990s, investors who dismissed renewable energy as niche missed the early compounding of what is now a multi-trillion-dollar global sector. Those who chose to divest from tobacco faced scepticism about sacrificing dividends, yet the long arc of regulatory tightening and litigation reshaped the industry's profitability. Similarly, financial institutions exposed to fossil fuels found themselves subject to stranded asset risks once climate policies began to shift. The evidence is clear: *decisions that appeared to sacrifice immediate gains were, with time, vindicated as prudent and even prescient.* Ethical investing demands this perspective because its returns are not always captured in short-term metrics; they are embedded in long-term structural realignments.

The psychology of markets, however, often works against patience. Human beings are wired to prefer instant feedback. Investors track indexes daily, compare fund performance quarterly, and make decisions under the pressure of peers or clients demanding results. Ethical strategies therefore require a reframing of what constitutes "success." Instead of benchmarking only against peers in the same reporting window, investors must learn to judge the trajectory of their holdings against longer, more consequential time frames: regulatory cycles, generational demographic shifts, and systemic risks such as climate change. A company that underperforms its industry in a quarter but positions itself for regulatory compliance in the coming decade is, in this frame, outperforming in the metrics that matter most.

The long horizon also forces us to think about the compounding of non-financial returns. Consider reputation: a company that avoids scandal by practising transparency does not merely protect itself from legal penalties; it compounds trust over time. Similarly, investment in employee wellbeing generates compounding loyalty, reducing turnover costs and nurturing innovation cultures that bear fruit years later. These benefits rarely appear in standard financial statements, but they are no less real. Ethical investors who recognise them understand that capital compounds not only through reinvested profits but also through reputational capital, stakeholder goodwill, and resilience to shocks. *These intangibles accumulate quietly, but when tested in crisis, they reveal their full weight.*

Patience, however, is not passive. To extend one's horizon is not to adopt complacency but to accept that disciplined allocation requires active conviction. Investors must often endure periods where their ethical stance is unfashionable or contrarian. The decision to avoid fossil fuel exposure, for example, looked premature during the oil price booms of the early 2000s. Yet those who held firm avoided exposure to volatility and stranded asset write-downs in the following decades. The long horizon therefore demands a mindset prepared to appear "wrong" in the short term in order to be right over the span that matters. This can be uncomfortable, but it is precisely the discomfort that separates patient capital from speculative capital.

There is also a philosophical dimension to this discipline. The long horizon invites investors to see themselves not merely as traders of financial instruments but as custodians of future outcomes. The patience required in ethical investing mirrors the patience required in stewarding ecosystems, nurturing education, or cultivating healthy institutions. Each involves deferring immediate gratification for enduring returns. In this sense, *ethical investing is not only a financial strategy but also a moral practice in long-term thinking.* By resisting the allure of rapid extraction, investors affirm a deeper commitment to sustainability—not as branding, but as a temporal ethic that recognises wealth as intergenerational by nature.

Of course, critics will argue that patience can disguise underperformance, and that long horizons may simply enable managers to excuse poor returns. This is a real risk. The defence lies in rigorous measurement and accountability. Ethical investing cannot mean abandoning scrutiny; it requires sharper tools for evaluating long-term performance. Metrics such as carbon-adjusted returns, employee productivity ratios, and governance scores provide ways to ensure that patience is not confused with complacency. The long horizon should sharpen standards, not relax them. It is about shifting the yardstick, not discarding it.

Practical applications of this perspective are increasingly visible. Sovereign wealth funds, pension funds, and university endowments—all institutions with inherently long-term obligations—are leading the integration of ethical criteria precisely because they cannot afford to chase quarterly gains at the expense of future stability. Norway's Government Pension Fund Global, one of the world's largest, excludes companies on ethical grounds not as political theatre but as risk management across a century-scale time horizon. Likewise, family offices that think generationally are often among the first to embrace sustainable strategies. Their time frames liberate them from short-term pressures, allowing them to align investment with principle in ways that compound steadily across decades.

The discipline required for long-horizon ethical investing is demanding. It requires courage in the face of peer pressure, the humility to accept slower returns in the short run, and the conviction to trust in the compounding of values as well as value. Yet the reward for this patience is profound. Investors who extend their horizon discover that ethical strategies are not fragile compromises but robust engines of resilience. They create wealth that endures not only because it grows mathematically through compounding, but because it avoids the corrosive risks of exploiting people or planet. Over time, these portfolios demonstrate that the most enduring profits are those earned in alignment with principle. *Patience, discipline, and conscience are not obstacles to compounding; they are its purest expression.*

Resilience Over Returns

The true test of an investment strategy does not occur during years of steady growth but in the crucible of crisis. When markets stumble, liquidity dries, or geopolitical shocks unsettle the financial system, portfolios are exposed for what they are: fragile constructions chasing yield or robust frameworks built on durable principles. Value-aligned portfolios—those guided by environmental, social, and governance criteria—often reveal an unexpected strength in these moments. Their resilience is not an accident but the logical outcome of aligning capital with long-term sustainability rather than short-term extraction. *It is in downturns, not in booms, that the hidden virtues of ethical investing become most visible.*

The financial crises of the past two decades provide abundant evidence. During the global financial crisis of 2008, funds overweight in highly leveraged financial instruments collapsed under pressure, while portfolios that had avoided exposure to predatory lending practices or opaque derivatives fared relatively better. In the COVID-19 market shock of early 2020, indices of companies with strong ESG ratings outperformed broader benchmarks. While the broader market plummeted, firms with demonstrable commitments to employee welfare, supply chain responsibility, and adaptive governance weathered the storm with fewer losses. The lesson is not that values immunise investors against volatility, but that they *reduce exposure to self-inflicted fragility*. Ethical screens tend to filter out businesses built on exploitation, poor risk governance, or environmental negligence—the very features that transform volatility into disaster.

Resilience, however, is more than the avoidance of harm; it is the capacity to adapt and recover. Companies embedded in value-aligned portfolios often possess structures that enable faster recovery post-crisis. Strong governance fosters transparent decision-making, which reassures markets and stakeholders alike. Investment in employee welfare cultivates loyalty and adaptability, which become invaluable when rapid operational shifts are necessary. Environmental stewardship reduces exposure to regulatory tightening that often follows crises, such as carbon taxes or stricter emissions standards. In this sense, resilience is not a defensive posture but an active capability: the ability to absorb shocks and then harness them for transformation.

The traditional model of investment optimisation prioritised return maximisation with risk framed primarily as volatility. Yet volatility is not synonymous with vulnerability. A company that produces steady earnings at the expense of environmental degradation is, in fact, harbouring long-term risks that may be invisible in short-term return metrics. Oil and gas majors, for instance, once considered safe dividend payers, now carry heightened exposure to stranded assets as the world transitions to renewables. By contrast, firms that invested early in sustainable technologies endured years of modest returns but emerged with positioning that cushioned them when regulatory and consumer preferences shifted. *The deeper lesson is that risk is multidimensional: resilience cannot be captured by beta coefficients alone.*

Critics often argue that ethical portfolios underperform because they exclude profitable but controversial sectors. Tobacco, arms, and fossil fuels have historically delivered strong margins, leading to concerns that excluding them is self-defeating. Yet this critique misunderstands resilience as a trade-off rather than an asset. These industries may offer high short-term returns, but they are disproportionately exposed to litigation, reputational collapse, regulatory constraints, and consumer backlash. When shocks occur, these vulnerabilities magnify losses. The exclusion of such sectors is not merely a moral stance but a recognition that fragility masquerading as profitability is a dangerous foundation for compounding wealth.

Case studies reinforce the point. After the Deepwater Horizon oil spill in 2010, BP lost more than half of its market capitalisation and spent over $60 billion in fines, settlements, and clean-up costs. Investors who had excluded high-environmental-risk companies avoided this catastrophic drawdown. Similarly, garment manufacturers exposed in the Rana Plaza factory collapse of 2013 suffered reputational and financial fallout, while companies with stronger labour oversight remained insulated. These are not isolated incidents; they exemplify a broader pattern where firms with poor social and environmental practices transform operational risks into systemic crises. Portfolios that screen for these risks, even at the expense of foregoing short-term profits, demonstrate superior resilience when crises inevitably arise.

There is also a psychological dimension to resilience. Investors aligned with their values are less likely to capitulate in moments of panic. When a portfolio reflects deeply held convictions about climate responsibility or social justice, it provides an anchor that stabilises behaviour under duress. This behavioural resilience—staying invested rather than liquidating during downturns—compounds financial resilience by avoiding costly market-timing errors. *In this way, values do not merely protect against external shocks; they also guard against the internal hazards of fear and greed.*

Resilience also reframes the meaning of performance. The question is not solely whether a portfolio delivers the highest return in a given year, but whether it delivers durable returns over decades without eroding the conditions that sustain them. Portfolios driven purely by profit can resemble athletes using performance-enhancing drugs: dazzling in the short run but unsustainable over time. Value-aligned portfolios resemble disciplined training: progress may appear slower, but it is sustainable, repeatable, and protective of long-term health. For pension funds, university endowments, and sovereign wealth vehicles—investors with multi-generational obligations—this distinction is decisive.

The academic literature increasingly supports this perspective. Studies by institutions such as MSCI and

Morningstar have documented that ESG-integrated funds exhibit lower downside risk during market crises. They may not always outperform in bull markets, but their defensive qualities prove invaluable in protecting capital during downturns. The compounding effect of avoiding large drawdowns is significant: a portfolio that loses 50 per cent must double simply to recover, while one that loses 20 per cent needs only a 25 per cent gain. Over decades, this asymmetry means that *resilience often outpaces raw return-chasing in producing enduring wealth.*

Still, resilience must be approached with nuance. Not all ESG funds are equally robust, and greenwashing remains a threat. Investors cannot assume that labels guarantee resilience; they must interrogate methodologies, scrutinise holdings, and demand transparency. True resilience arises not from branding but from substantive commitments embedded in governance, operations, and capital allocation. The burden on ethical investors is therefore twofold: to hold fast to principles and to ensure that those principles are implemented rigorously. Without this diligence, the promise of resilience risks becoming hollow.

Ultimately, resilience over returns is not an argument against profitability but a reordering of priorities. By privileging resilience, investors accept that their portfolios may not top short-term performance charts, but they gain something far more valuable: protection against catastrophic loss, adaptability in crisis, and alignment with the forces reshaping markets. Ethical investing demonstrates that the pursuit of resilience is itself a strategy for superior long-term returns. *What appears to be a sacrifice of speed is, in fact, an investment in staying power.* Over time, it is the portfolios that endure shocks, adapt, and compound steadily that generate not only wealth but also legitimacy—the most essential currency of all in modern finance.

A Mental Model for Investors

The prevailing assumption in finance has long been that principle and profit exist in uneasy tension. Ethical considerations, many argue, are an add-on, a noble but secondary concern that inevitably dilutes returns. Yet this framing is not only outdated; it is intellectually misleading. Principle and profit are not competing imperatives but interdependent forces. *When structured correctly, they reinforce each other, creating a virtuous cycle of trust, resilience, and compounding value.* What is needed is a mental model—a framework that recasts ethical investing not as a constraint on profit but as a more complete and enduring conception of it.

The starting point is to recognise that financial returns are inseparable from the systems that generate them. Profit cannot exist in a vacuum; it is drawn from labour, natural resources, social trust, and institutional stability. When those foundations are eroded, profits may persist in the short run but decay in the long run. A company that pollutes a river may inflate margins today, but it externalises costs onto communities, regulators, and future generations. Eventually, those costs rebound—through fines, reputational collapse, or a drying up of social licence to operate. The supposed "conflict" between principle and profit is thus often a misperception of time horizon. *Principle is profit extended into the future; profit without principle is simply borrowing against tomorrow.*

This is not a theoretical claim but one borne out in practice. Consider Unilever, which embraced sustainability as a core business model rather than a marketing exercise. Its Sustainable Living brands, from Dove to Hellmann's, consistently outperformed the rest of its portfolio in growth and margins, precisely because consumers rewarded authenticity and long-term stewardship. On the other hand, Volkswagen's emissions scandal showed the inverse: short-term profits derived from cheating environmental standards triggered billions in losses, criminal penalties, and a reputational scar that continues to constrain the company. The same logic applies across sectors: in pharmaceuticals, technology, energy, and finance, firms that align profit with principle enjoy more stable earnings, stronger customer loyalty, and reduced regulatory risk.

For investors, the challenge is to rewire decision-making around this insight. Traditional portfolio theory treats risk and return as the sole coordinates of analysis. A mental model that incorporates conscience adds a third axis: legitimacy. Legitimacy is not captured by volatility measures or quarterly reports but by whether a company's business practices are aligned with the broader currents of social expectation and ecological survival. When legitimacy is ignored, investors find themselves complicit in accumulating hidden risks—risks that crystallise violently when scandals, crises, or cultural shifts erupt. By contrast, portfolios that price legitimacy as a fundamental dimension of value are less fragile and better positioned to capture the reallocation of capital as markets evolve.

One can think of this model as a triangle: profit, principle, and legitimacy. At its strongest, each side reinforces the others. Profit provides the resources for sustained investment in ethical practices. Principle shapes the long-term orientation that prevents extractive behaviours from corroding trust. Legitimacy sustains the social and regulatory permissions that allow enterprises to operate. The triangle is not symmetrical at all times—there may be years where profit lags principle, or principle is tested by shareholder impatience. Yet when held together, the structure endures, while portfolios that optimise only for one side risk collapse.

Sceptics may counter that markets reward efficiency, not virtue. Yet this is to misunderstand the changing definition of efficiency itself. Efficiency once meant squeezing the most output from inputs with little regard for side effects. Today, efficiency increasingly includes carbon intensity, water usage, data privacy, and supply chain integrity. These are not "extras" but metrics of whether a business can sustain operations in a world of climate risk, geopolitical tension, and hyper-transparent digital scrutiny. *What looks like principle is, in fact, the most modern understanding of efficiency.* Investors who persist in divorcing ethics from economics are not hard-nosed realists but practitioners of an outdated model.

The mental model also requires humility about time. Ethical investing does not guarantee linear or immediate outperformance. There will be quarters when tobacco or fossil fuel stocks surge while renewable energy firms or socially responsible funds lag. But to judge principle by quarterly performance is to misapply the yardstick. A value-aligned portfolio is less about chasing every market swing than about compounding steadily over decades. The mental discipline required is akin to that of patient capitalists like Warren Buffett, who prize durability of competitive advantage over quarterly surprises. Ethical investors extend that same patience to values: they accept that the market may misprice principle in the short run but trust that resilience, consumer preference, and regulatory alignment will reward it over time.

Examples of this principle-profit synthesis are multiplying. Tesla, once derided as a niche automaker bleeding cash, catalysed a global shift towards electric vehicles that forced incumbents into transformative investments. Its early backers were not philanthropists but investors who recognised that principle—accelerating the transition to sustainable energy—was also the most powerful driver of profit in the automotive sector's future. Similarly, funds that integrated climate risk into asset allocation a decade ago are now better protected against stranded asset exposure as coal plants shutter and oil demand peaks. These are not acts of charity; they are acts of foresight.

To apply this model practically, investors must ask three interlinked questions of every opportunity. First: *what is the true source of this company's profit, and is it sustainable under future environmental, social, and regulatory conditions?* Second: *what principles guide this company's decisions, and are they consistent with preserving long-term value?* Third: *does this company enjoy legitimacy among its stakeholders, or is it accruing silent liabilities that may one day implode?* These questions do not replace traditional analysis but elevate it, ensuring that portfolios are built on deeper foundations than financial engineering alone.

The convergence of principle and profit also reframes the role of the investor. Investors are not passive recipients of market outcomes but active participants shaping the incentives that guide corporate behaviour. By directing capital towards firms that embody the triangle of profit, principle, and legitimacy, investors do not merely manage portfolios; they influence the architecture of the economy. This influence is not abstract. Shareholder engagement, proxy voting, capital allocation—all of these decisions send signals that reshape industries. When investors integrate principle into their model, they are exercising power not just to protect their wealth but to guide the future contours of commerce.

A mental model where principle and profit reinforce each other is not simply a strategy for investing; it is a philosophy for how capital operates in society. It insists that the purpose of investing is not only to grow wealth but to ensure that the mechanisms of wealth creation are compatible with human flourishing and ecological survival. It recognises that while the pursuit of profit alone can generate impressive bursts of growth, only when profit is tethered to principle can it sustain legitimacy across generations. And it provides the investor with a framework that is at once intellectually rigorous, practically applicable, and morally coherent. *To invest with such a model is not to compromise but to clarify: to see that the strongest portfolios are those in which conscience and compounding are aligned.*

The Investor's New Role

For much of modern financial history, the investor has been cast as a passive figure—an observer of markets, reacting to price signals, allocating capital based on risk and reward, and treating companies as abstract vehicles for returns. Yet this conception is increasingly inadequate. The role of the investor is no longer confined to interpreting markets but extends to shaping them. *Every allocation decision is a vote for the kind of economy we are building.* In this sense, investors are no longer spectators; they are architects of the structures that will define wealth, opportunity, and sustainability for generations.

The transition from spectator to architect is rooted in a simple but profound recognition: capital is not neutral. Where money flows, activity follows. Industries expand, innovations are accelerated, and social norms are reinforced or undermined. When investors back extractive models, they are not simply chasing returns; they are underwriting systems that degrade ecological stability and erode trust. When they fund enterprises that prioritise fairness, innovation, and resilience, they help embed those values into the scaffolding of the global economy. This agency is not incidental. It is the essence of investment. *To deploy capital is to express a vision of the future.*

Examples abound of how investors' choices have already shaped society at scale. Consider the growth of renewable energy: once marginal, it is now mainstream, catalysed by investors who saw not only the environmental imperative but also the long-term business case. The acceleration of solar and wind deployment, the rapid decline in battery costs, and the emergence of electric mobility are not simply technological stories; they are financial stories. They are the result of trillions of dollars redirected towards clean energy, guided by investors who understood that profit and principle could align. By contrast, industries that once dominated—coal, tobacco, asbestos—have shrunk under the weight of capital flight, with investors recognising both the moral hazards and financial risks of staying involved.

The investor's new role demands a reframing of fiduciary duty. Traditional fiduciary logic has often been defined narrowly as maximising financial returns for clients or shareholders. But as climate risk, social unrest, and governance failures prove material to long-term performance, fiduciary responsibility must also include stewardship of the conditions that make returns possible. A pension fund manager who invests solely in high-yield fossil fuel assets may capture returns in the short term but simultaneously undermine the climate stability required for beneficiaries to enjoy those pensions in the future. The most rigorous interpretation of fiduciary duty is therefore not short-term maximisation but long-term preservation—ensuring that the system in which wealth is compounded remains viable.

This expanded role also requires a shift in mindset from extraction to partnership. Investors are not external to the enterprises they fund; they are participants in shaping their direction. Engagement—through proxy voting, dialogue with management, and the exercise of ownership rights—becomes a core responsibility, not an optional add-on. The choice between divestment and engagement, explored in debates over fossil fuels, arms, or social media platforms, is emblematic of this new role. Sometimes exit sends the strongest signal; sometimes staying invested and pushing for reform yields greater change. Both strategies rely on recognising that investors are not passive bystanders but active shapers of corporate conduct.

The technology-driven transparency of modern finance amplifies this responsibility. Digital platforms, shareholder databases, and ESG analytics ensure that the decisions of large asset managers and even retail investors are more visible than ever. Capital markets are no longer opaque channels; they are scrutinised ecosystems where flows of money are mapped, analysed, and judged in real time. Investors can no longer pretend their choices are detached or invisible. They are accountable to clients, to regulators, to society—and increasingly, to younger generations who demand that capital reflect conscience. *The invisibility cloak has been lifted; investors must now act in the open, with consistency and integrity.*

Critics may argue that it is not the job of investors to fix social or environmental problems. Their role, they insist, is to generate returns and let governments and civil society handle the rest. But this separation of spheres collapses under scrutiny. Governments cannot decarbonise the economy without massive private investment. Communities cannot scale innovation without access to venture funding. Global challenges—from pandemics to data ethics to resource scarcity—require capital flows aligned with solutions. Investors may not be sole agents of change, but their withdrawal or apathy guarantees inertia. Inaction is not neutral; it entrenches the status quo.

The implications of this reframing are profound. It changes how we view risk: no longer as volatility measured against benchmarks but as the possibility of undermining the very systems that sustain markets. It changes how we view returns: not as numbers in isolation but as signals of whether wealth is being built on durable foundations or borrowed from future stability. And it changes how we view the purpose of investing itself: not simply to accumulate but to construct, not simply to ride markets but to mould them. *The investor is not a consumer of markets but a co-creator of their trajectory.*

To embody this new role, investors need frameworks that integrate principle and profit without compromise. That means adopting investment theses that are resilient to systemic shocks, attuned to shifting cultural expectations, and transparent in their measurement of impact. It requires collaboration across asset managers, sovereign funds, family offices, and retail investors to ensure that conscience is not marginal but mainstream. It requires rejecting the myth that markets are mechanical systems detached from human values and embracing the reality that markets are social constructs, continually shaped by collective choices.

There is also a personal dimension to this new role. For individual investors, the decision to align portfolios with principles is not merely financial optimisation; it is an act of identity. It is a way of declaring what one believes wealth is for and what kind of world one wishes to see compounded into the future. For institutional investors, the stakes are magnified but the logic is the same: every allocation reflects a worldview. To accept the role of architect is to recognise that wealth is not an end but a means—a lever through which the future can be tilted towards sustainability, justice, and shared prosperity.

The investor's new role is therefore not a burden but an invitation. It invites investors to step beyond the narrow calculus of quarterly earnings and to see themselves as participants in history. It invites them to understand that the privilege of allocating capital comes with the power to shape its consequences. And it invites them to recognise that the most enduring legacy of investment is not the returns booked in one's lifetime but the systems and structures left for those who follow. *To invest is to imagine the future—and to decide, consciously, what that future will be.*

About the Author

Zayn Elric writes about money with both clarity and conscience. His work explores how everyday decisions about saving and investing shape not only personal wealth but also the world we leave behind. Known for combining accessible financial wisdom with a values-driven perspective, his books challenge readers to think about profit and principle in the same breath. Through his writing, Elric makes a compelling case that investing is not just a financial act but a moral one—an opportunity to compound wealth while aligning capital with conscience. He lives by the conviction that finance is most powerful when it reflects the values of those who use it.

www.ingramcontent.com/pod-product-compliance
Lightning Source LLC
Chambersburg PA
CBHW031337230926
51848CB00002B/270
9789371770378